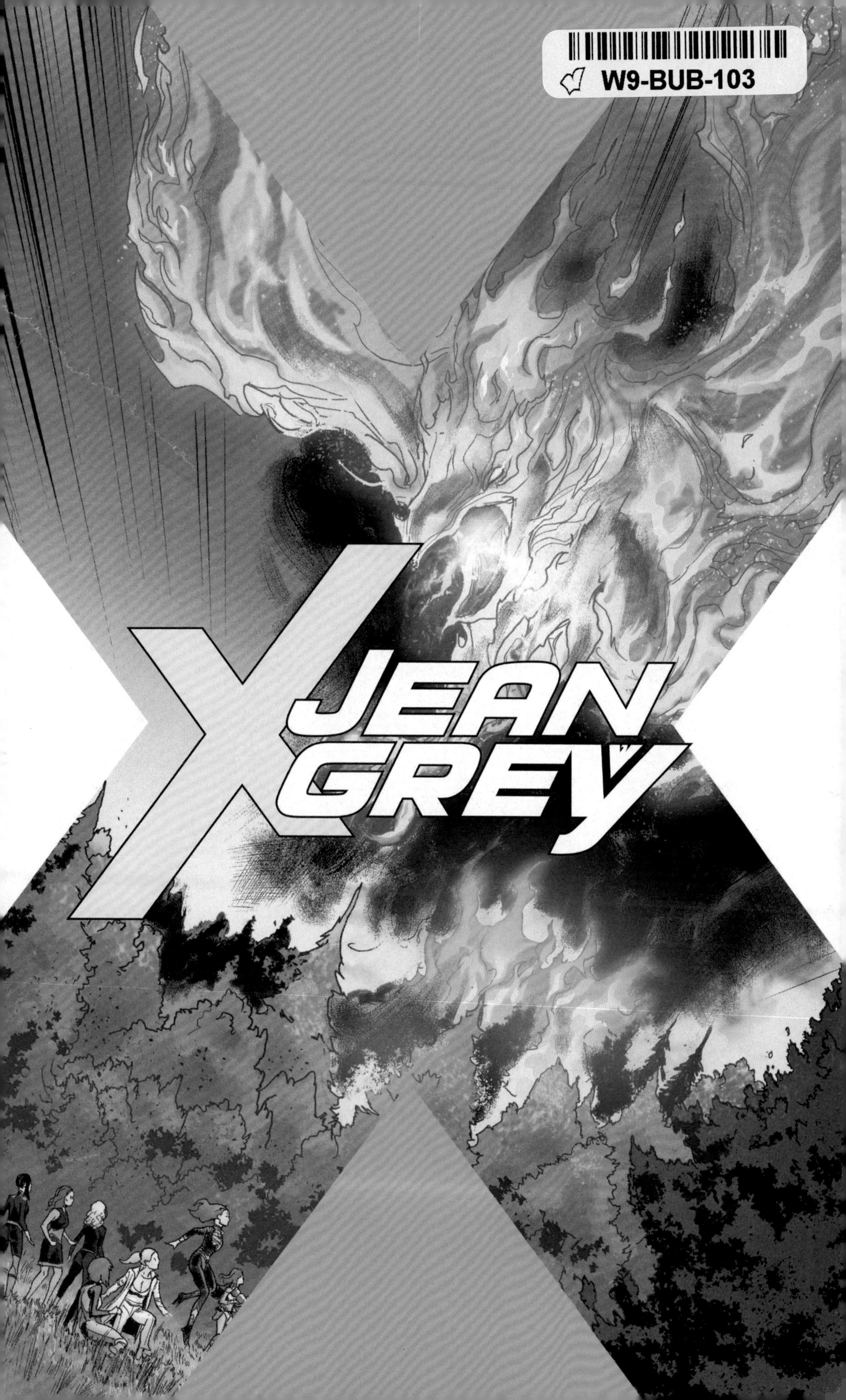
JEAN
GREY

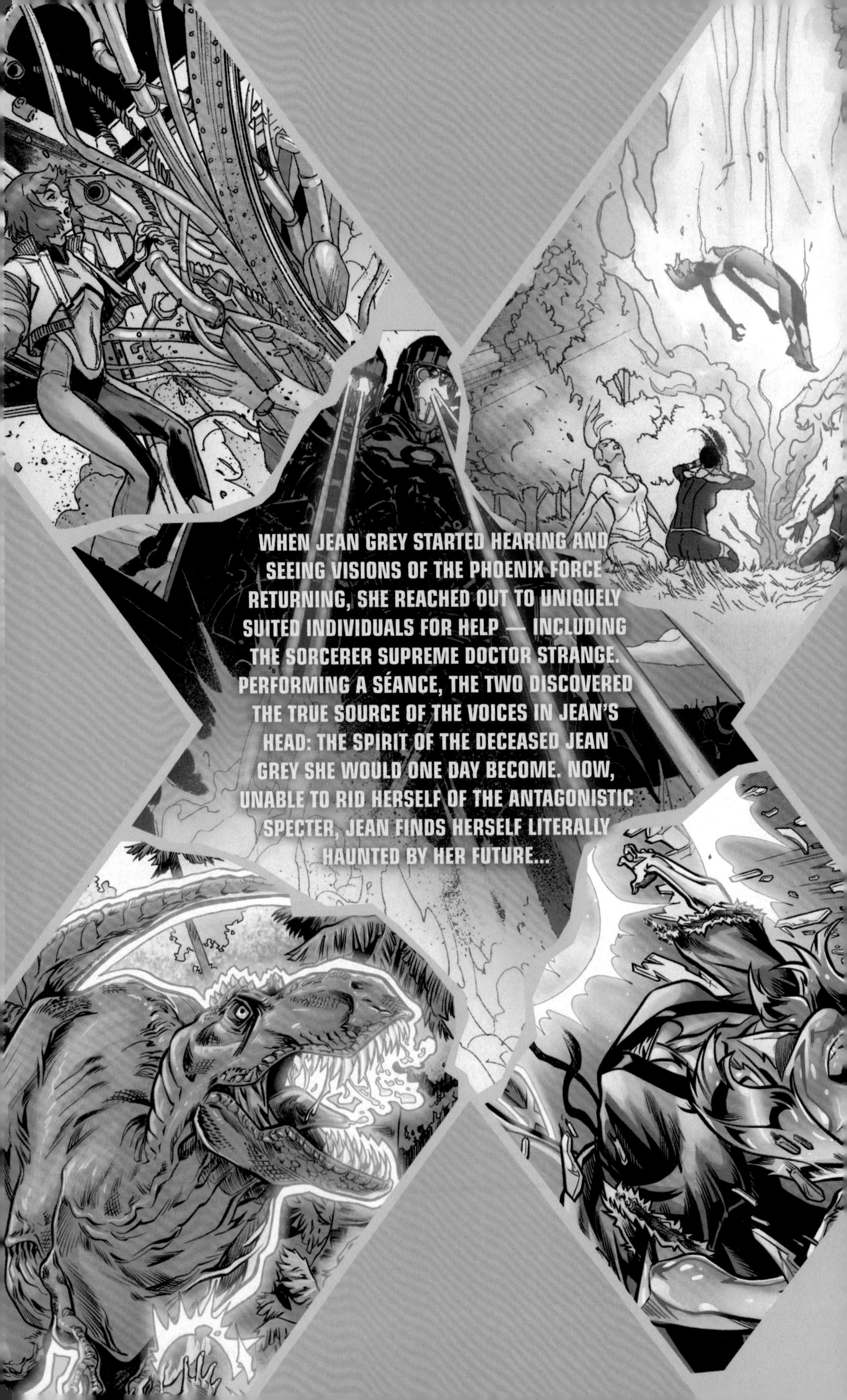

WHEN JEAN GREY STARTED HEARING AND SEEING VISIONS OF THE PHOENIX FORCE RETURNING, SHE REACHED OUT TO UNIQUELY SUITED INDIVIDUALS FOR HELP — INCLUDING THE SORCERER SUPREME DOCTOR STRANGE. PERFORMING A SÉANCE, THE TWO DISCOVERED THE TRUE SOURCE OF THE VOICES IN JEAN'S HEAD: THE SPIRIT OF THE DECEASED JEAN GREY SHE WOULD ONE DAY BECOME. NOW, UNABLE TO RID HERSELF OF THE ANTAGONISTIC SPECTER, JEAN FINDS HERSELF LITERALLY HAUNTED BY HER FUTURE...

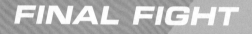

X JEAN GREY

FINAL FIGHT

Writer/**DENNIS HOPELESS**

Artists/**ALBERTO ALBURQUERQUE** (#7, #10-11)
& **VICTOR IBÁÑEZ** (#8-9, #11)

Color Artists/**JAY DAVIS RAMOS** (#7, #9-11)
& **CHRIS SOTOMAYOR** (#8)

Letterer/**VC'S TRAVIS LANHAM**

Cover Art/**DAVID YARDIN**

Assistant Editor/**CHRIS ROBINSON**
Editor/**DARREN SHAN**
X-Men Group Editor/**MARK PANICCIA**

JEAN GREY CREATED BY **STAN LEE** & **JACK KIRBY**

Collection Editor/**JENNIFER GRÜNWALD** • Assistant Editor/**CAITLIN O'CONNELL**
Associate Managing Editor/**KATERI WOODY** • Editor, Special Projects/**MARK D. BEAZLEY**
VP Production & Special Projects/**JEFF YOUNGQUIST** • SVP Print, Sales & Marketing/**DAVID GABRIEL**
Book Designer/**JAY BOWEN**

Editor in Chief/**C.B. CEBULSKI** • Chief Creative Officer/**JOE QUESADA**
President/**DAN BUCKLEY** • Executive Producer/**ALAN FINE**

JEAN GREY VOL. 2: FINAL FIGHT. Contains material originally published in magazine form as JEAN GREY #7-11. First printing 2018. ISBN 978-1-302-90878-2. Published by MARVEL WORLDWIDE, INC., a subsidiary of MARVEL ENTERTAINMENT, LLC. OFFICE OF PUBLICATION: 135 West 50th Street, New York, NY 10020. **Printed in Canada.** DAN BUCKLEY, President, Marvel Entertainment; JOHN NEE, Publisher; JOE QUESADA, Chief Creative Officer; TOM BREVOORT, SVP of Publishing; DAVID BOGART, SVP of Business Affairs & Operations, Publishing & Partnership; DAVID GABRIEL, SVP of Sales & Marketing, Publishing; JEFF YOUNGQUIST, VP of Production & Special Projects; DAN CARR, Executive Director of Publishing Technology; ALEX MORALES, Director of Publishing Operations; SUSAN CRESPI, Production Manager; STAN LEE, Chairman Emeritus. For information regarding advertising in Marvel Comics or on Marvel.com, please contact Vit DeBellis, Custom Solutions & Integrated Advertising Manager, at vdebellis@marvel.com. For Marvel subscription inquiries, please call 888-511-5480. **Manufactured between 2/16/2018 and 3/20/2018 by SOLISCO PRINTERS, SCOTT, QC, CANADA.**

10 9 8 7 6 5 4 3 2 1

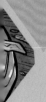

7

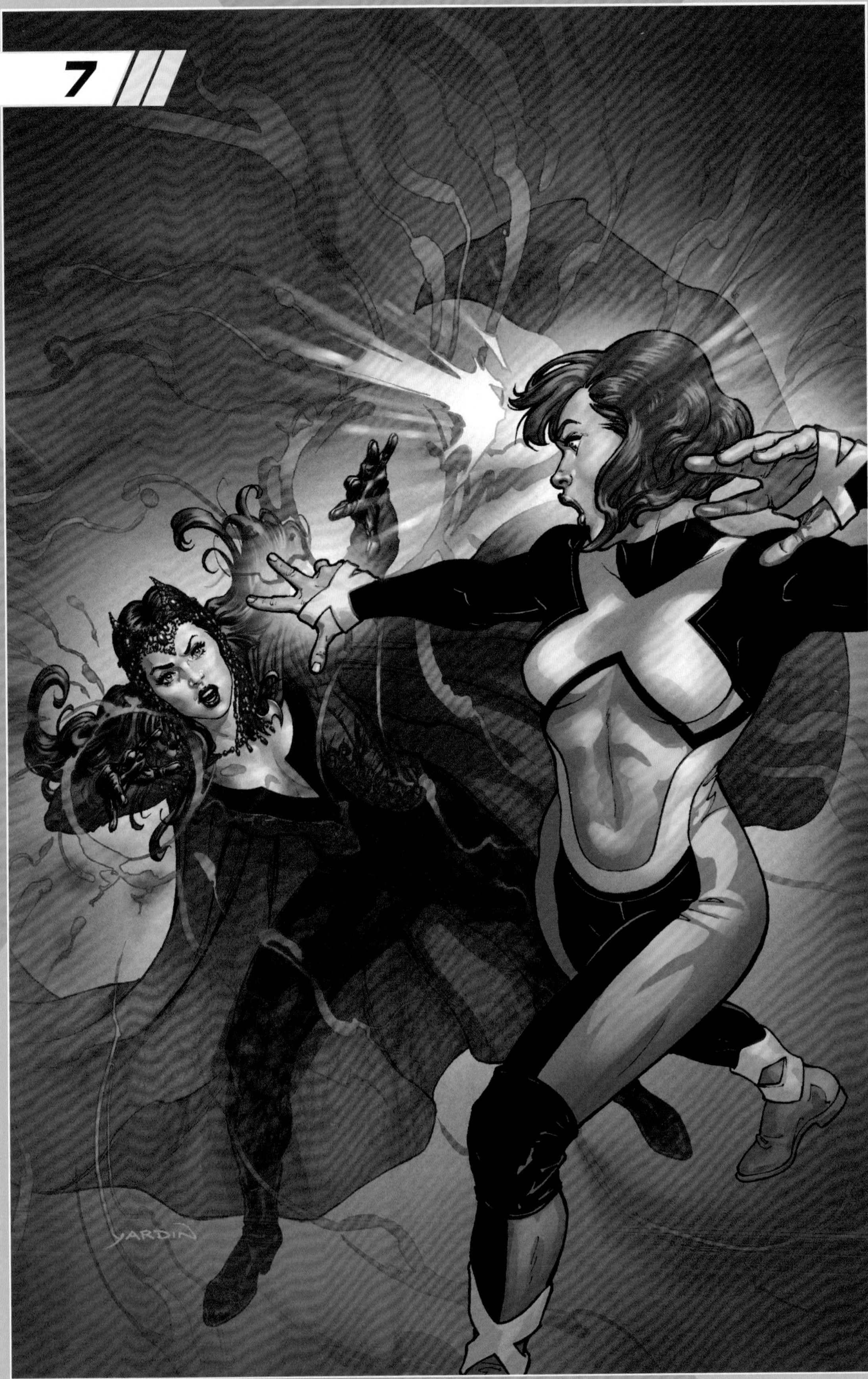
YARDIN

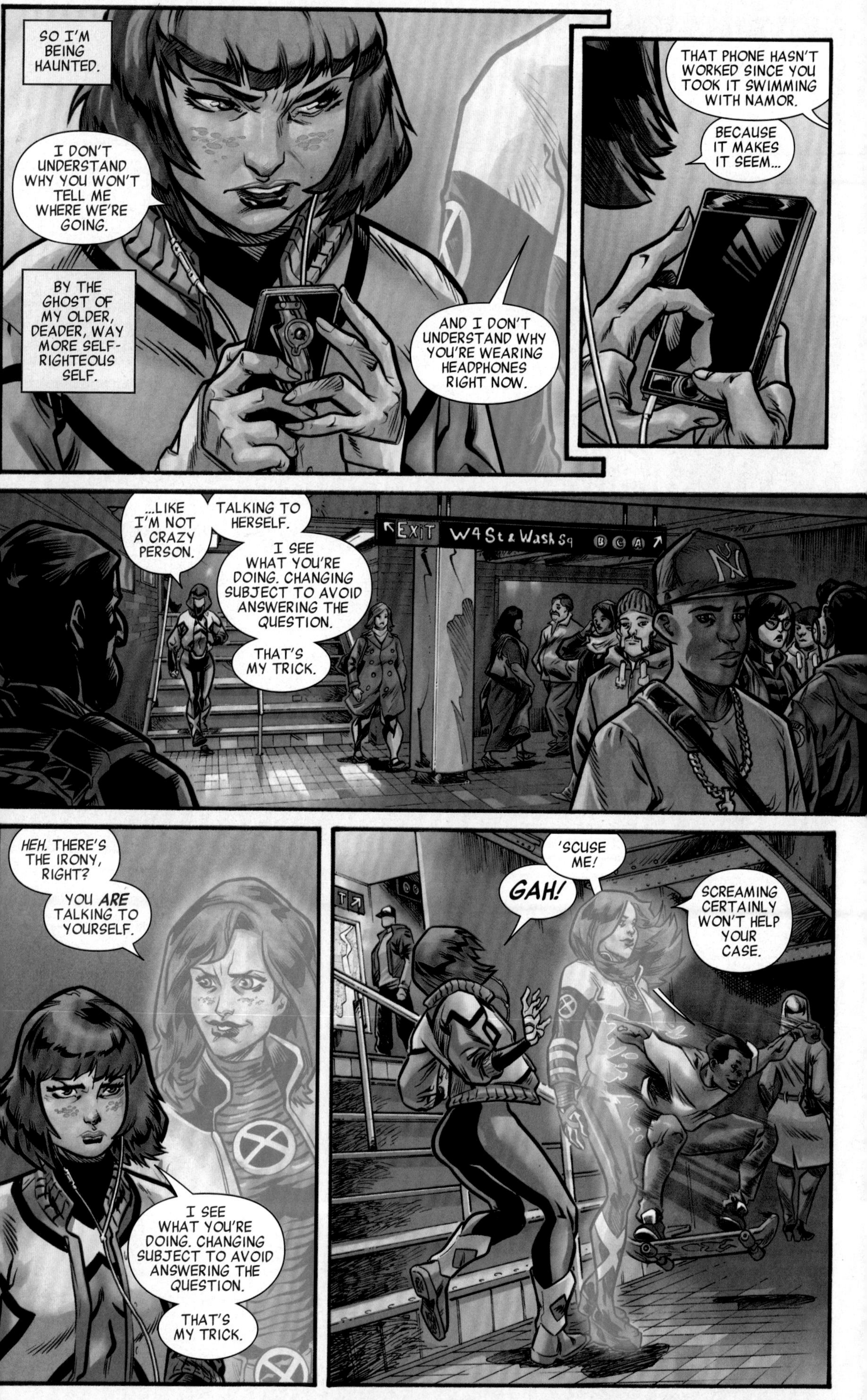
SO I'M BEING HAUNTED.
I DON'T UNDERSTAND WHY YOU WON'T TELL ME WHERE WE'RE GOING.
BY THE GHOST OF MY OLDER, DEADER, WAY MORE SELF-RIGHTEOUS SELF.
AND I DON'T UNDERSTAND WHY YOU'RE WEARING HEADPHONES RIGHT NOW.
THAT PHONE HASN'T WORKED SINCE YOU TOOK IT SWIMMING WITH NAMOR.
BECAUSE IT MAKES IT SEEM...
...LIKE I'M NOT A CRAZY PERSON.
TALKING TO HERSELF.
I SEE WHAT YOU'RE DOING. CHANGING SUBJECT TO AVOID ANSWERING THE QUESTION.
THAT'S MY TRICK.
EXIT W4 St & Wash Sq B C A
HEH. THERE'S THE IRONY, RIGHT?
YOU *ARE* TALKING TO YOURSELF.
I SEE WHAT YOU'RE DOING. CHANGING SUBJECT TO AVOID ANSWERING THE QUESTION.
THAT'S MY TRICK.
'SCUSE ME!
GAH!
SCREAMING CERTAINLY WON'T HELP YOUR CASE.

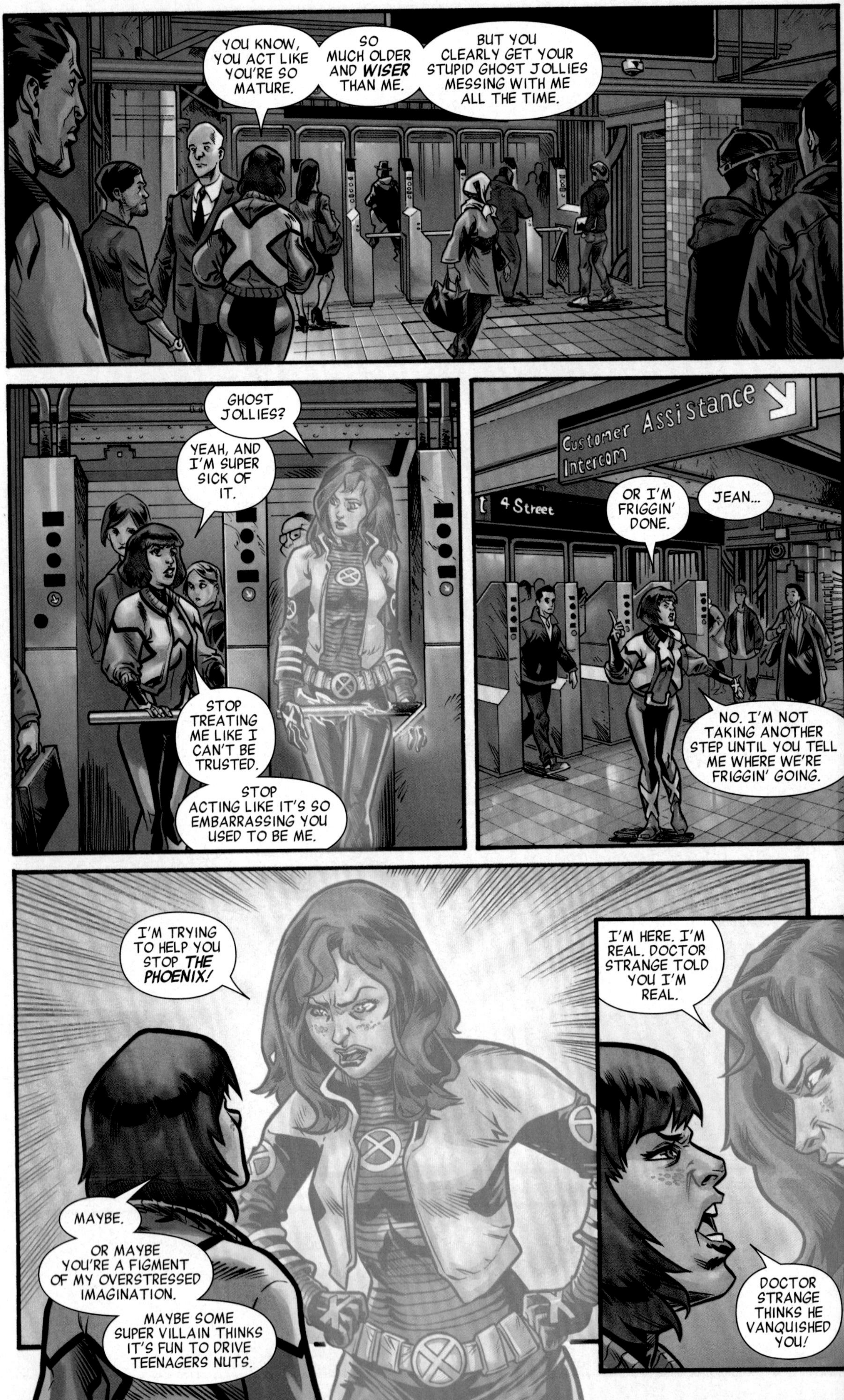

YOU KNOW, YOU ACT LIKE YOU'RE SO MATURE.
SO MUCH OLDER AND WISER THAN ME.
BUT YOU CLEARLY GET YOUR STUPID GHOST JOLLIES MESSING WITH ME ALL THE TIME.
GHOST JOLLIES?
YEAH, AND I'M SUPER SICK OF IT.
STOP TREATING ME LIKE I CAN'T BE TRUSTED.
STOP ACTING LIKE IT'S SO EMBARRASSING YOU USED TO BE ME.
Customer Assistance Intercom
4 Street
OR I'M FRIGGIN' DONE.
JEAN...
NO. I'M NOT TAKING ANOTHER STEP UNTIL YOU TELL ME WHERE WE'RE FRIGGIN' GOING.
I'M TRYING TO HELP YOU STOP THE PHOENIX!
MAYBE.
OR MAYBE YOU'RE A FIGMENT OF MY OVERSTRESSED IMAGINATION.
MAYBE SOME SUPER VILLAIN THINKS IT'S FUN TO DRIVE TEENAGERS NUTS.
I'M HERE. I'M REAL. DOCTOR STRANGE TOLD YOU I'M REAL.
DOCTOR STRANGE THINKS HE VANQUISHED YOU!

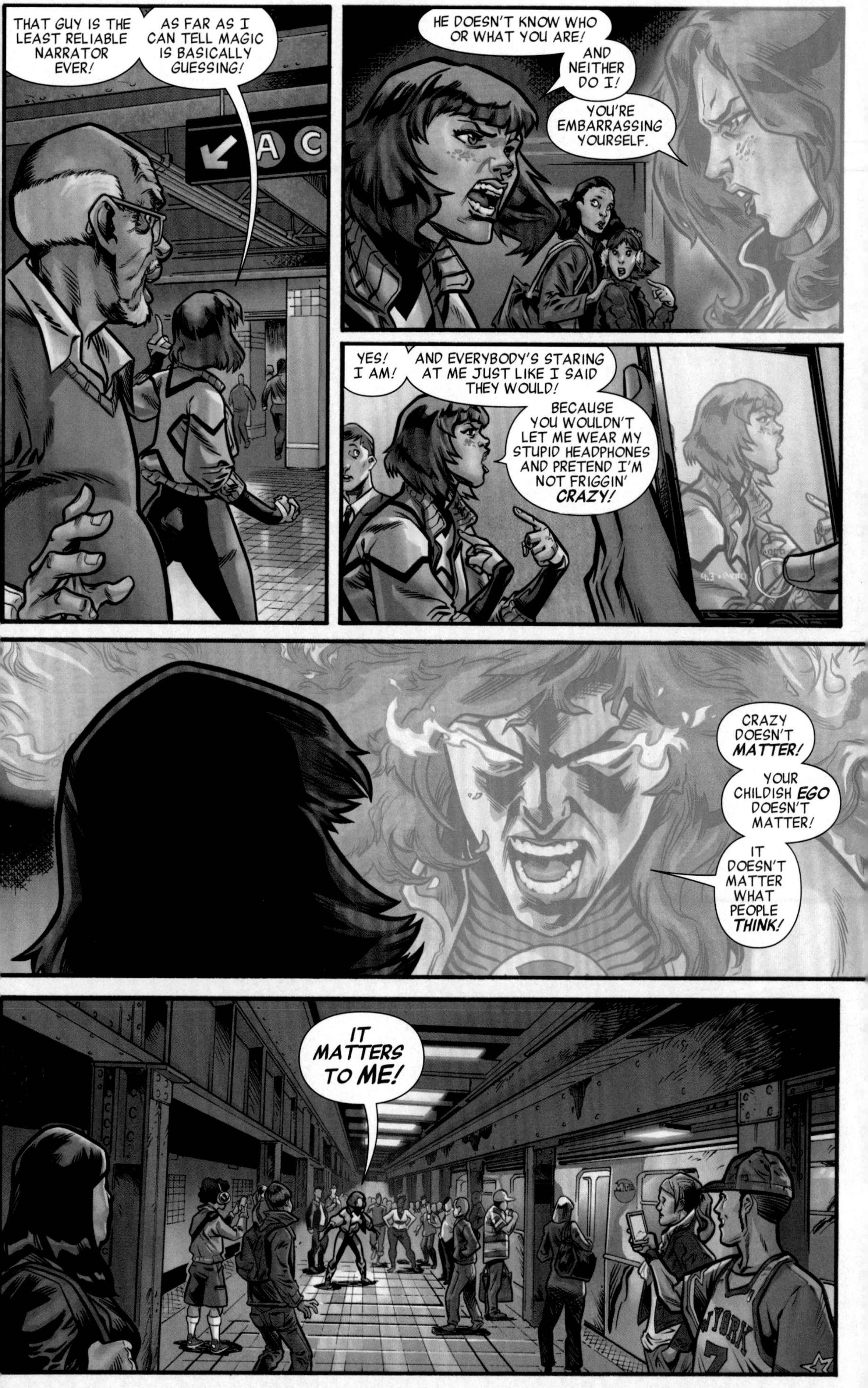
THAT GUY IS THE LEAST RELIABLE NARRATOR EVER!
AS FAR AS I CAN TELL MAGIC IS BASICALLY GUESSING!
A
C
HE DOESN'T KNOW WHO OR WHAT YOU ARE!
AND NEITHER DO I!
YOU'RE EMBARRASSING YOURSELF.
YES! I AM!
AND EVERYBODY'S STARING AT ME JUST LIKE I SAID THEY WOULD!
BECAUSE YOU WOULDN'T LET ME WEAR MY STUPID HEADPHONES AND PRETEND I'M NOT FRIGGIN' CRAZY!
CRAZY DOESN'T MATTER!
YOUR CHILDISH EGO DOESN'T MATTER!
IT DOESN'T MATTER WHAT PEOPLE THINK!
IT MATTERS TO ME!

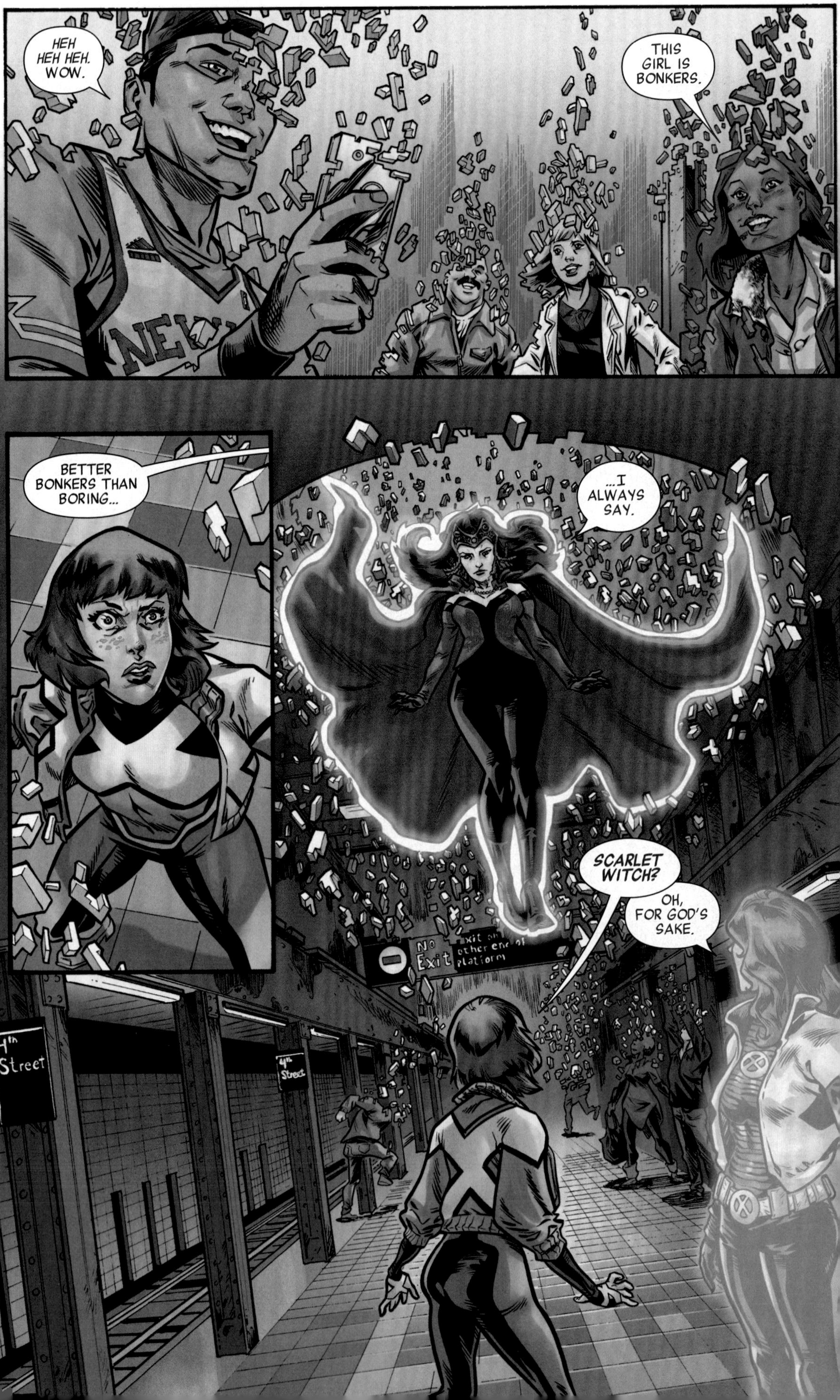
HEH HEH HEH. WOW.
THIS GIRL IS BONKERS.
BETTER BONKERS THAN BORING...
...I ALWAYS SAY.
SCARLET WITCH?
OH, FOR GOD'S SAKE.
No Exit
xit on other end of platform
4th Street
4th Street

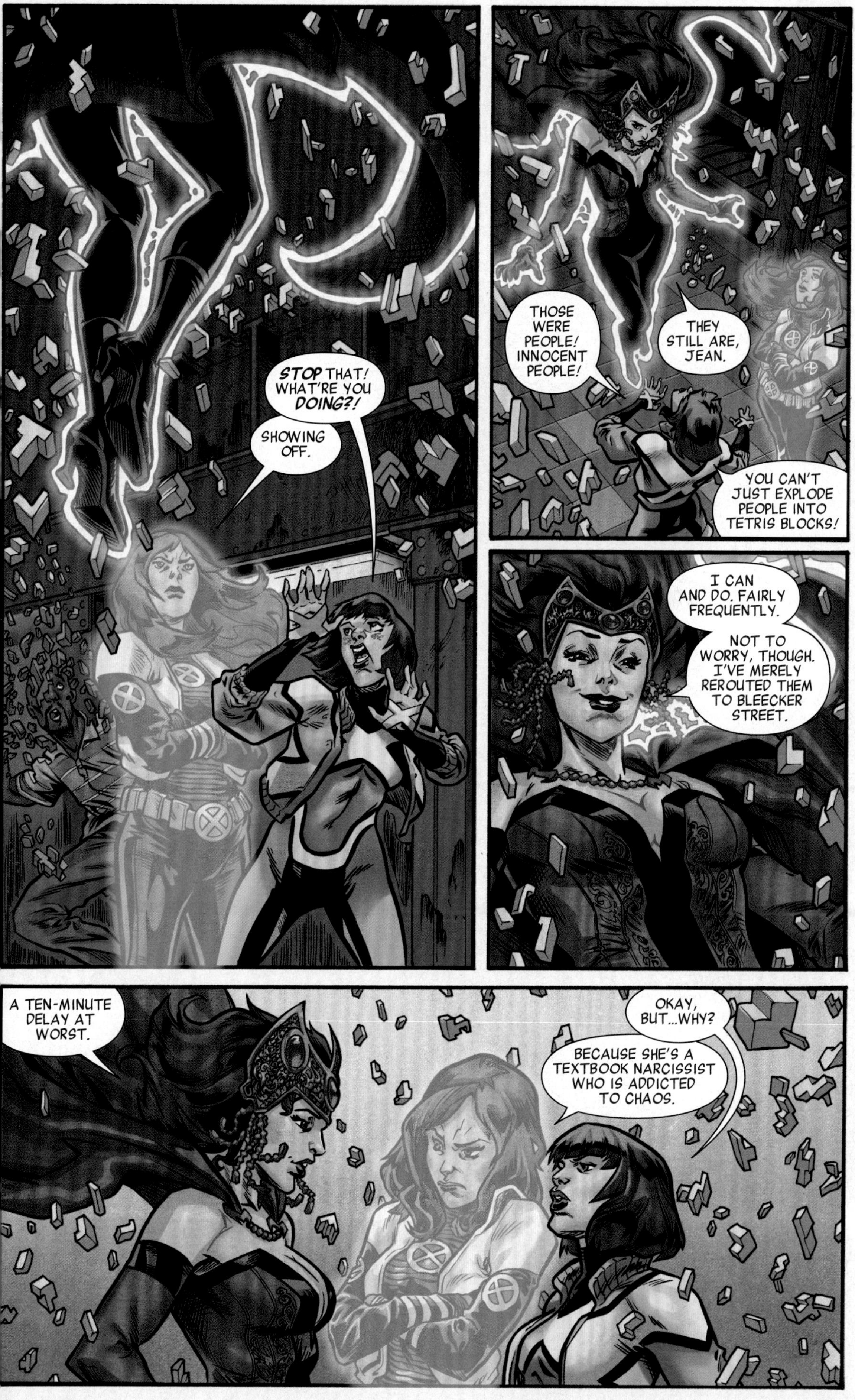
STOP THAT! WHAT'RE YOU DOING?!
SHOWING OFF.
THOSE WERE PEOPLE! INNOCENT PEOPLE!
THEY STILL ARE, JEAN.
YOU CAN'T JUST EXPLODE PEOPLE INTO TETRIS BLOCKS!
I CAN AND DO. FAIRLY FREQUENTLY.
NOT TO WORRY, THOUGH. I'VE MERELY REROUTED THEM TO BLEECKER STREET.
A TEN-MINUTE DELAY AT WORST.
OKAY, BUT...WHY?
BECAUSE SHE'S A TEXTBOOK NARCISSIST WHO IS ADDICTED TO CHAOS.

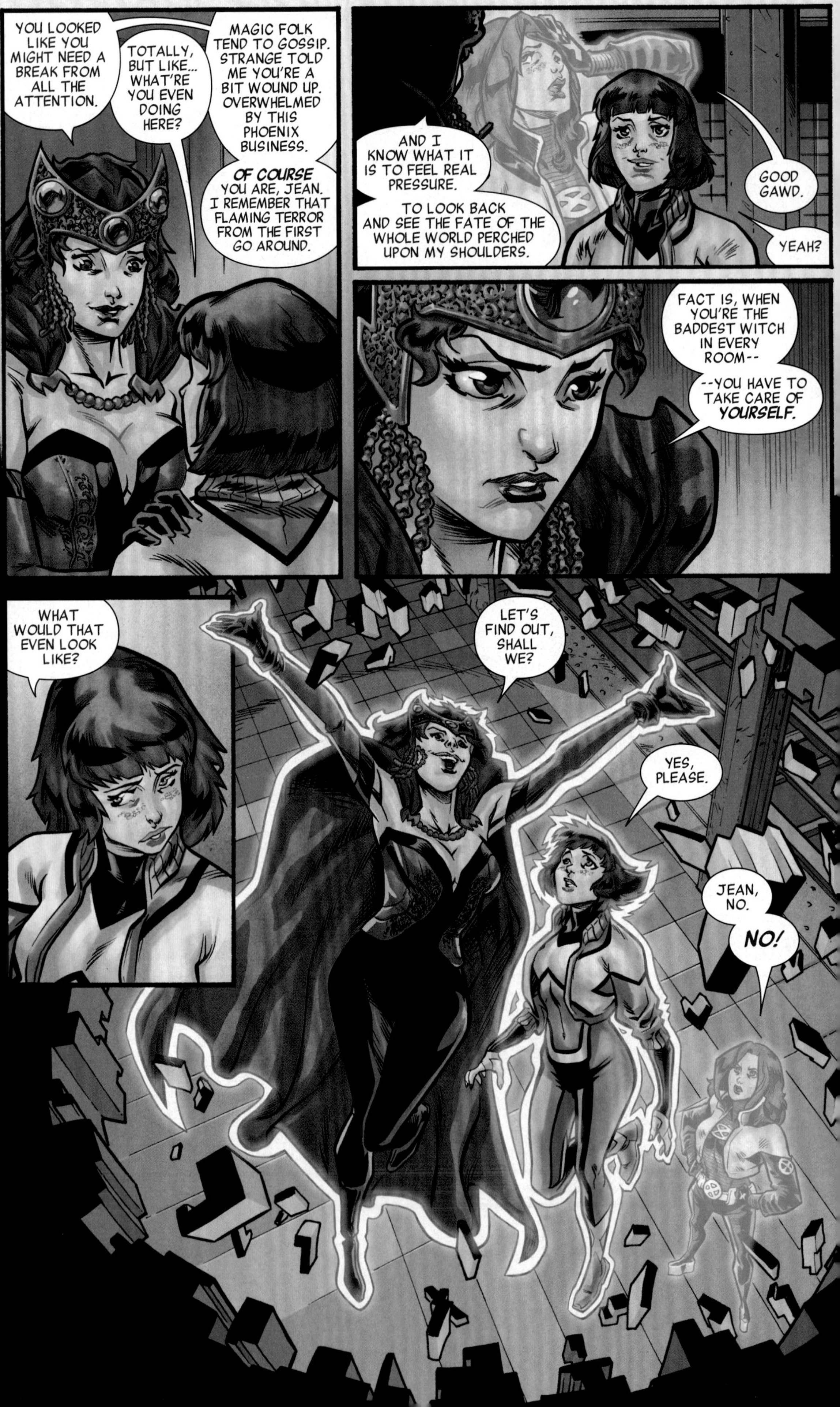

YOU LOOKED LIKE YOU MIGHT NEED A BREAK FROM ALL THE ATTENTION.
TOTALLY, BUT LIKE... WHAT'RE YOU EVEN DOING HERE?
MAGIC FOLK TEND TO GOSSIP. STRANGE TOLD ME YOU'RE A BIT WOUND UP. OVERWHELMED BY THIS PHOENIX BUSINESS.
OF COURSE YOU ARE, JEAN. I REMEMBER THAT FLAMING TERROR FROM THE FIRST GO AROUND.
AND I KNOW WHAT IT IS TO FEEL REAL PRESSURE.
TO LOOK BACK AND SEE THE FATE OF THE WHOLE WORLD PERCHED UPON MY SHOULDERS.
GOOD GAWD.
YEAH?
FACT IS, WHEN YOU'RE THE BADDEST WITCH IN EVERY ROOM--
--YOU HAVE TO TAKE CARE OF YOURSELF.
WHAT WOULD THAT EVEN LOOK LIKE?
LET'S FIND OUT, SHALL WE?
YES, PLEASE.
JEAN, NO.
NO!

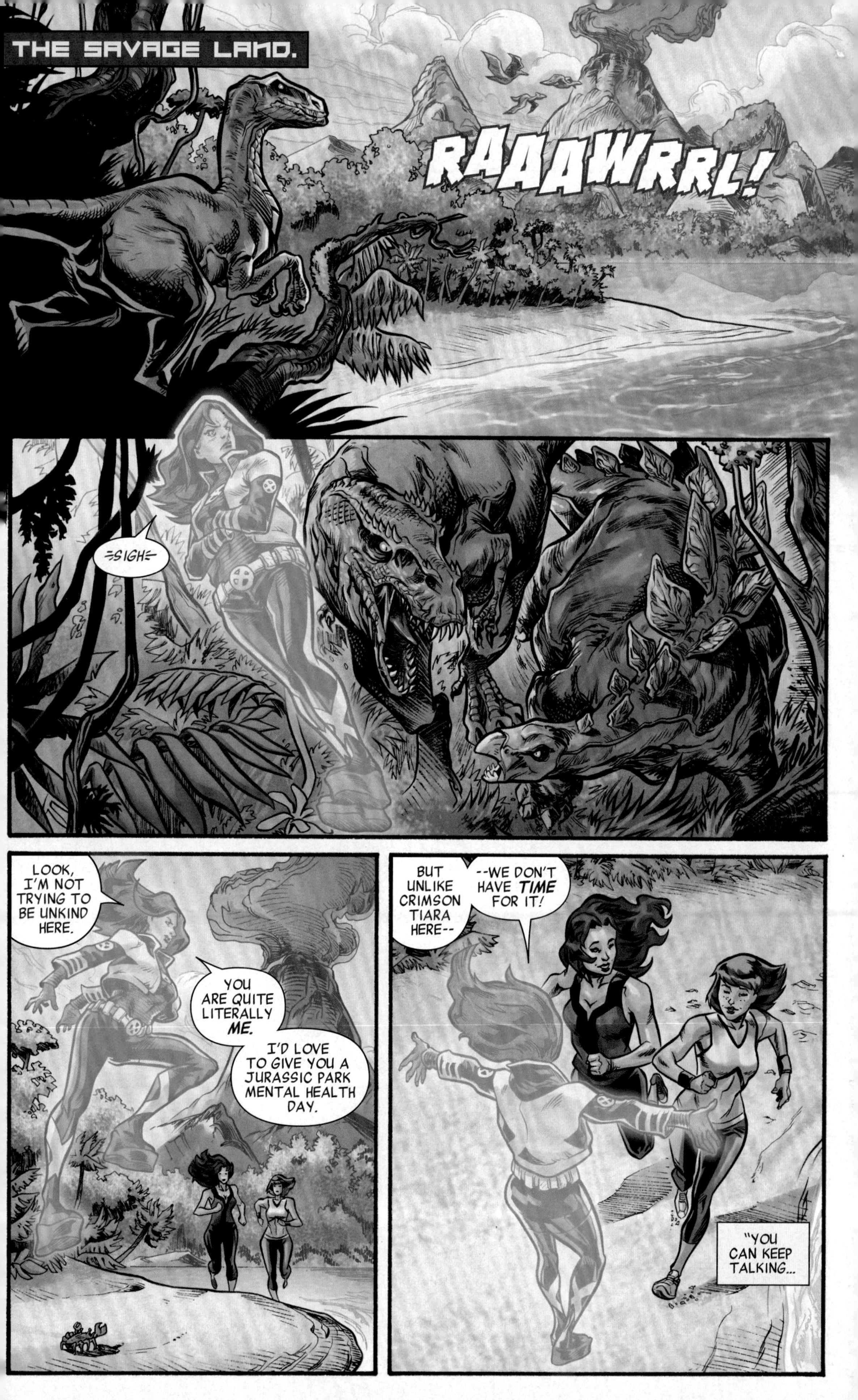
THE SAVAGE LAND.
RAAAWRRL!
=SIGH=
LOOK, I'M NOT TRYING TO BE UNKIND HERE.
YOU ARE QUITE LITERALLY ME.
I'D LOVE TO GIVE YOU A JURASSIC PARK MENTAL HEALTH DAY.
BUT UNLIKE CRIMSON TIARA HERE--
--WE DON'T HAVE TIME FOR IT!
"YOU CAN KEEP TALKING...

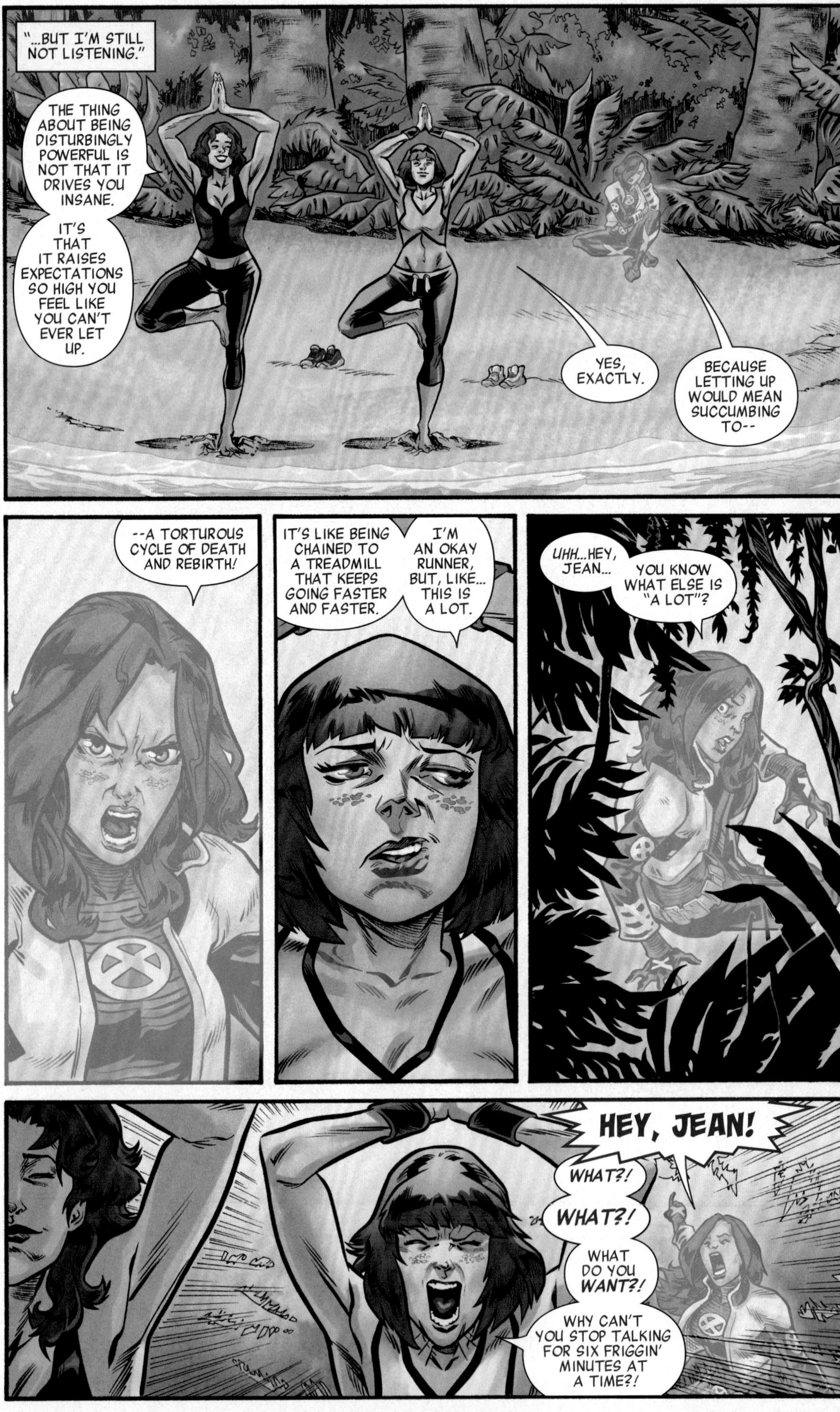
"...BUT I'M STILL NOT LISTENING."
THE THING ABOUT BEING DISTURBINGLY POWERFUL IS NOT THAT IT DRIVES YOU INSANE.
IT'S THAT IT RAISES EXPECTATIONS SO HIGH YOU FEEL LIKE YOU CAN'T EVER LET UP.
YES, EXACTLY.
BECAUSE LETTING UP WOULD MEAN SUCCUMBING TO--
--A TORTUROUS CYCLE OF DEATH AND REBIRTH!
IT'S LIKE BEING CHAINED TO A TREADMILL THAT KEEPS GOING FASTER AND FASTER.
I'M AN OKAY RUNNER, BUT, LIKE... THIS IS A LOT.
UHH...HEY, JEAN...
YOU KNOW WHAT ELSE IS "A LOT"?
HEY, JEAN!
WHAT?!
WHAT?!
WHAT DO YOU WANT?!
WHY CAN'T YOU STOP TALKING FOR SIX FRIGGIN' MINUTES AT A TIME?!

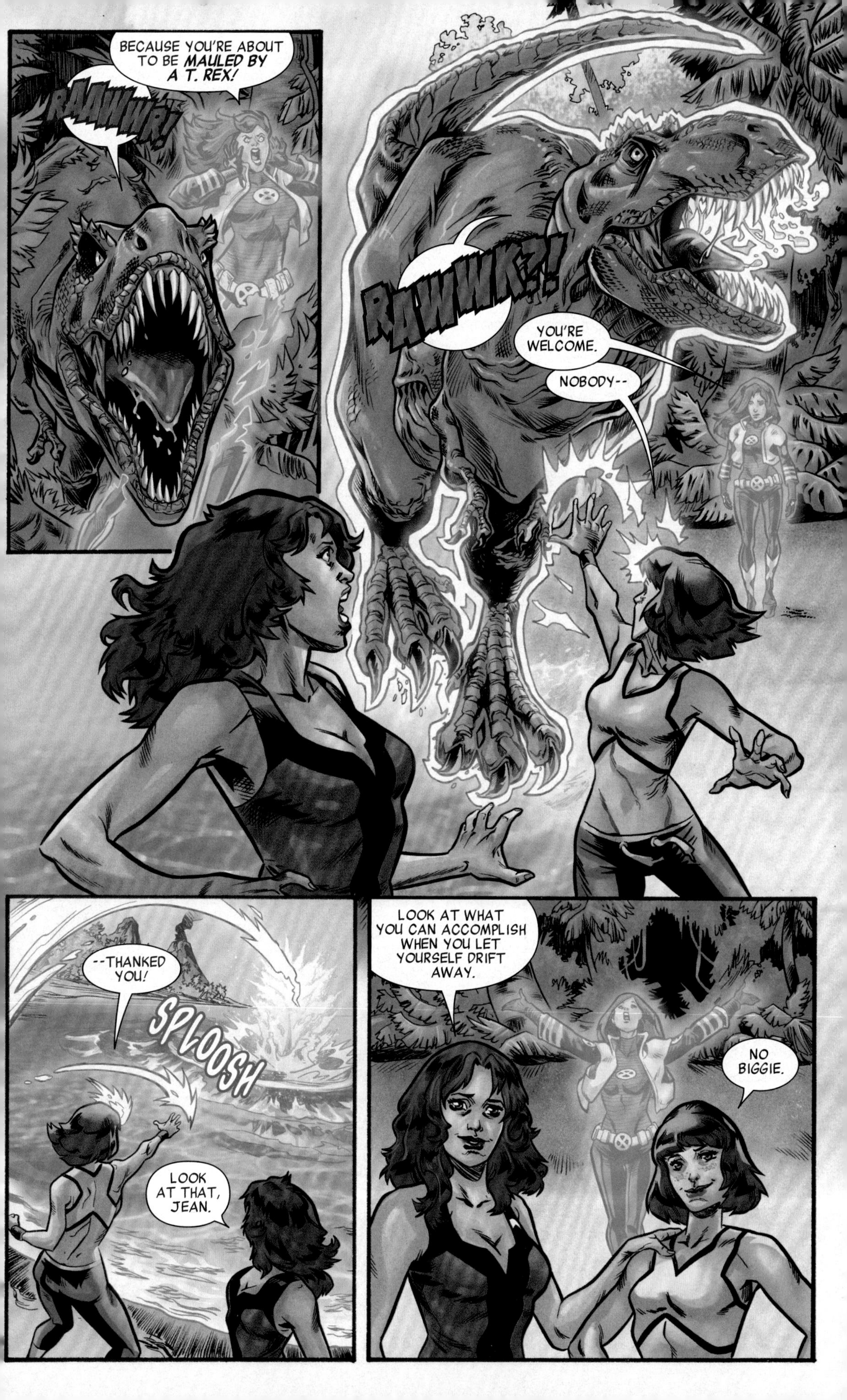
BECAUSE YOU'RE ABOUT TO BE MAULED BY A T. REX!
RAAWWR!
RAWWK?!
YOU'RE WELCOME.
NOBODY--
--THANKED YOU!
SPLOOSH
LOOK AT THAT, JEAN.
LOOK AT WHAT YOU CAN ACCOMPLISH WHEN YOU LET YOURSELF DRIFT AWAY.
NO BIGGIE.

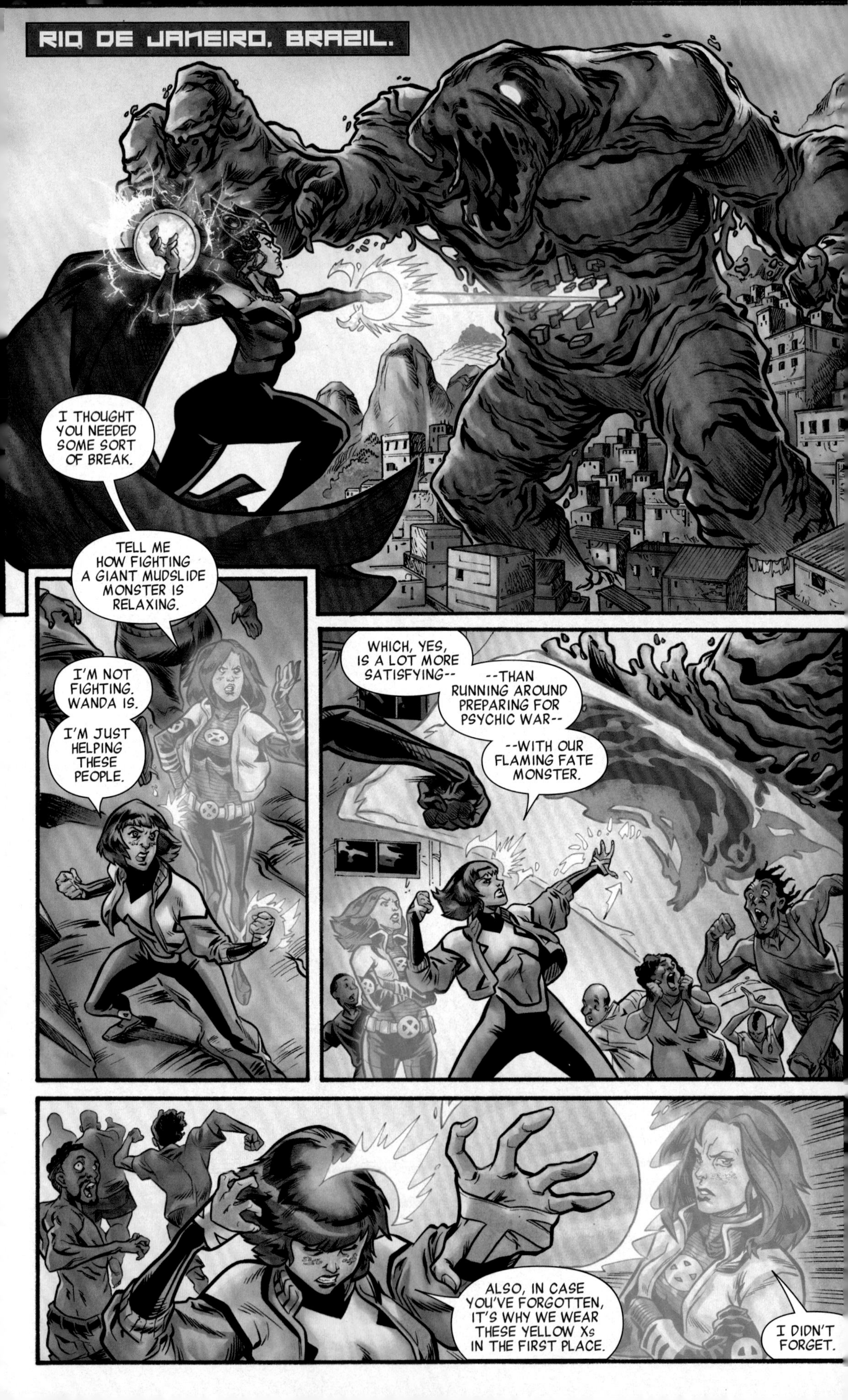
RIO DE JANEIRO, BRAZIL.
I THOUGHT YOU NEEDED SOME SORT OF BREAK.
TELL ME HOW FIGHTING A GIANT MUDSLIDE MONSTER IS RELAXING.
I'M NOT FIGHTING. WANDA IS.
I'M JUST HELPING THESE PEOPLE.
WHICH, YES, IS A LOT MORE SATISFYING--
--THAN RUNNING AROUND PREPARING FOR PSYCHIC WAR--
--WITH OUR FLAMING FATE MONSTER.
ALSO, IN CASE YOU'VE FORGOTTEN, IT'S WHY WE WEAR THESE YELLOW Xs IN THE FIRST PLACE.
I DIDN'T FORGET.

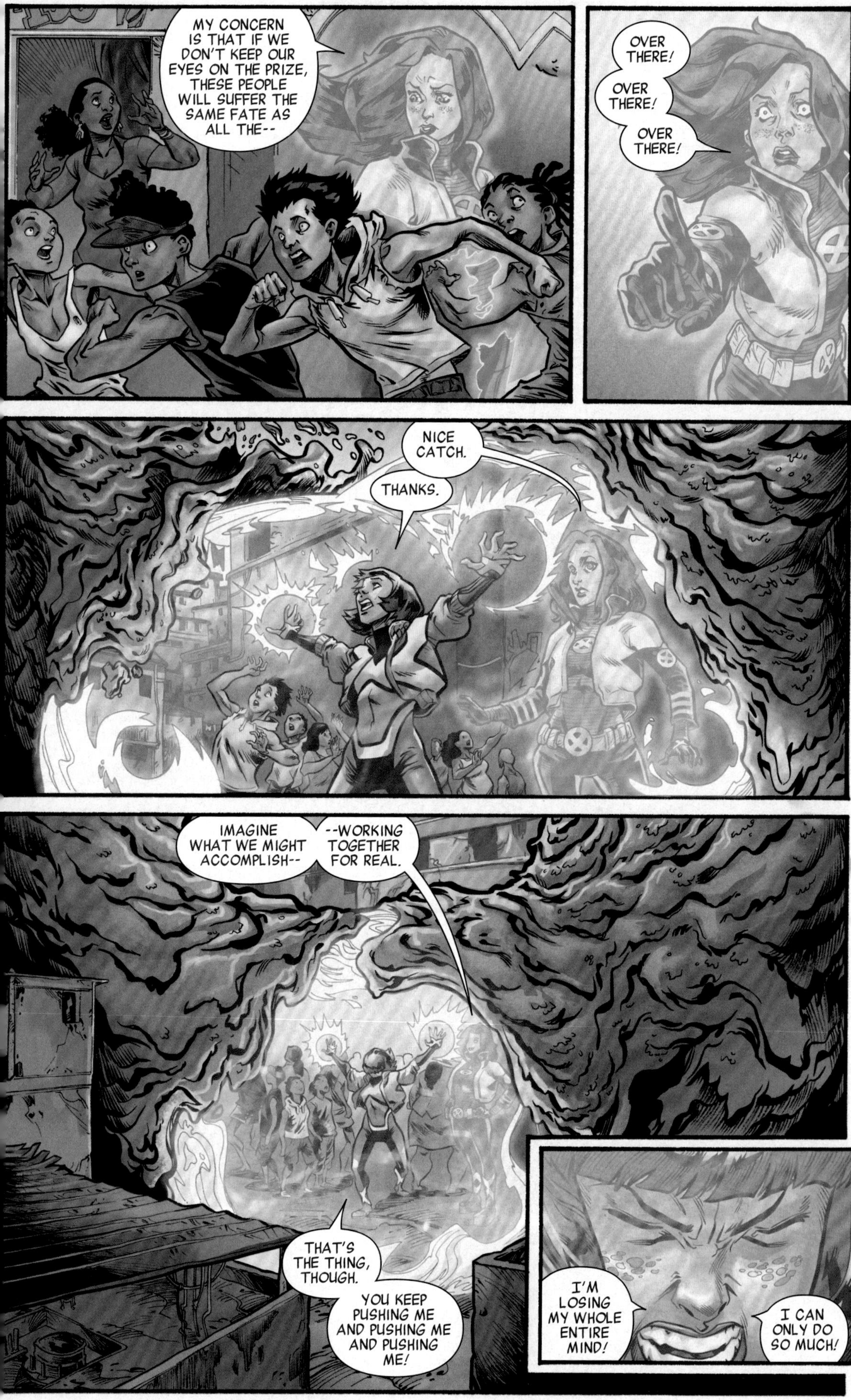
MY CONCERN IS THAT IF WE DON'T KEEP OUR EYES ON THE PRIZE, THESE PEOPLE WILL SUFFER THE SAME FATE AS ALL THE--
OVER THERE!
OVER THERE!
OVER THERE!
NICE CATCH.
THANKS.
IMAGINE WHAT WE MIGHT ACCOMPLISH--
--WORKING TOGETHER FOR REAL.
THAT'S THE THING, THOUGH.
YOU KEEP PUSHING ME AND PUSHING ME AND PUSHING ME!
I'M LOSING MY WHOLE ENTIRE MIND!
I CAN ONLY DO SO MUCH!

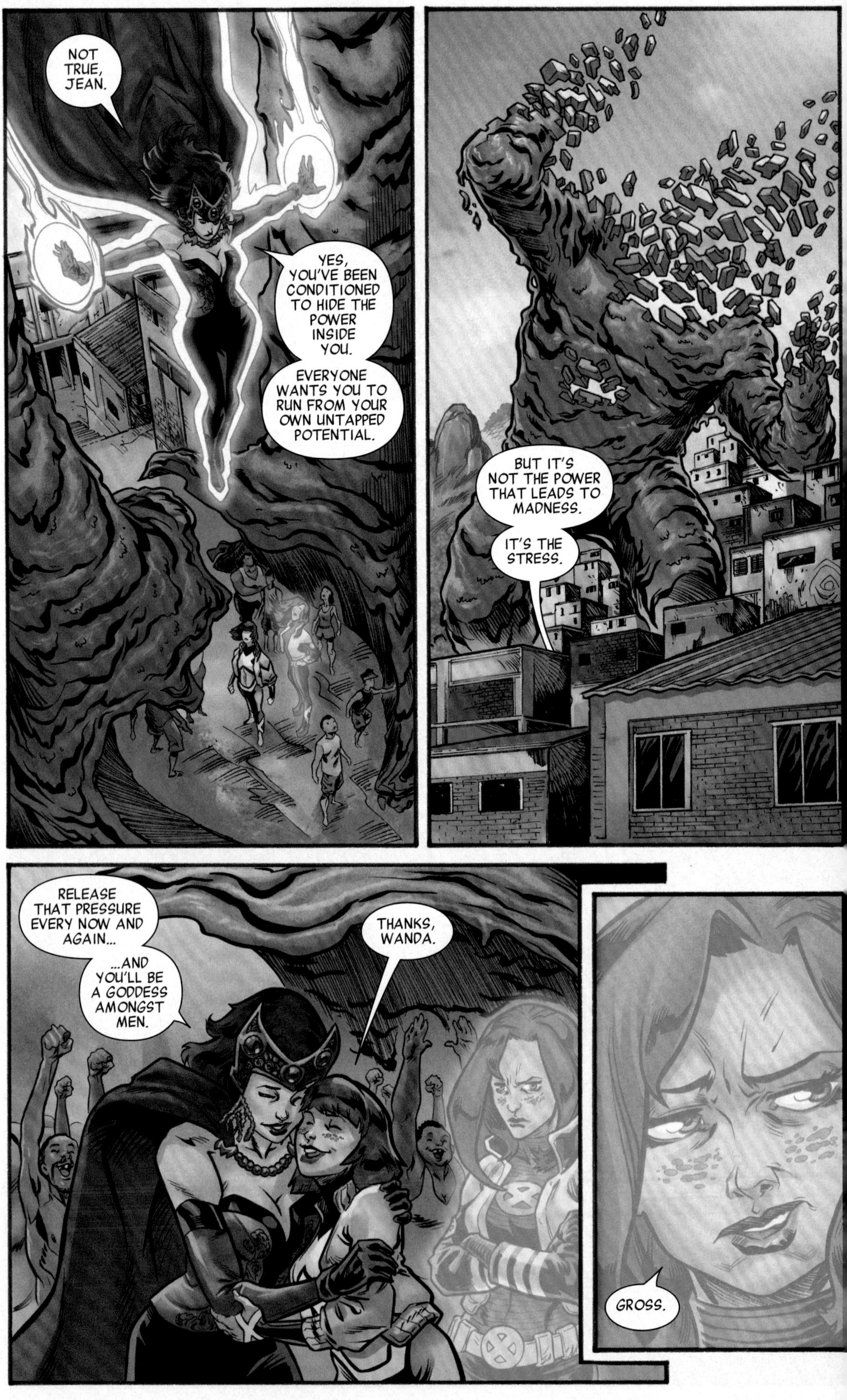
NOT TRUE, JEAN.
YES, YOU'VE BEEN CONDITIONED TO HIDE THE POWER INSIDE YOU.
EVERYONE WANTS YOU TO RUN FROM YOUR OWN UNTAPPED POTENTIAL.
BUT IT'S NOT THE POWER THAT LEADS TO MADNESS.
IT'S THE STRESS.
RELEASE THAT PRESSURE EVERY NOW AND AGAIN...
...AND YOU'LL BE A GODDESS AMONGST MEN.
THANKS, WANDA.
GROSS.

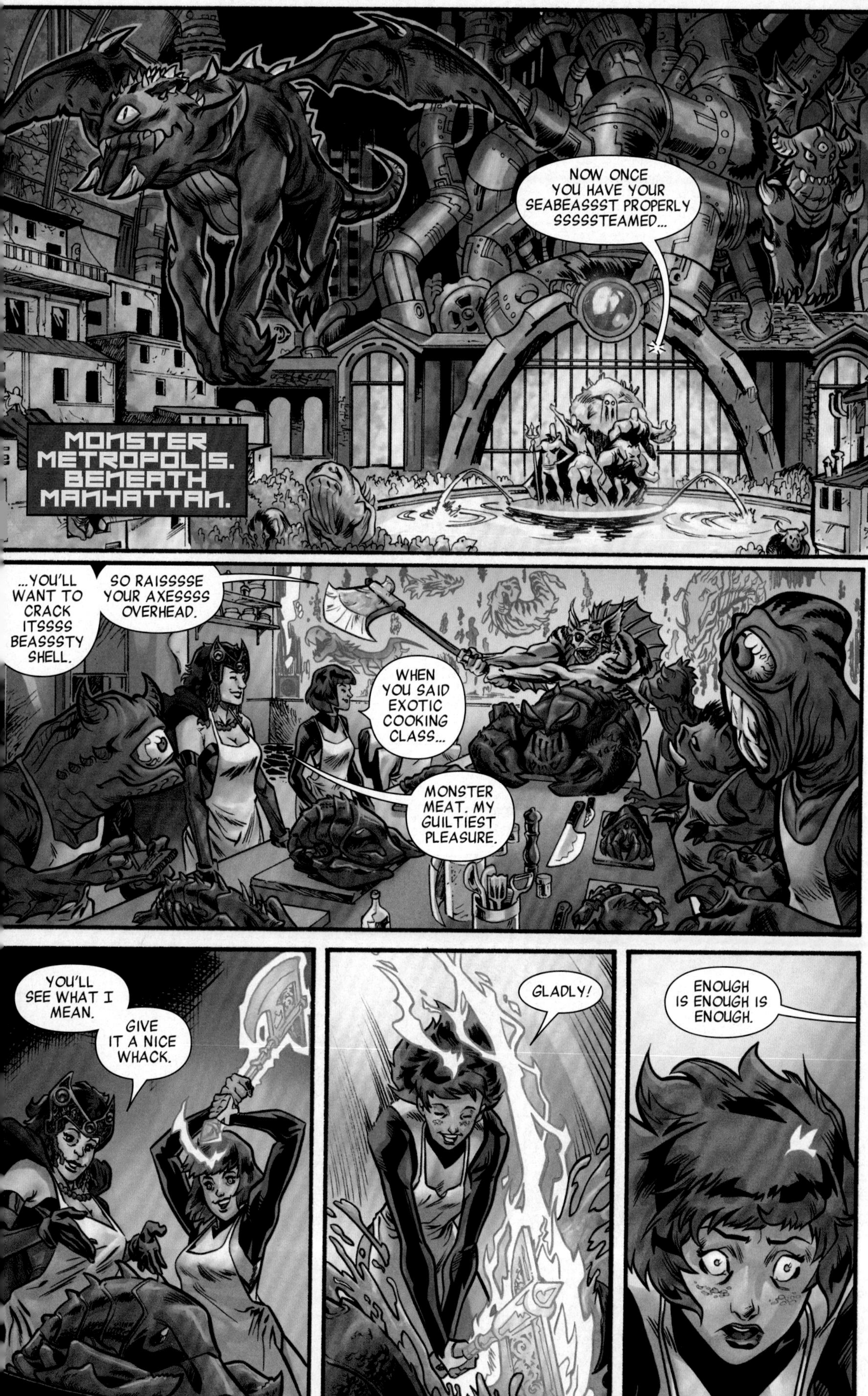
NOW ONCE YOU HAVE YOUR SEABEASSST PROPERLY SSSSSTEAMED...
MONSTER METROPOLIS. BENEATH MANHATTAN.
...YOU'LL WANT TO CRACK ITSSSS BEASSSTY SHELL.
SO RAISSSSE YOUR AXESSSS OVERHEAD.
WHEN YOU SAID EXOTIC COOKING CLASS...
MONSTER MEAT. MY GUILTIEST PLEASURE.
YOU'LL SEE WHAT I MEAN.
GIVE IT A NICE WHACK.
GLADLY!
ENOUGH IS ENOUGH IS ENOUGH.

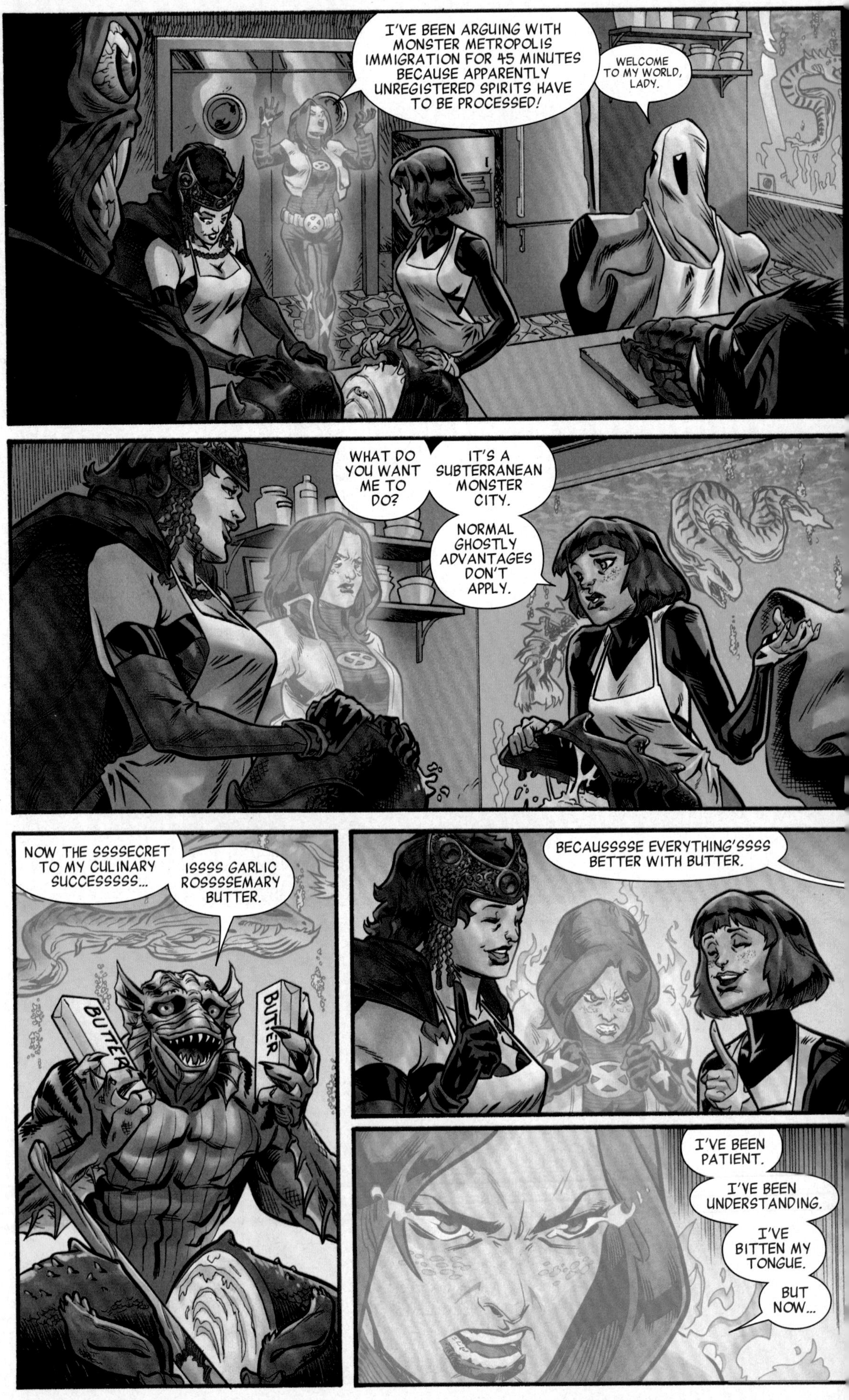

I'VE BEEN ARGUING WITH MONSTER METROPOLIS IMMIGRATION FOR 45 MINUTES BECAUSE APPARENTLY UNREGISTERED SPIRITS HAVE TO BE PROCESSED!
WELCOME TO MY WORLD, LADY.
WHAT DO YOU WANT ME TO DO?
IT'S A SUBTERRANEAN MONSTER CITY.
NORMAL GHOSTLY ADVANTAGES DON'T APPLY.
NOW THE SSSSECRET TO MY CULINARY SUCCESSSSS...
ISSSS GARLIC ROSSSSEMARY BUTTER.
BUTTER
BUTTER
BECAUSSSSE EVERYTHING'SSSS BETTER WITH BUTTER.
I'VE BEEN PATIENT.
I'VE BEEN UNDERSTANDING.
I'VE BITTEN MY TONGUE.
BUT NOW...

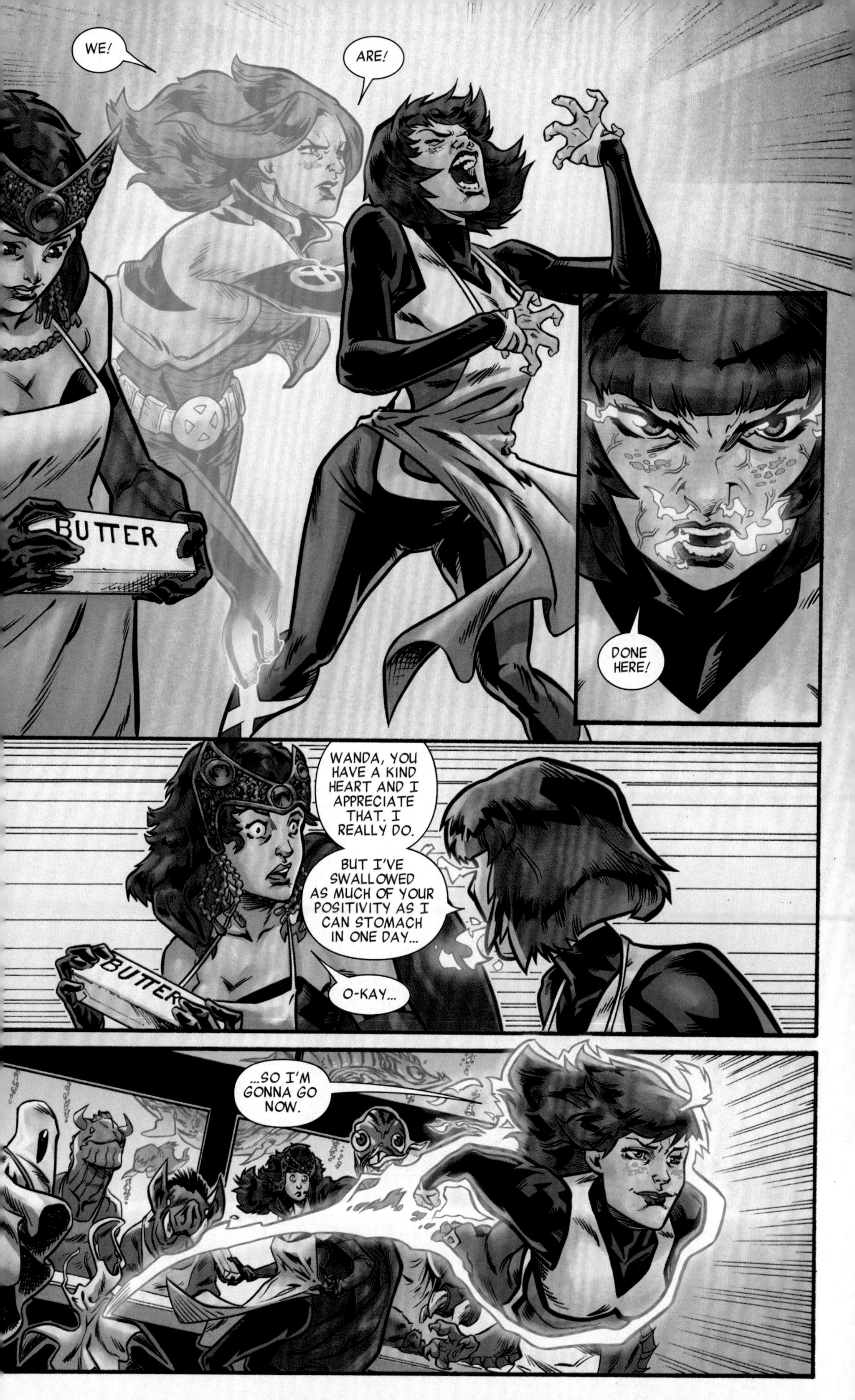

WE!
ARE!
DONE HERE!
WANDA, YOU HAVE A KIND HEART AND I APPRECIATE THAT. I REALLY DO.
BUT I'VE SWALLOWED AS MUCH OF YOUR POSITIVITY AS I CAN STOMACH IN ONE DAY...
O-KAY...
...SO I'M GONNA GO NOW.

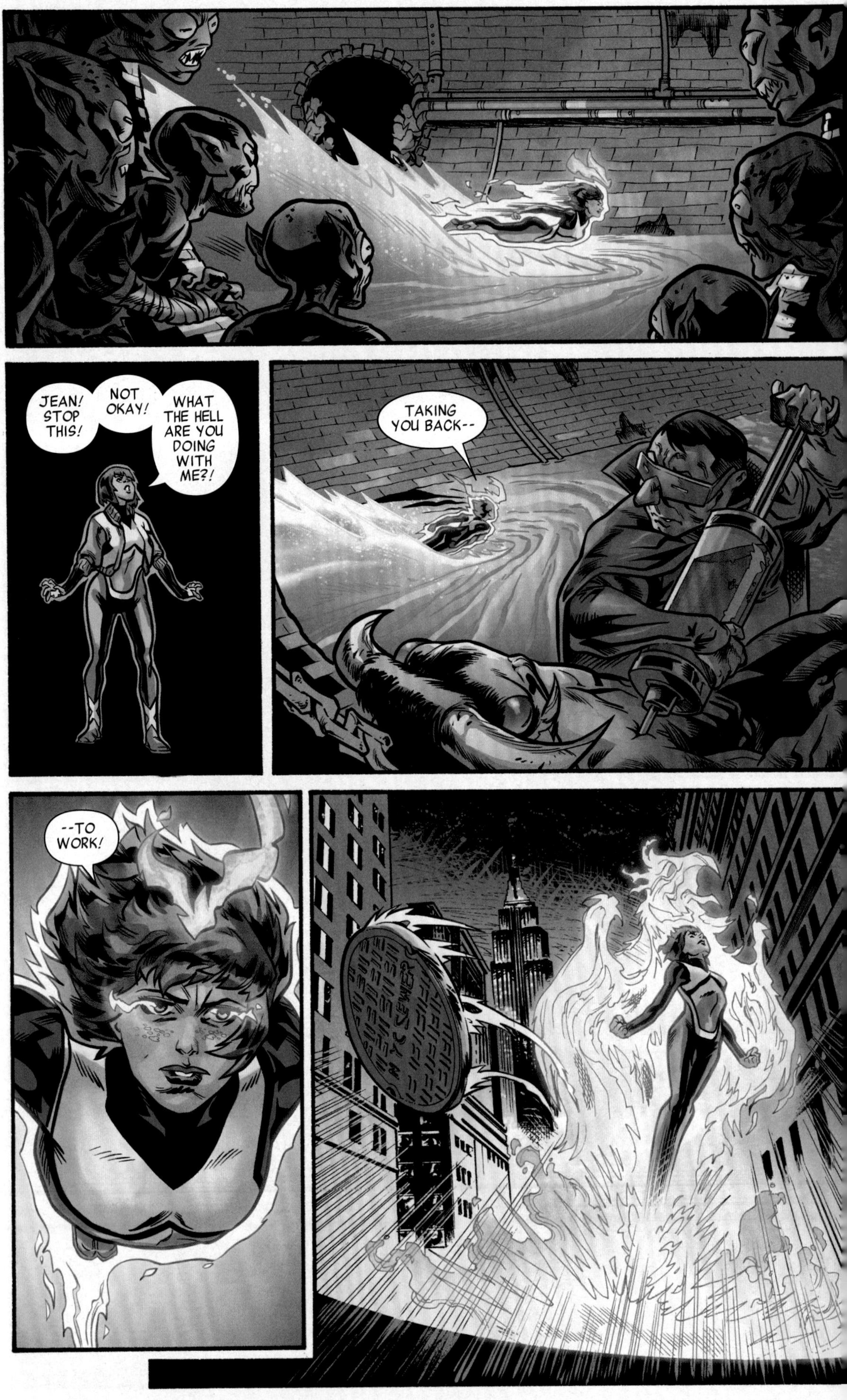
JEAN! STOP THIS!
NOT OKAY!
WHAT THE HELL ARE YOU DOING WITH ME?!
TAKING YOU BACK--
--TO WORK!

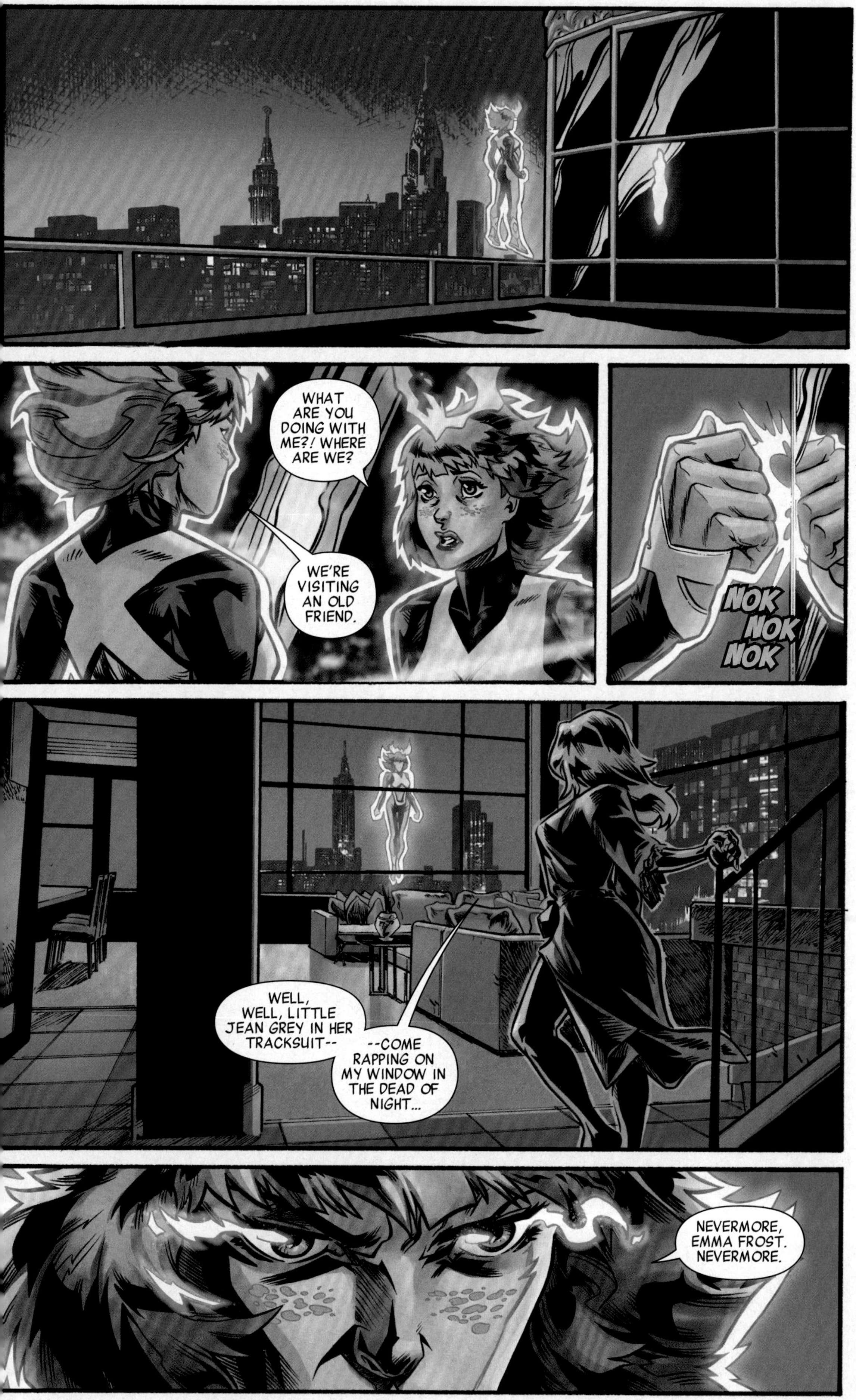
WHAT ARE YOU DOING WITH ME?! WHERE ARE WE?
WE'RE VISITING AN OLD FRIEND.
NOK NOK NOK
WELL, WELL, LITTLE JEAN GREY IN HER TRACKSUIT--
--COME RAPPING ON MY WINDOW IN THE DEAD OF NIGHT...
NEVERMORE, EMMA FROST. NEVERMORE.

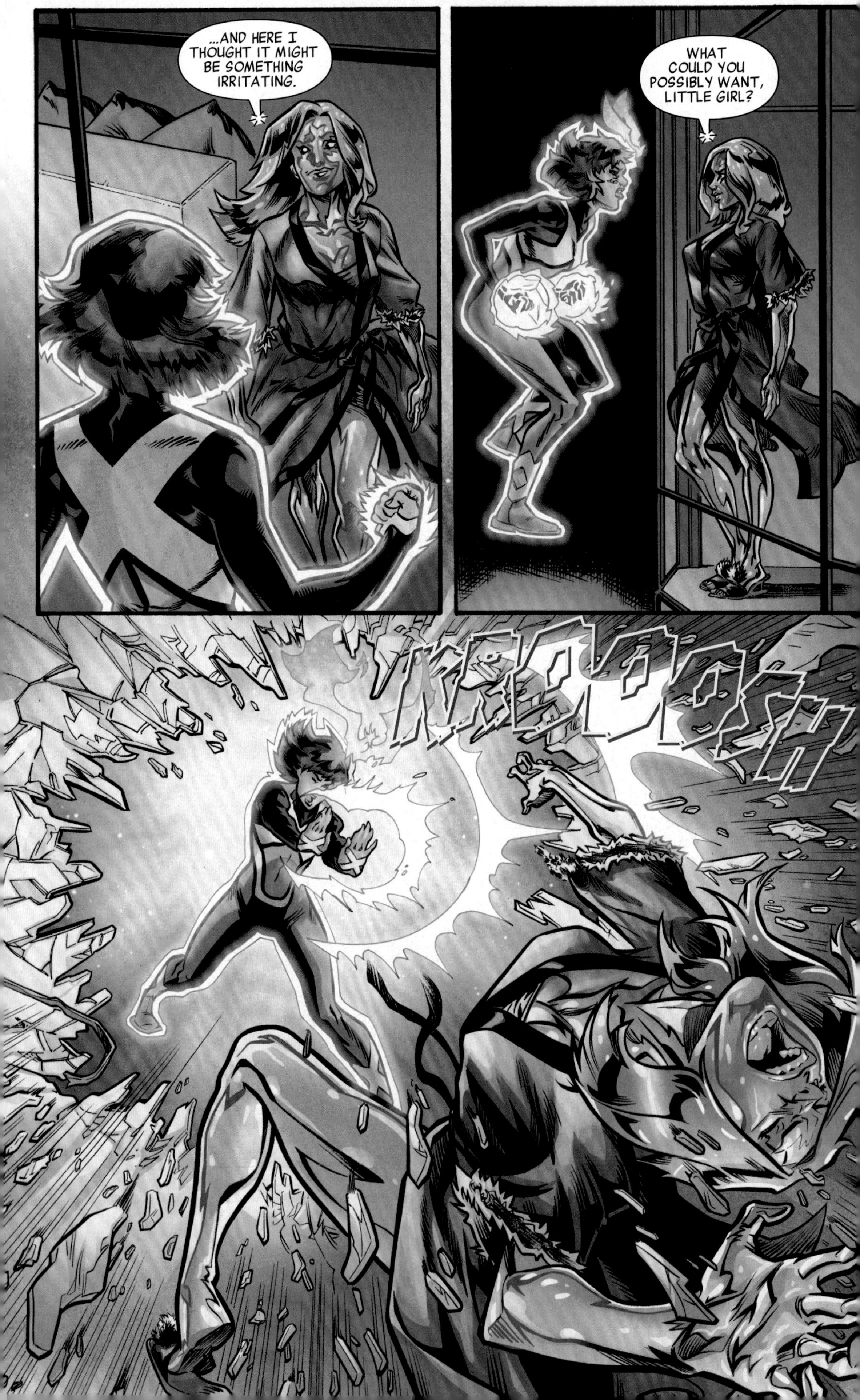

...AND HERE I THOUGHT IT MIGHT BE SOMETHING IRRITATING.
WHAT COULD YOU POSSIBLY WANT, LITTLE GIRL?
KROOOSH

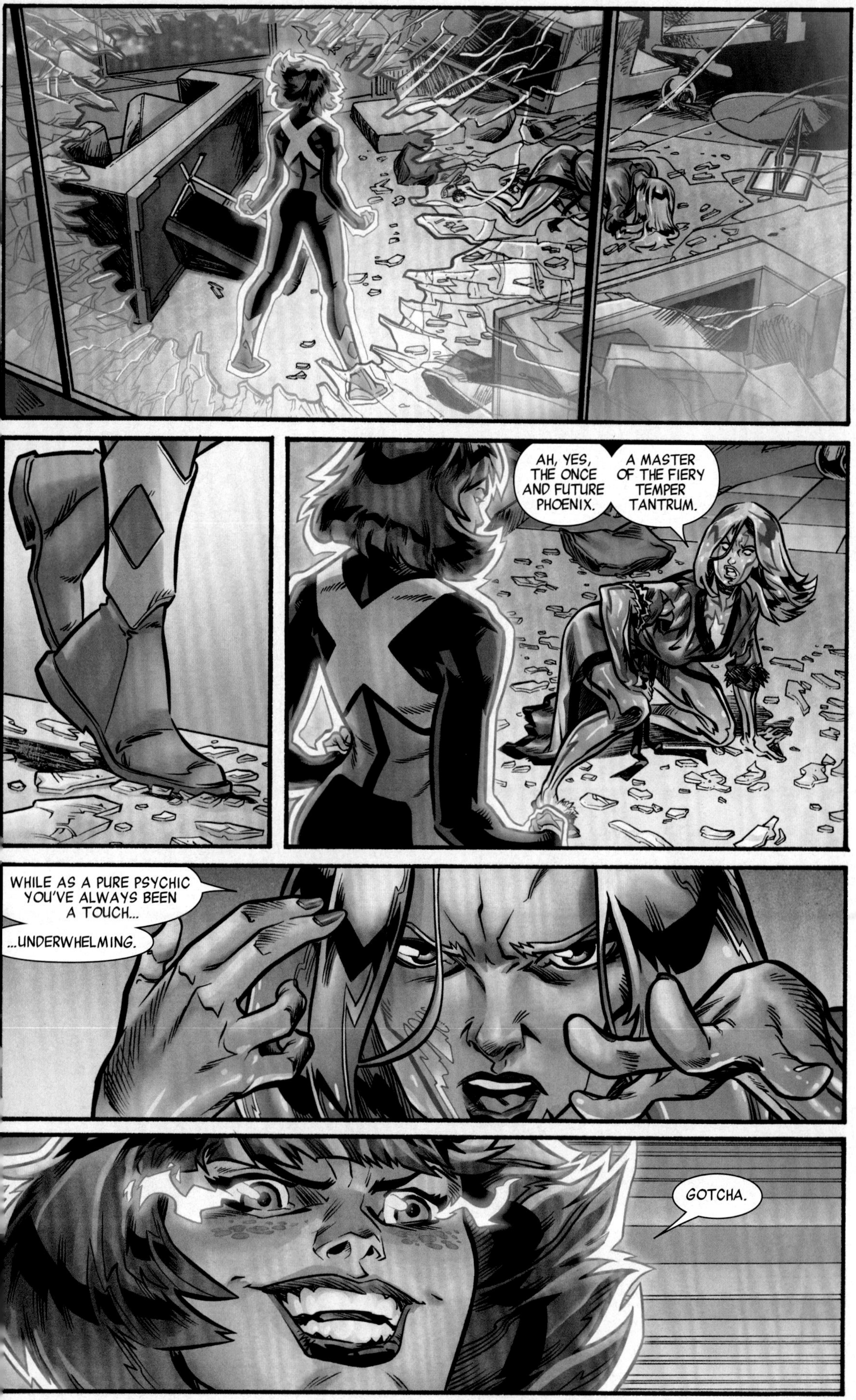
AH, YES, THE ONCE AND FUTURE PHOENIX.
A MASTER OF THE FIERY TEMPER TANTRUM.
WHILE AS A PURE PSYCHIC YOU'VE ALWAYS BEEN A TOUCH...
...UNDERWHELMING.
GOTCHA.

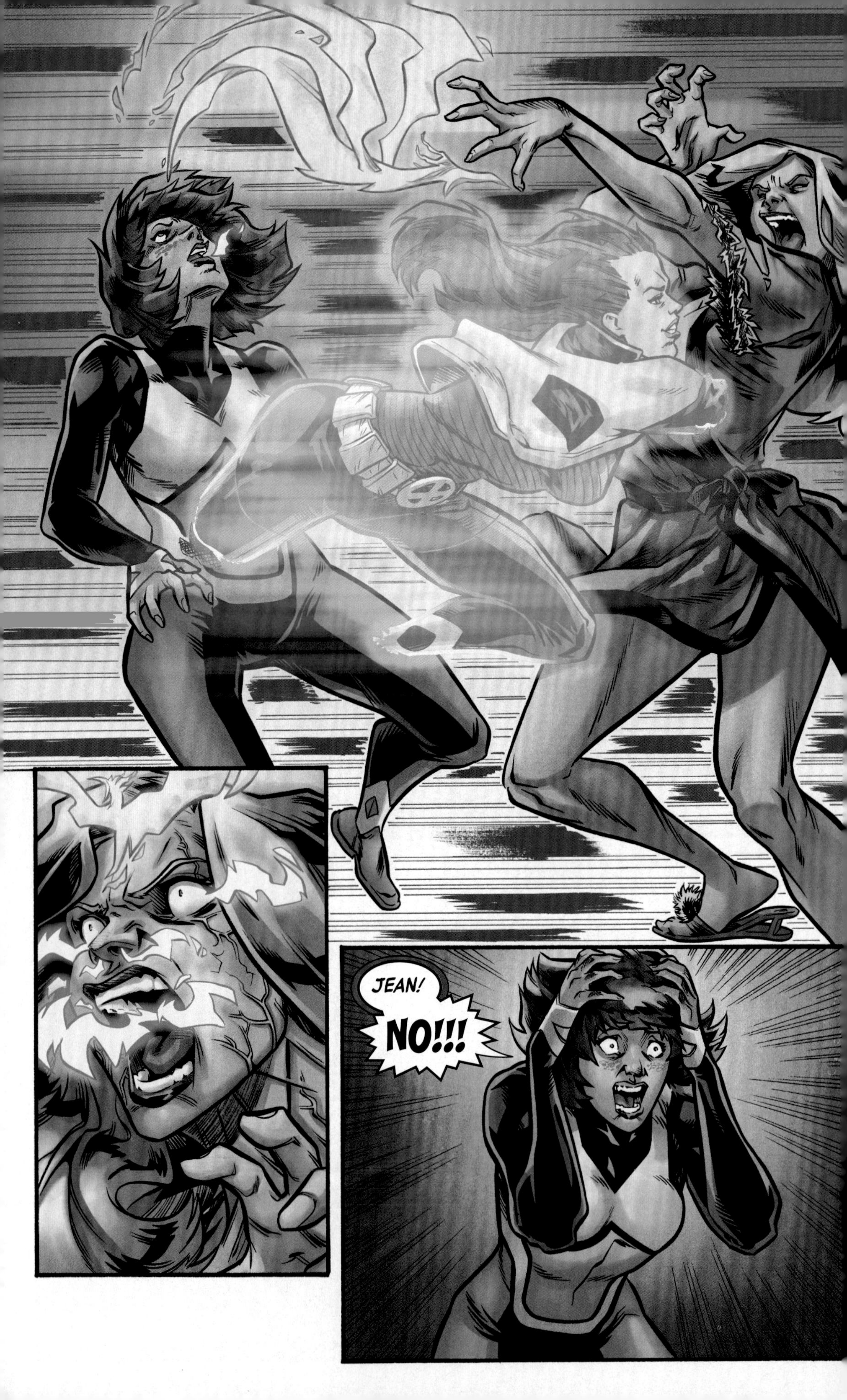
JEAN!
NO!!!

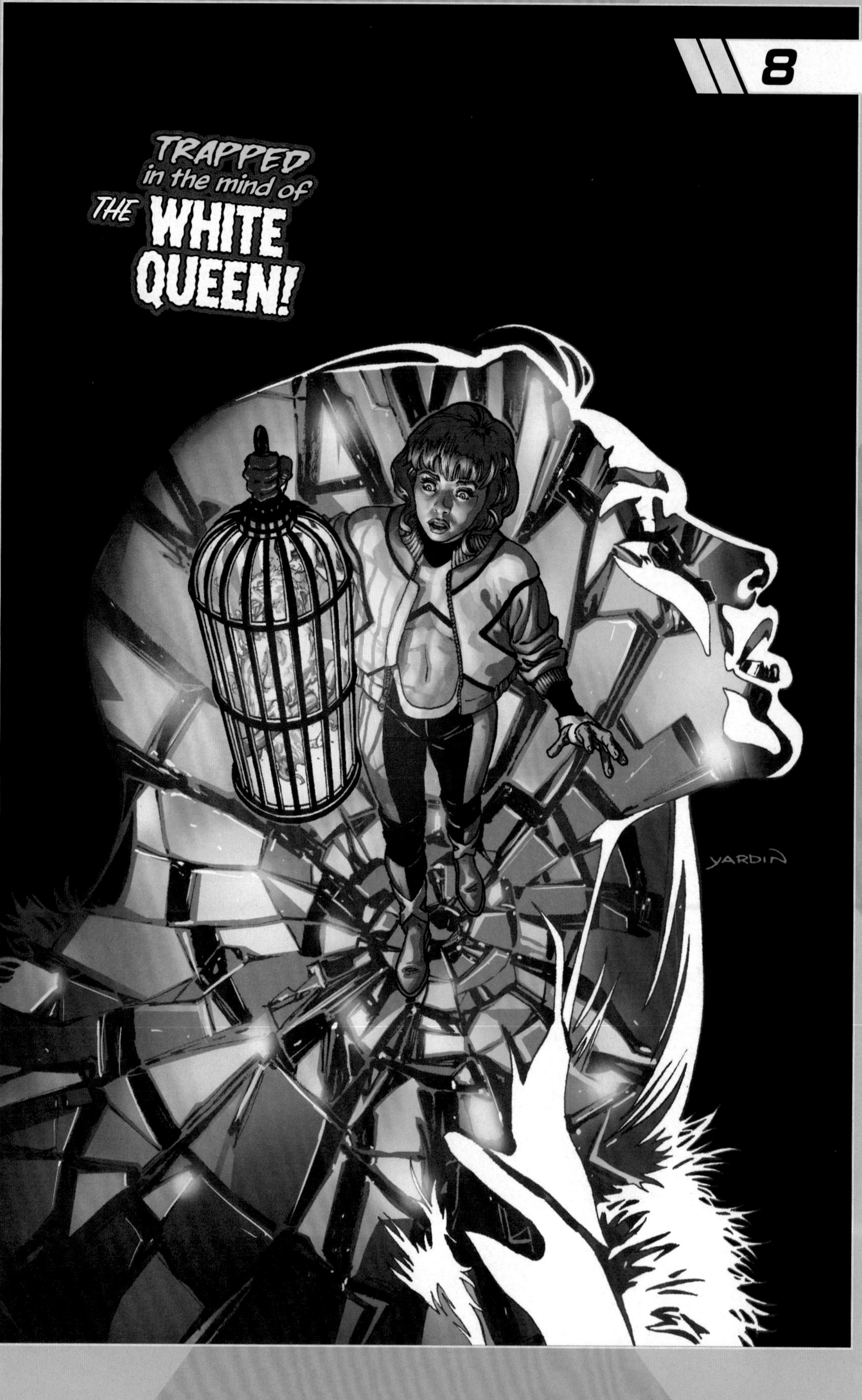
TRAPPED in the mind of THE WHITE QUEEN!
YARDIN

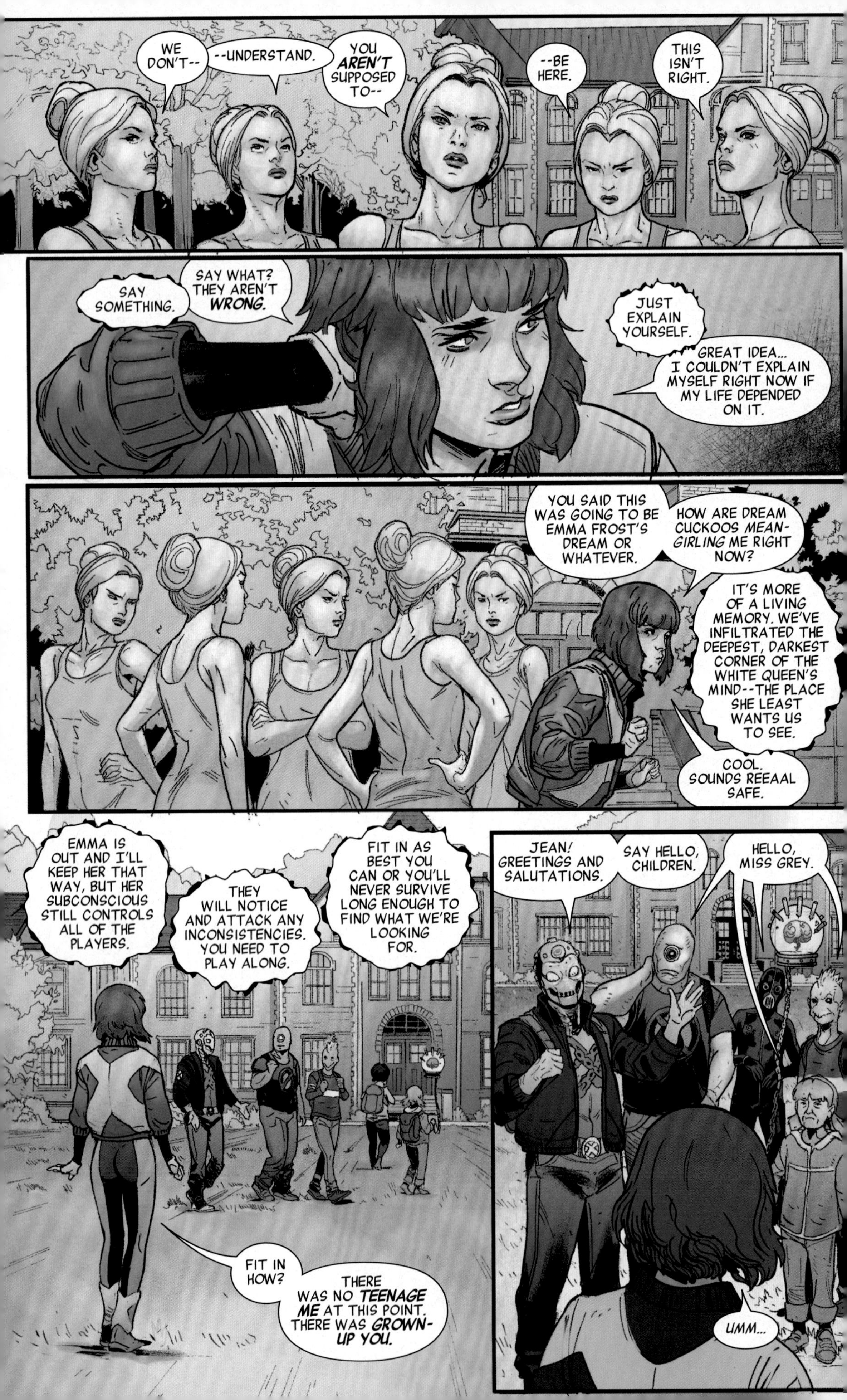
WE DON'T--
--UNDERSTAND.
YOU AREN'T SUPPOSED TO--
--BE HERE.
THIS ISN'T RIGHT.
SAY SOMETHING.
SAY WHAT? THEY AREN'T WRONG.
JUST EXPLAIN YOURSELF.
GREAT IDEA... I COULDN'T EXPLAIN MYSELF RIGHT NOW IF MY LIFE DEPENDED ON IT.
YOU SAID THIS WAS GOING TO BE EMMA FROST'S DREAM OR WHATEVER.
HOW ARE DREAM CUCKOOS MEAN-GIRLING ME RIGHT NOW?
IT'S MORE OF A LIVING MEMORY. WE'VE INFILTRATED THE DEEPEST, DARKEST CORNER OF THE WHITE QUEEN'S MIND--THE PLACE SHE LEAST WANTS US TO SEE.
COOL. SOUNDS REEAAL SAFE.
EMMA IS OUT AND I'LL KEEP HER THAT WAY, BUT HER SUBCONSCIOUS STILL CONTROLS ALL OF THE PLAYERS.
THEY WILL NOTICE AND ATTACK ANY INCONSISTENCIES. YOU NEED TO PLAY ALONG.
FIT IN AS BEST YOU CAN OR YOU'LL NEVER SURVIVE LONG ENOUGH TO FIND WHAT WE'RE LOOKING FOR.
FIT IN HOW?
THERE WAS NO TEENAGE ME AT THIS POINT. THERE WAS GROWN-UP YOU.
JEAN! GREETINGS AND SALUTATIONS.
SAY HELLO, CHILDREN.
HELLO, MISS GREY.
UMM...

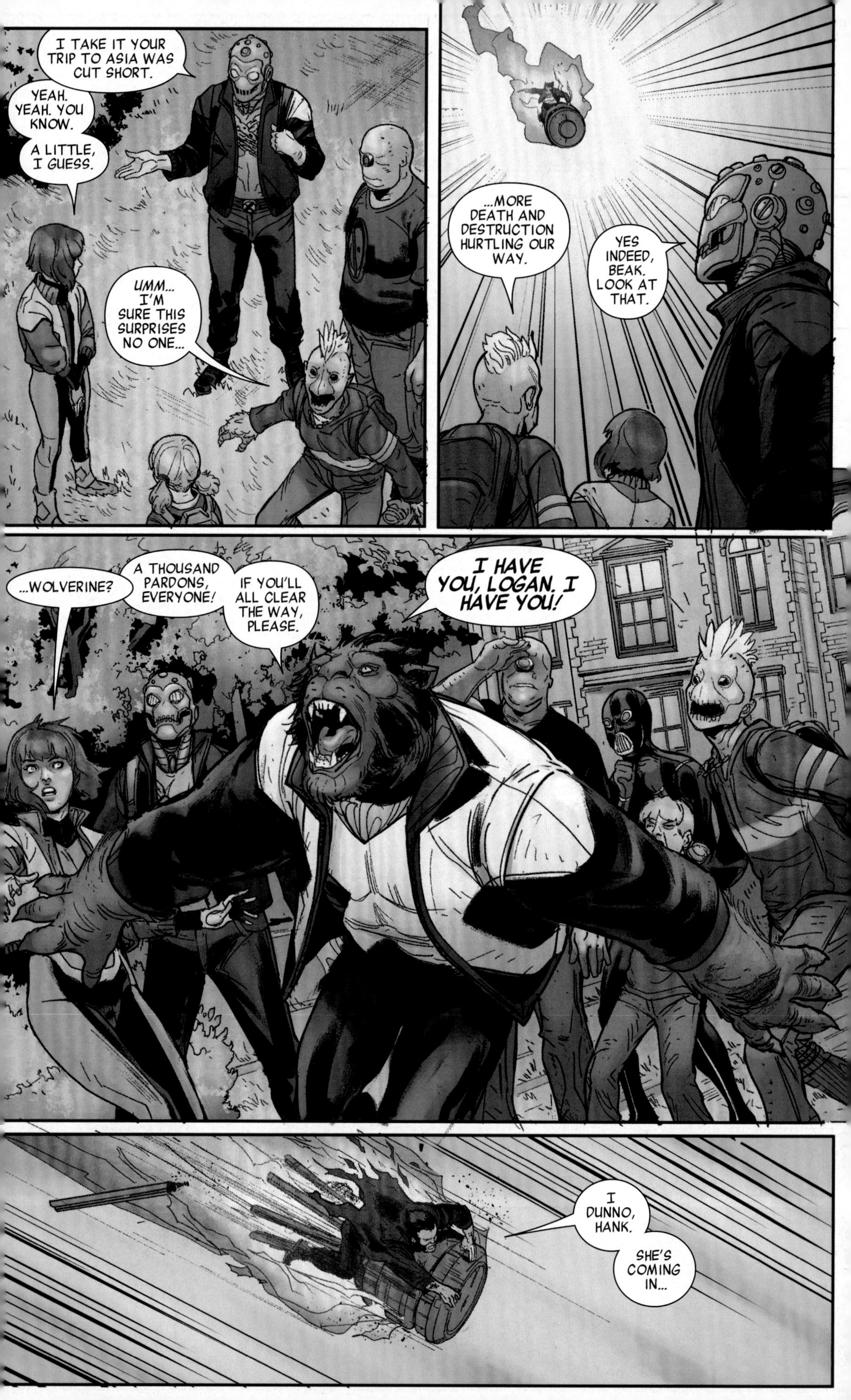
I TAKE IT YOUR TRIP TO ASIA WAS CUT SHORT.
YEAH. YEAH. YOU KNOW.
A LITTLE, I GUESS.
UMM... I'M SURE THIS SURPRISES NO ONE...
...MORE DEATH AND DESTRUCTION HURTLING OUR WAY.
YES INDEED, BEAK. LOOK AT THAT.
...WOLVERINE?
A THOUSAND PARDONS, EVERYONE!
IF YOU'LL ALL CLEAR THE WAY, PLEASE.
I HAVE YOU, LOGAN. I HAVE YOU!
I DUNNO, HANK.
SHE'S COMING IN...

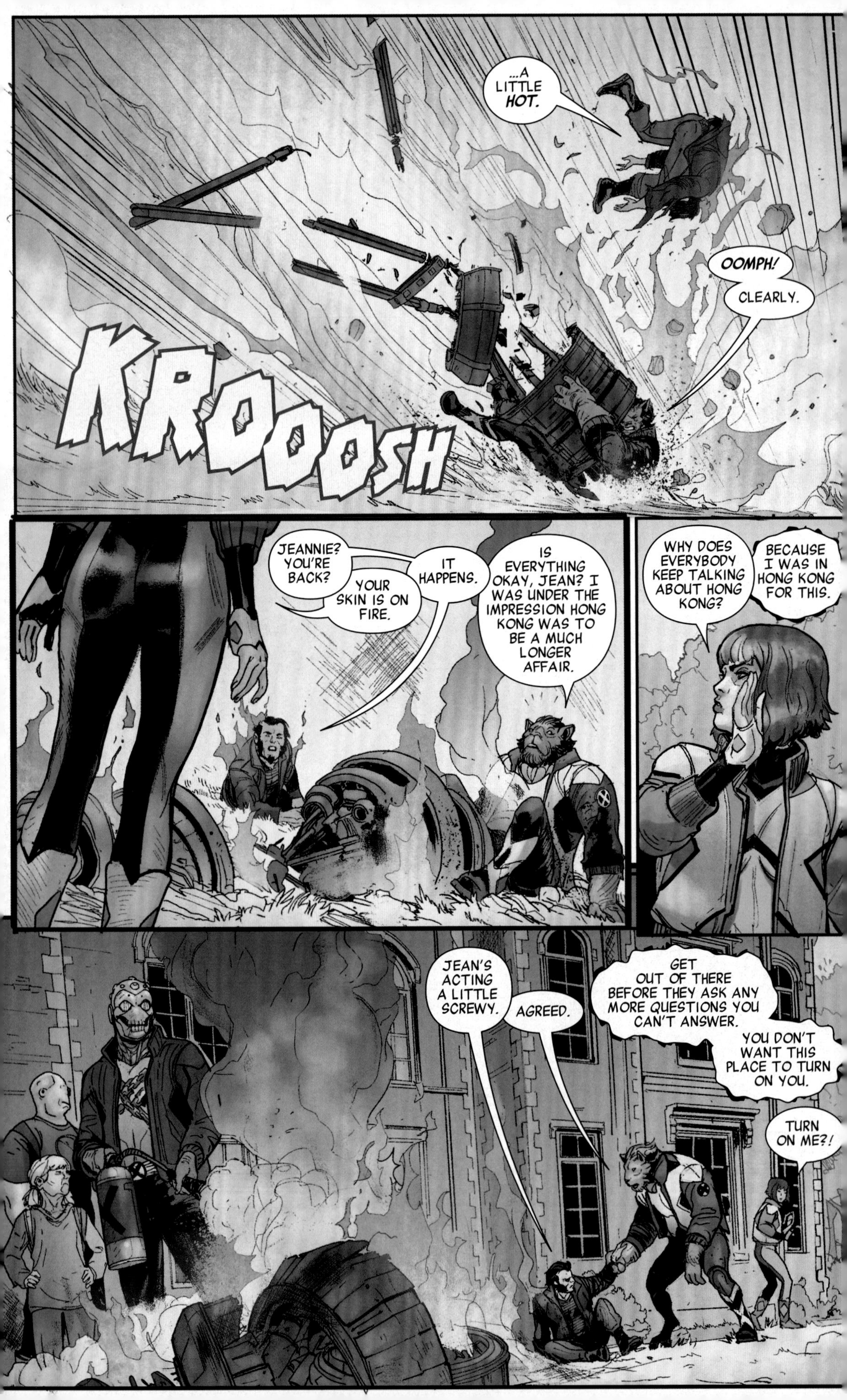
...A LITTLE HOT.
KROOOSH
OOMPH!
CLEARLY.
JEANNIE? YOU'RE BACK?
YOUR SKIN IS ON FIRE.
IT HAPPENS.
IS EVERYTHING OKAY, JEAN? I WAS UNDER THE IMPRESSION HONG KONG WAS TO BE A MUCH LONGER AFFAIR.
WHY DOES EVERYBODY KEEP TALKING ABOUT HONG KONG?
BECAUSE I WAS IN HONG KONG FOR THIS.
JEAN'S ACTING A LITTLE SCREWY.
AGREED.
GET OUT OF THERE BEFORE THEY ASK ANY MORE QUESTIONS YOU CAN'T ANSWER.
YOU DON'T WANT THIS PLACE TO TURN ON YOU.
TURN ON ME?!

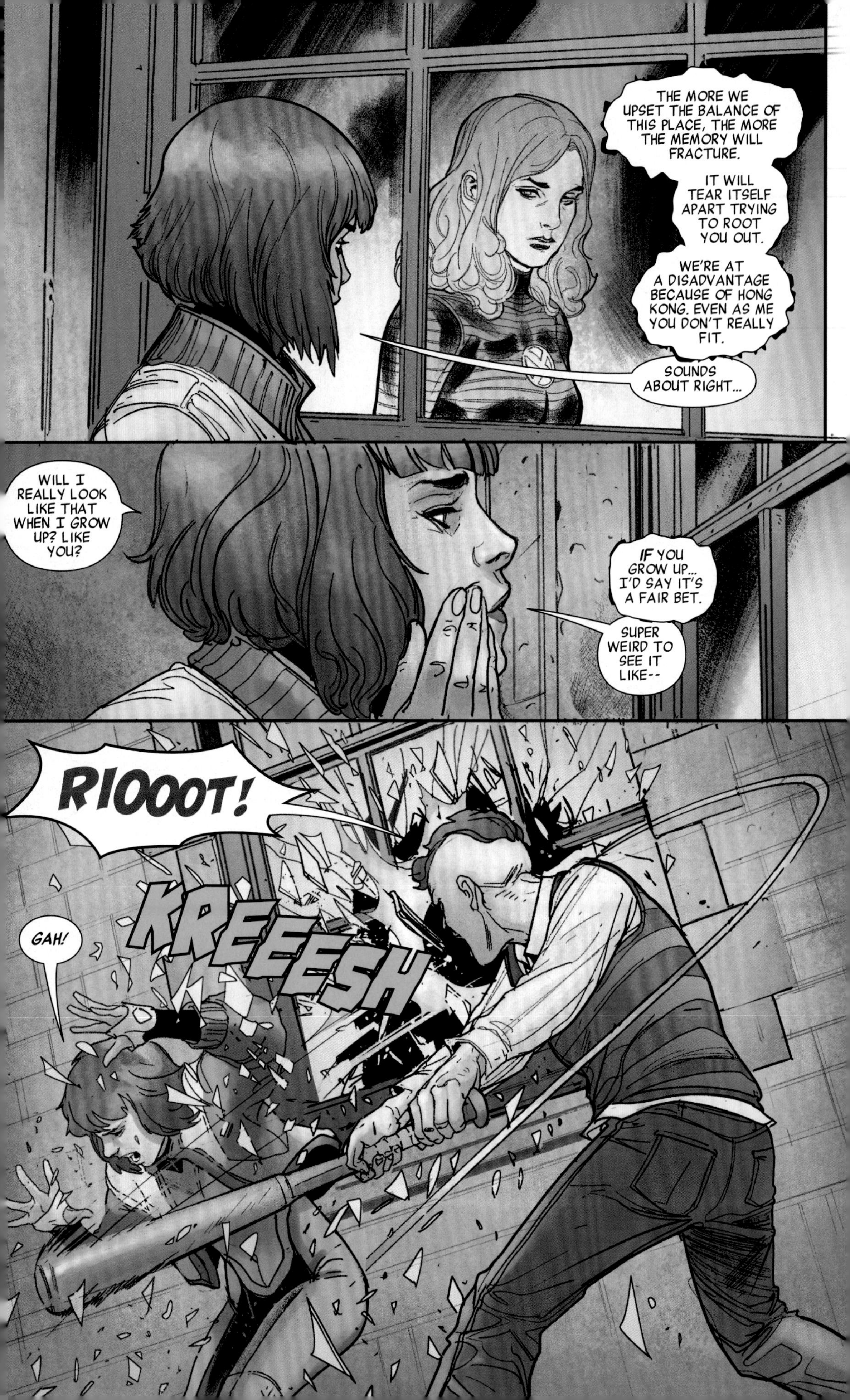
THE MORE WE UPSET THE BALANCE OF THIS PLACE, THE MORE THE MEMORY WILL FRACTURE.
IT WILL TEAR ITSELF APART TRYING TO ROOT YOU OUT.
WE'RE AT A DISADVANTAGE BECAUSE OF HONG KONG. EVEN AS ME YOU DON'T REALLY FIT.
SOUNDS ABOUT RIGHT...
WILL I REALLY LOOK LIKE THAT WHEN I GROW UP? LIKE YOU?
IF YOU GROW UP... I'D SAY IT'S A FAIR BET.
SUPER WEIRD TO SEE IT LIKE--
RIOOOT!
KREEESH
GAH!

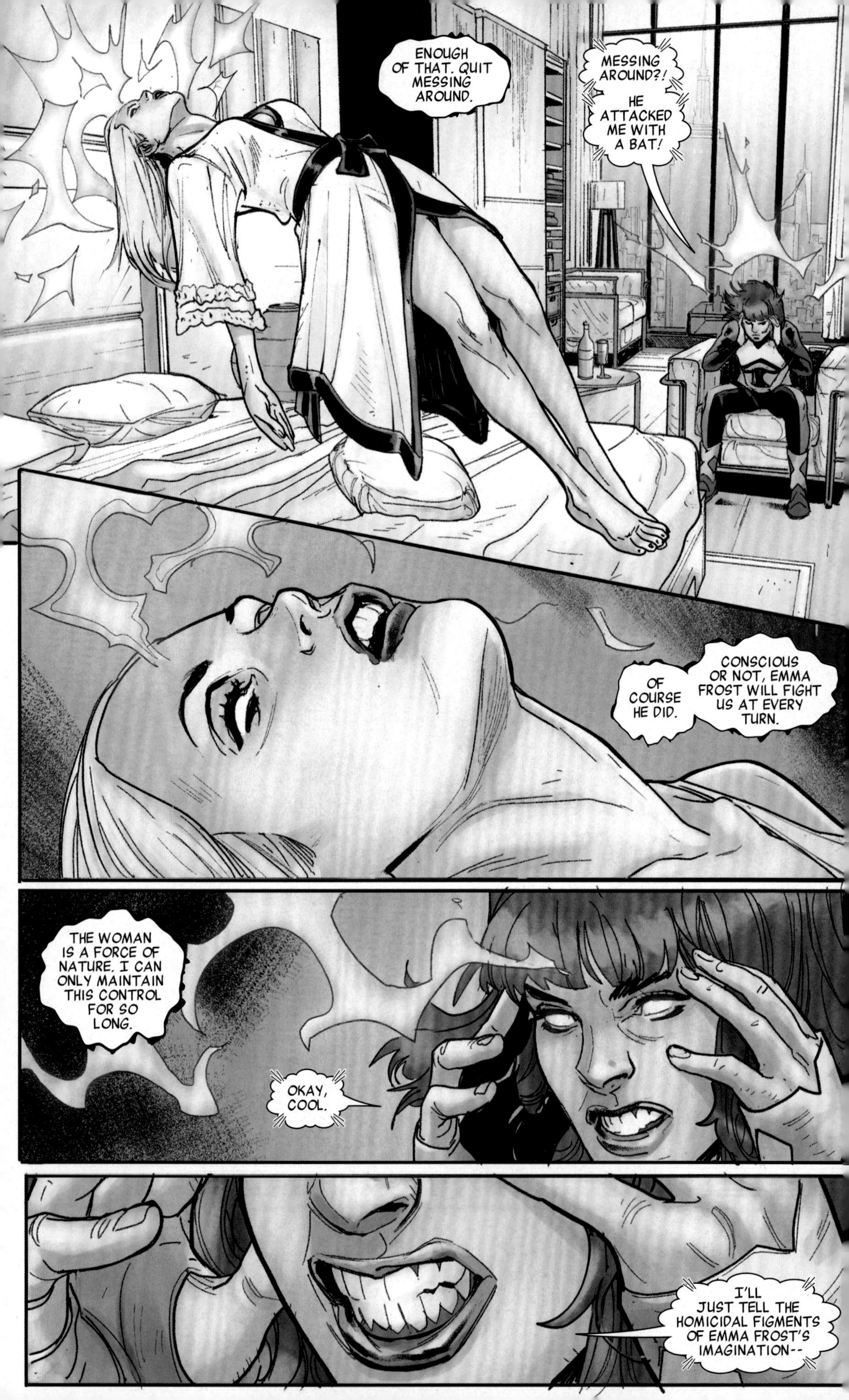
ENOUGH OF THAT. QUIT MESSING AROUND.
MESSING AROUND?! HE ATTACKED ME WITH A BAT!
OF COURSE HE DID.
CONSCIOUS OR NOT, EMMA FROST WILL FIGHT US AT EVERY TURN.
THE WOMAN IS A FORCE OF NATURE. I CAN ONLY MAINTAIN THIS CONTROL FOR SO LONG.
OKAY, COOL.
I'LL JUST TELL THE HOMICIDAL FIGMENTS OF EMMA FROST'S IMAGINATION--

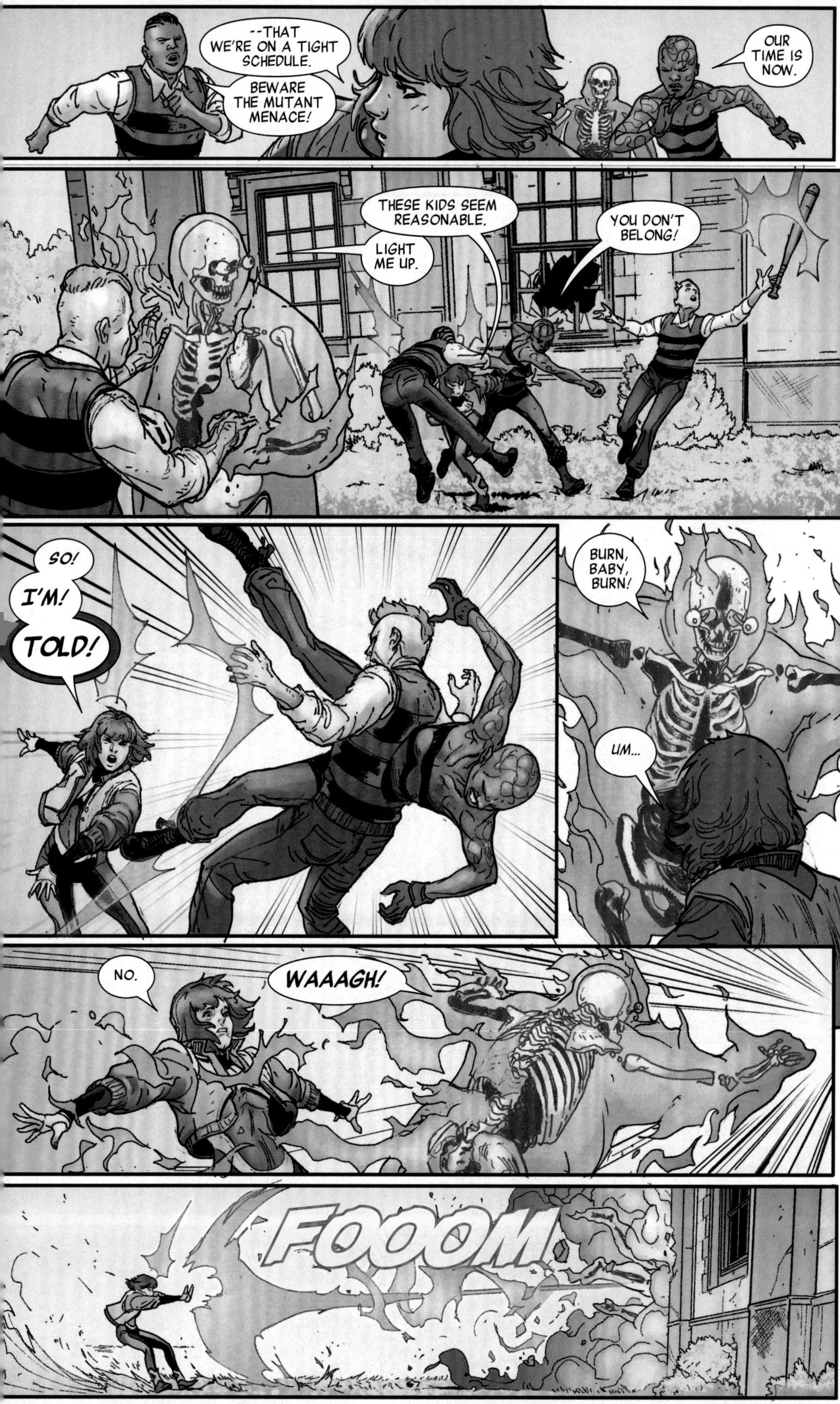
--THAT WE'RE ON A TIGHT SCHEDULE.
BEWARE THE MUTANT MENACE!
OUR TIME IS NOW.
THESE KIDS SEEM REASONABLE.
LIGHT ME UP.
YOU DON'T BELONG!
SO!
I'M!
TOLD!
BURN, BABY, BURN!
UM...
NO.
WAAAGH!
FOOOM

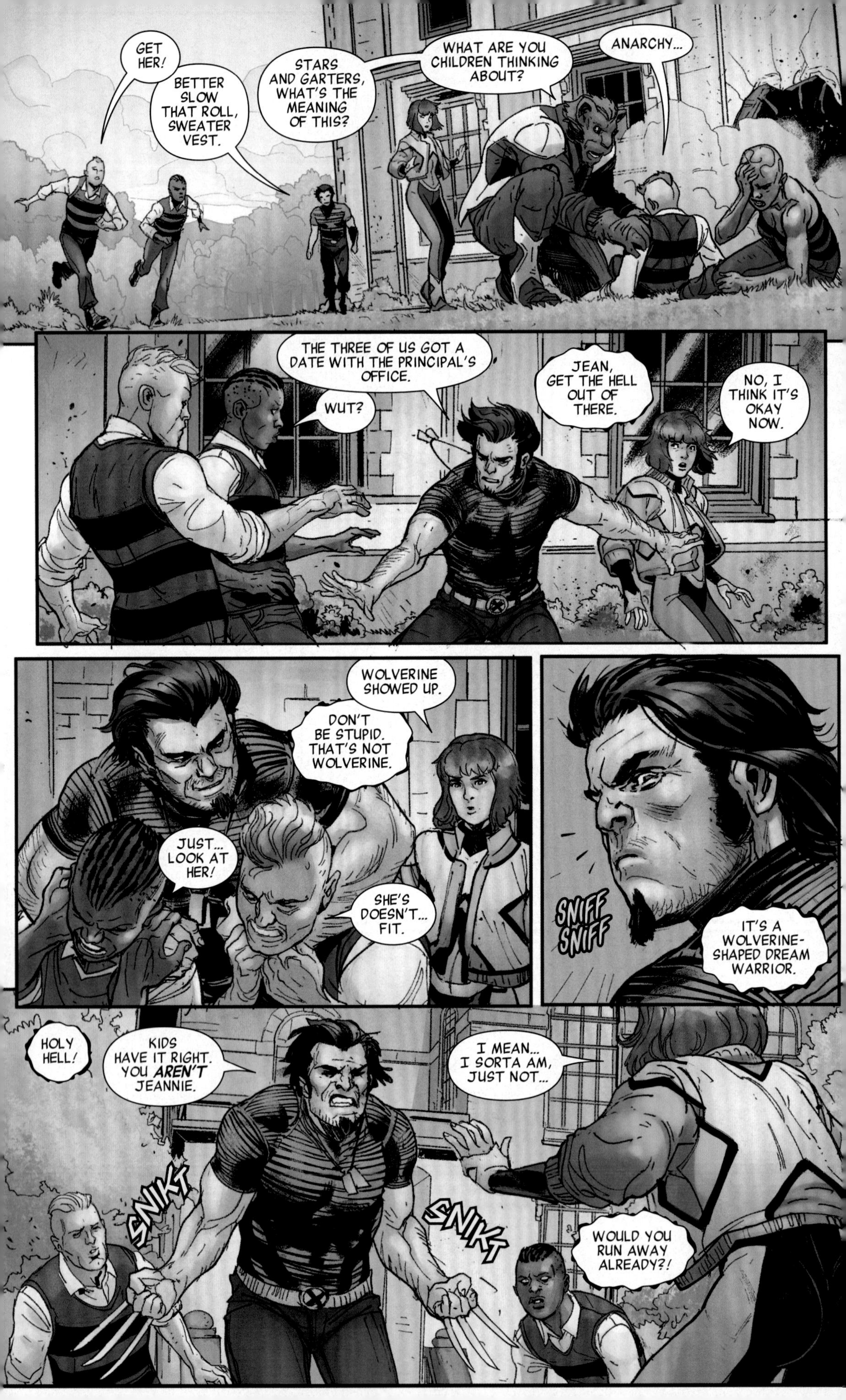
GET HER!
BETTER SLOW THAT ROLL, SWEATER VEST.
STARS AND GARTERS, WHAT'S THE MEANING OF THIS?
WHAT ARE YOU CHILDREN THINKING ABOUT?
ANARCHY...
THE THREE OF US GOT A DATE WITH THE PRINCIPAL'S OFFICE.
WUT?
JEAN, GET THE HELL OUT OF THERE.
NO, I THINK IT'S OKAY NOW.
WOLVERINE SHOWED UP.
DON'T BE STUPID. THAT'S NOT WOLVERINE.
JUST... LOOK AT HER!
SHE'S DOESN'T... FIT.
SNIFF SNIFF
IT'S A WOLVERINE-SHAPED DREAM WARRIOR.
HOLY HELL!
KIDS HAVE IT RIGHT. YOU AREN'T JEANNIE.
I MEAN... I SORTA AM, JUST NOT...
SNIKT
SNIKT
WOULD YOU RUN AWAY ALREADY?!

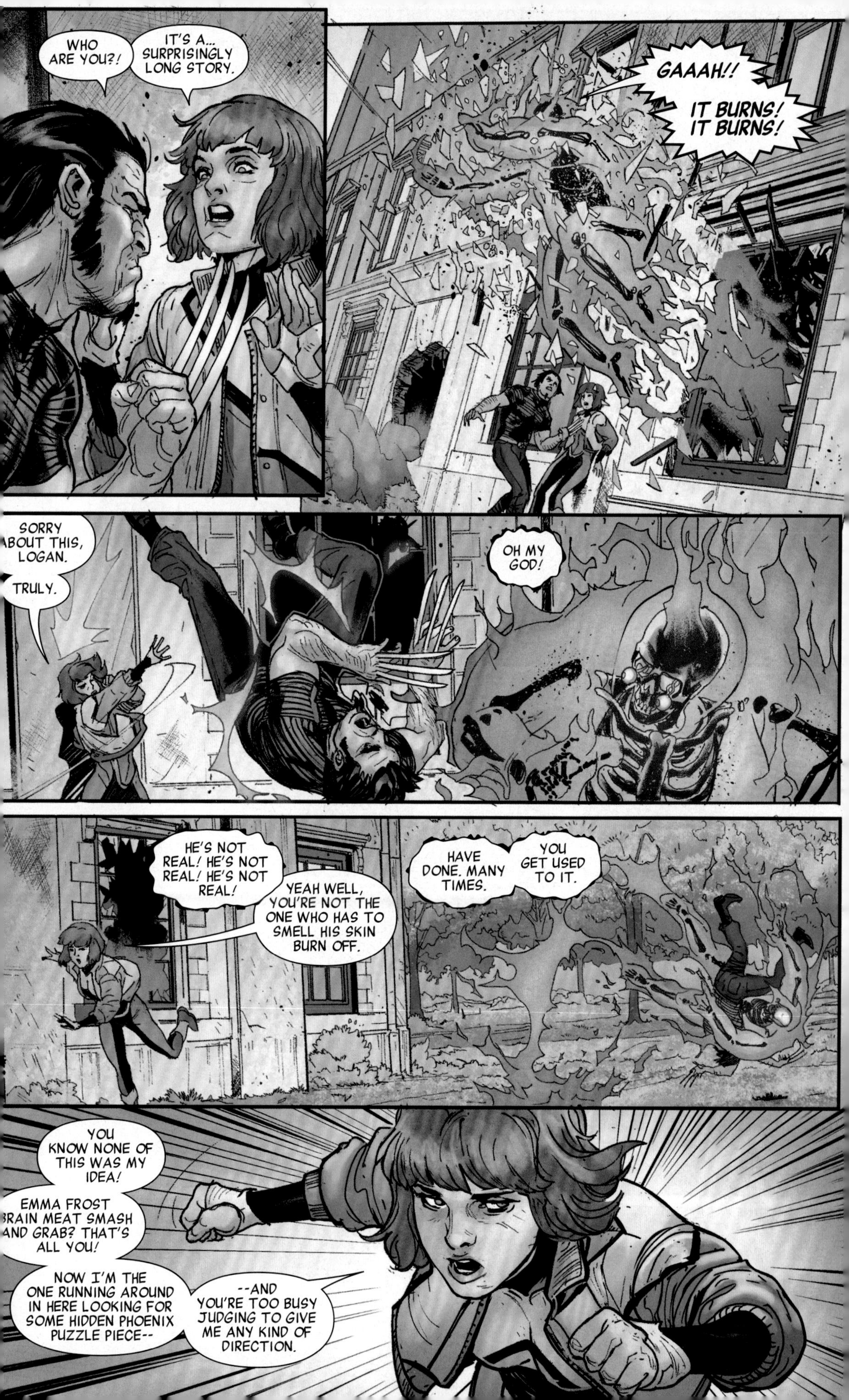
WHO ARE YOU?!
IT'S A... SURPRISINGLY LONG STORY.
GAAAH!!
IT BURNS! IT BURNS!
SORRY ABOUT THIS, LOGAN.
TRULY.
OH MY GOD!
HE'S NOT REAL! HE'S NOT REAL! HE'S NOT REAL!
YEAH WELL, YOU'RE NOT THE ONE WHO HAS TO SMELL HIS SKIN BURN OFF.
HAVE DONE. MANY TIMES.
YOU GET USED TO IT.
YOU KNOW NONE OF THIS WAS MY IDEA!
EMMA FROST BRAIN MEAT SMASH AND GRAB? THAT'S ALL YOU!
NOW I'M THE ONE RUNNING AROUND IN HERE LOOKING FOR SOME HIDDEN PHOENIX PUZZLE PIECE--
--AND YOU'RE TOO BUSY JUDGING TO GIVE ME ANY KIND OF DIRECTION.

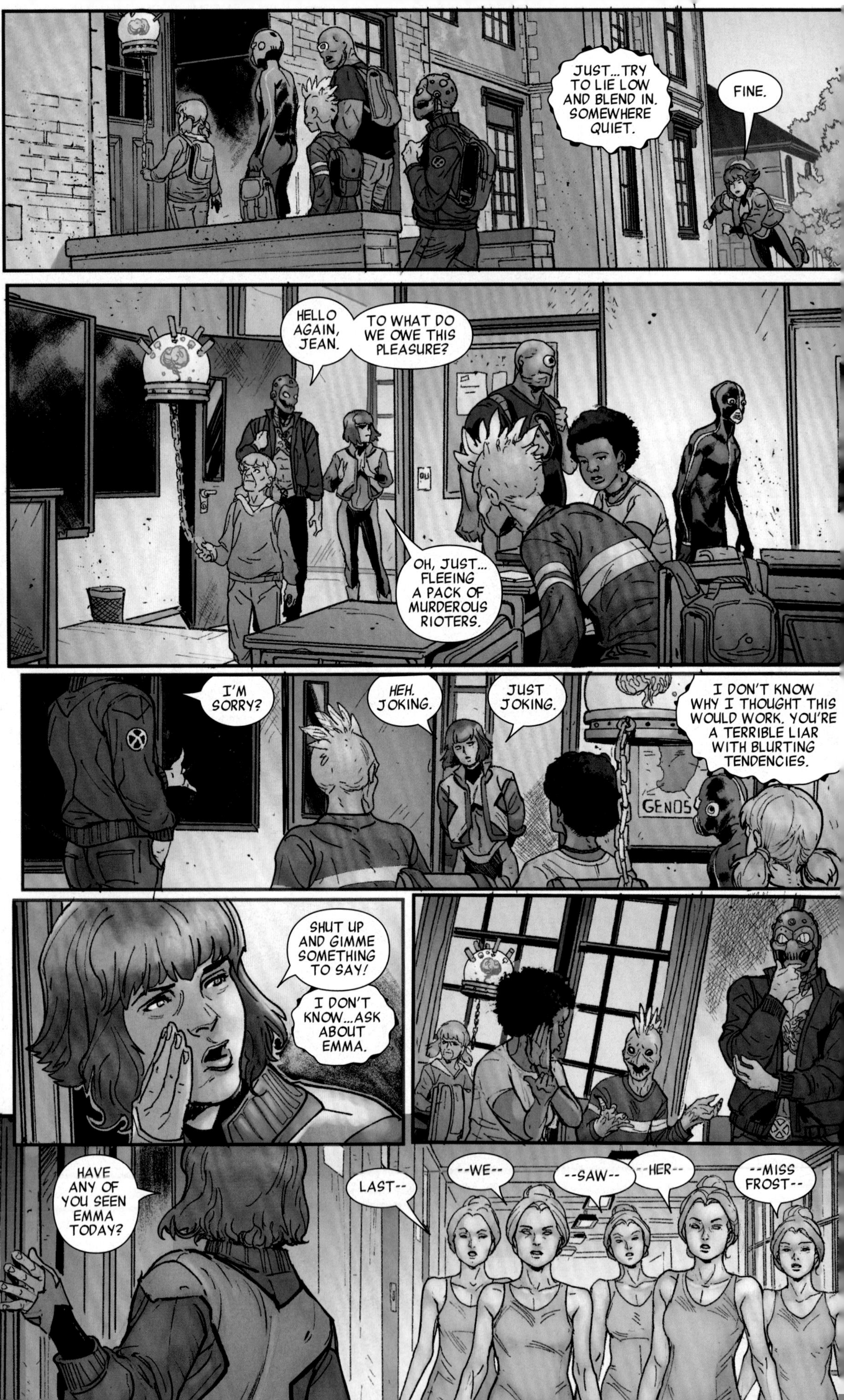
JUST...TRY TO LIE LOW AND BLEND IN. SOMEWHERE QUIET.
FINE.
HELLO AGAIN, JEAN.
TO WHAT DO WE OWE THIS PLEASURE?
OH, JUST... FLEEING A PACK OF MURDEROUS RIOTERS.
I'M SORRY?
HEH. JOKING.
JUST JOKING.
I DON'T KNOW WHY I THOUGHT THIS WOULD WORK. YOU'RE A TERRIBLE LIAR WITH BLURTING TENDENCIES.
GENOS
SHUT UP AND GIMME SOMETHING TO SAY!
I DON'T KNOW...ASK ABOUT EMMA.
HAVE ANY OF YOU SEEN EMMA TODAY?
LAST--
--WE--
--SAW--
--HER--
--MISS FROST--

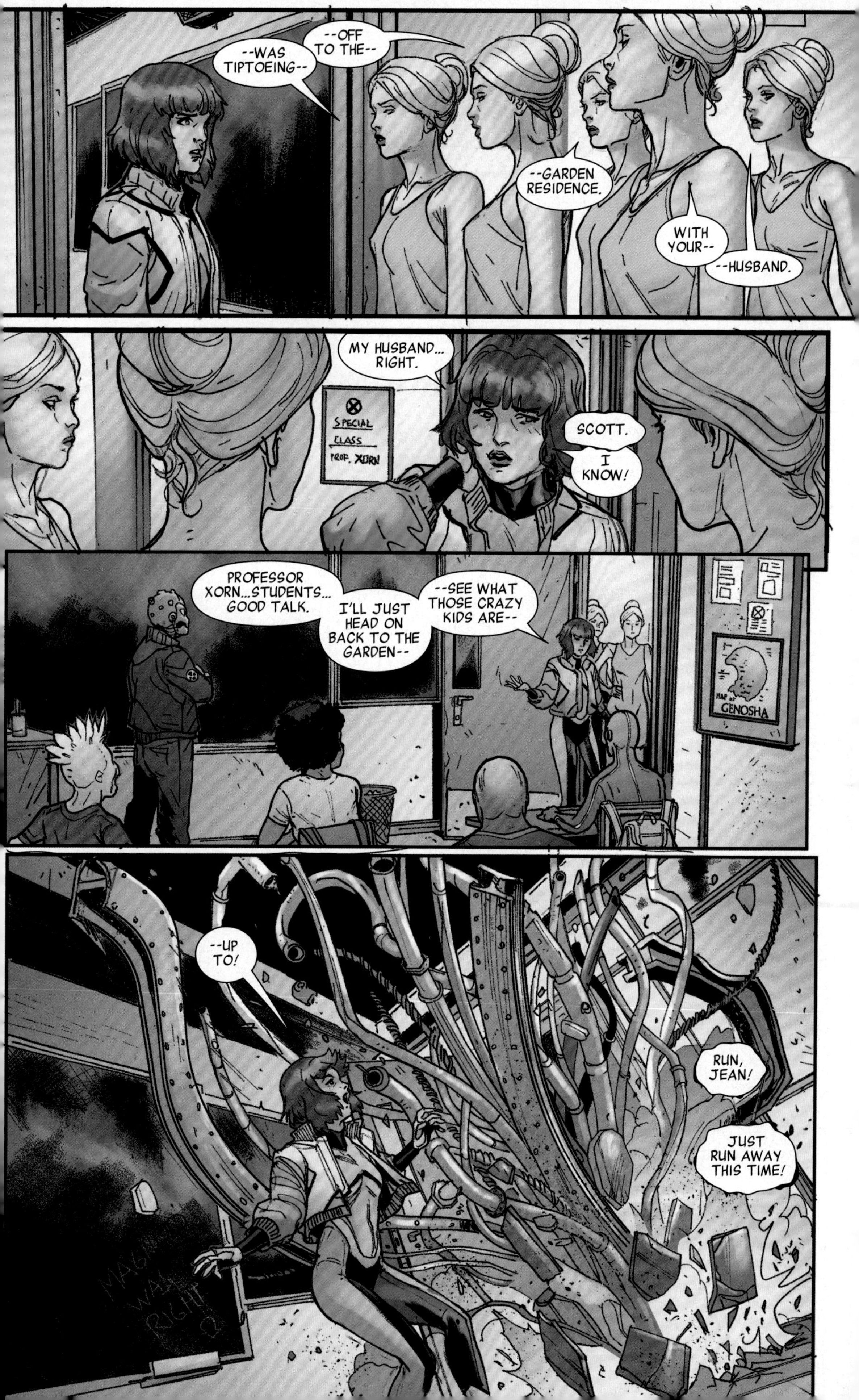
--WAS TIPTOEING--
--OFF TO THE--
--GARDEN RESIDENCE.
WITH YOUR--
--HUSBAND.
MY HUSBAND... RIGHT.
SPECIAL CLASS PROF. XORN
SCOTT.
I KNOW!
PROFESSOR XORN...STUDENTS... GOOD TALK.
I'LL JUST HEAD ON BACK TO THE GARDEN--
--SEE WHAT THOSE CRAZY KIDS ARE--
GENOSHA
--UP TO!
RUN, JEAN!
JUST RUN AWAY THIS TIME!

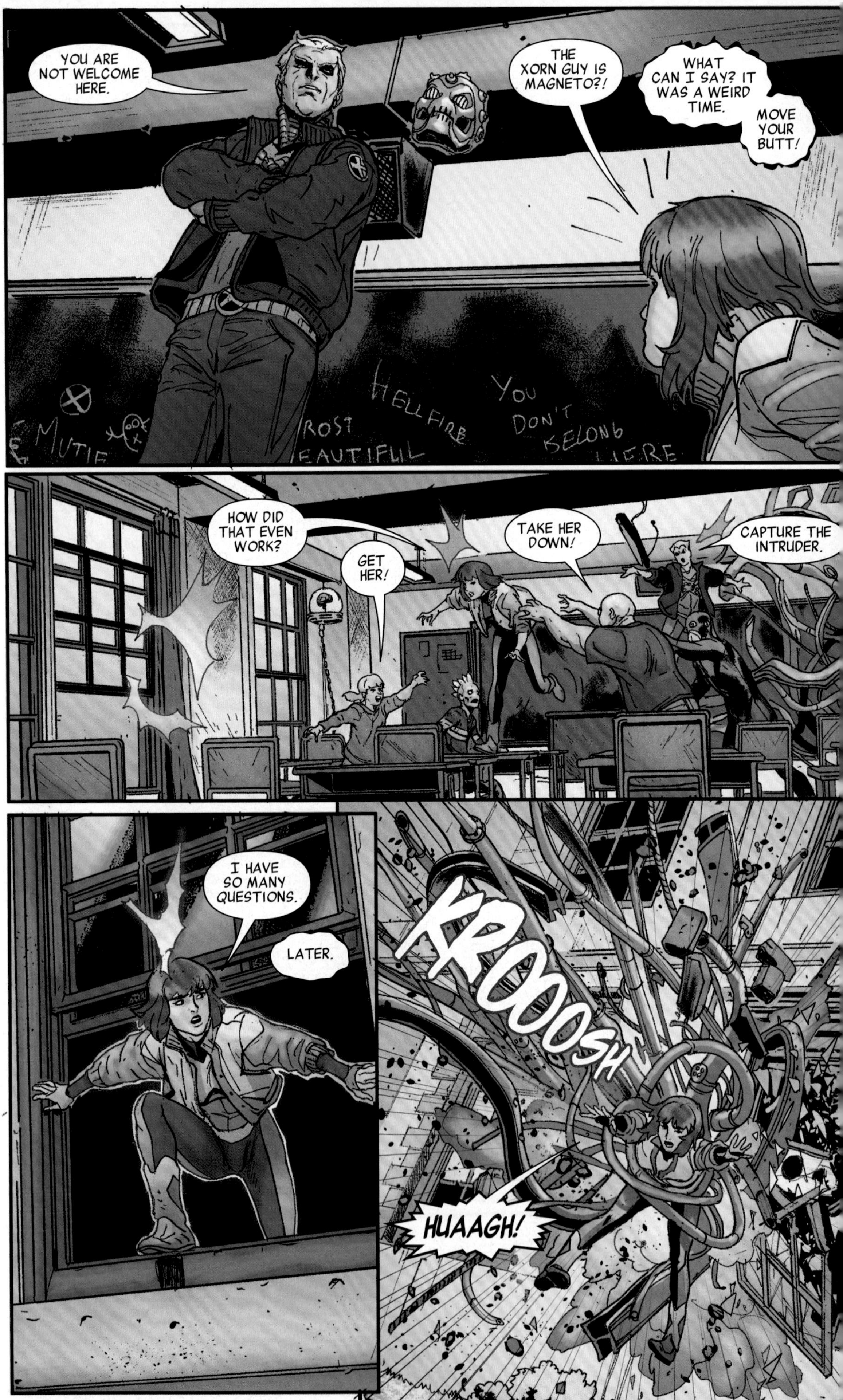
YOU ARE NOT WELCOME HERE.
THE XORN GUY IS MAGNETO?!
WHAT CAN I SAY? IT WAS A WEIRD TIME.
MOVE YOUR BUTT!
HELLFIRE
YOU DON'T BELONG
HOW DID THAT EVEN WORK?
GET HER!
TAKE HER DOWN!
CAPTURE THE INTRUDER.
I HAVE SO MANY QUESTIONS.
LATER.
KROOOOSH
HUAAGH!

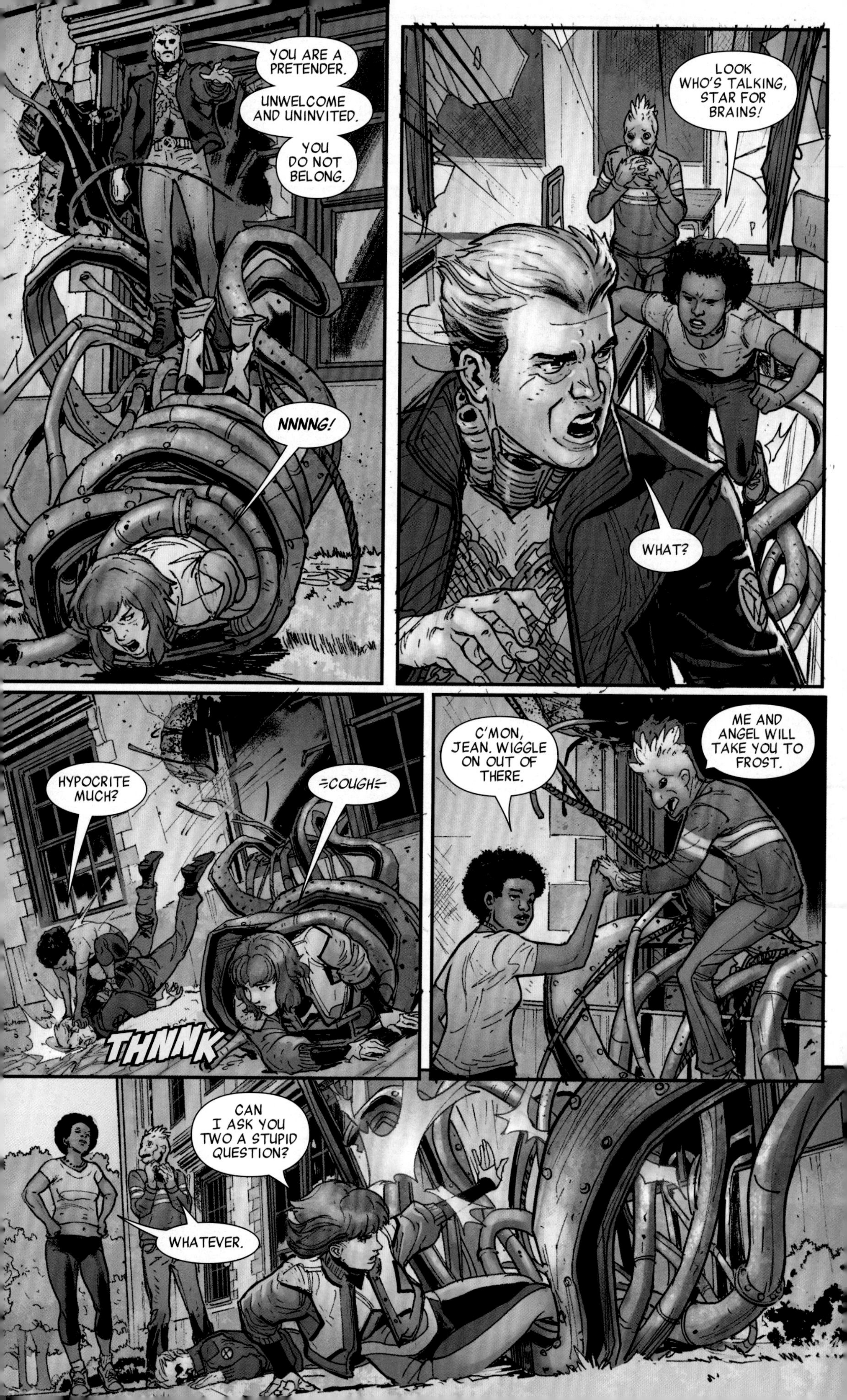
YOU ARE A PRETENDER.
UNWELCOME AND UNINVITED.
YOU DO NOT BELONG.
NNNNG!
LOOK WHO'S TALKING, STAR FOR BRAINS!
WHAT?
HYPOCRITE MUCH?
=COUGH=
THNNK
C'MON, JEAN. WIGGLE ON OUT OF THERE.
ME AND ANGEL WILL TAKE YOU TO FROST.
CAN I ASK YOU TWO A STUPID QUESTION?
WHATEVER.

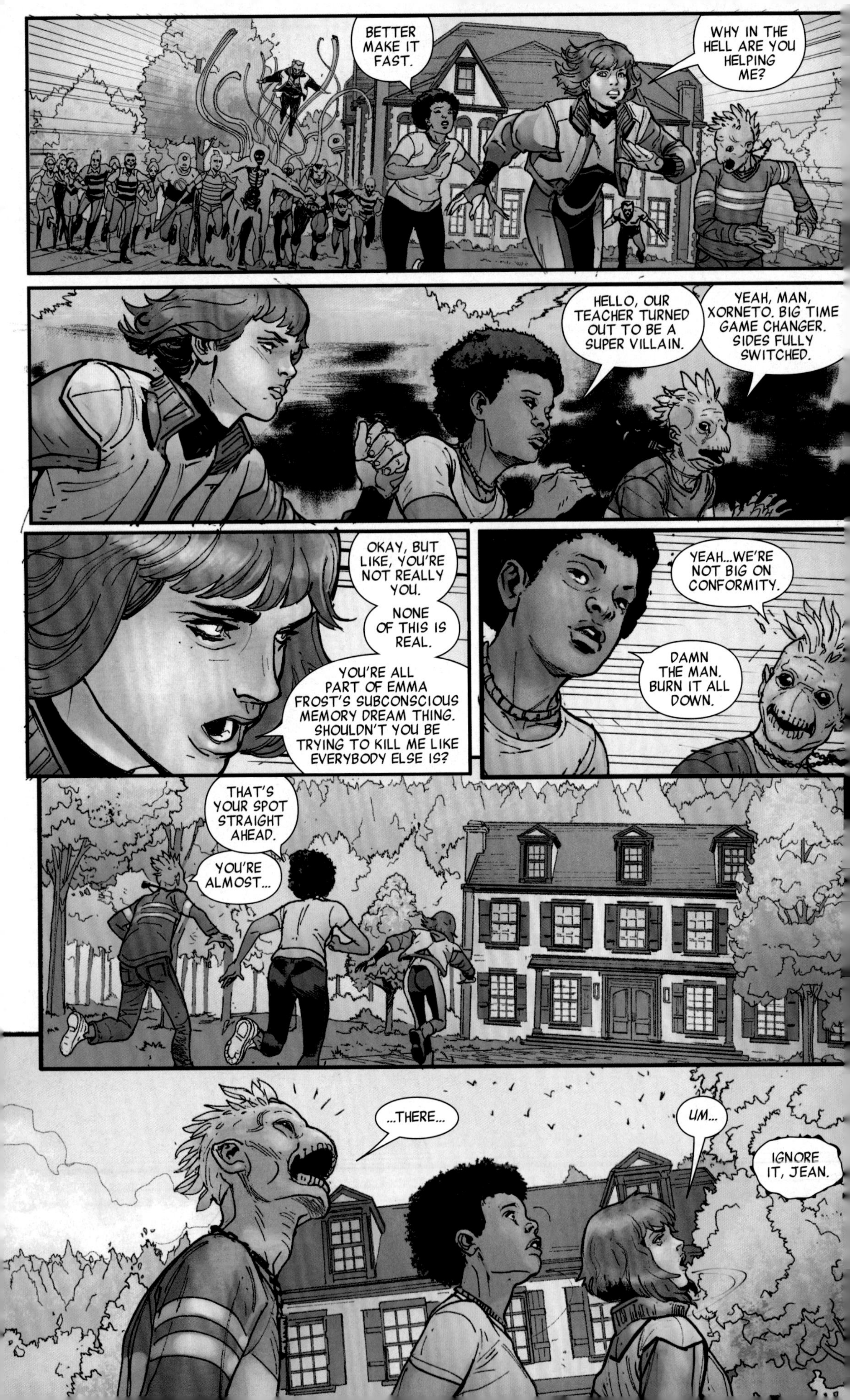
BETTER MAKE IT FAST.
WHY IN THE HELL ARE YOU HELPING ME?
HELLO, OUR TEACHER TURNED OUT TO BE A SUPER VILLAIN.
YEAH, MAN, XORNETO. BIG TIME GAME CHANGER. SIDES FULLY SWITCHED.
OKAY, BUT LIKE, YOU'RE NOT REALLY YOU.
NONE OF THIS IS REAL.
YOU'RE ALL PART OF EMMA FROST'S SUBCONSCIOUS MEMORY DREAM THING. SHOULDN'T YOU BE TRYING TO KILL ME LIKE EVERYBODY ELSE IS?
YEAH...WE'RE NOT BIG ON CONFORMITY.
DAMN THE MAN. BURN IT ALL DOWN.
THAT'S YOUR SPOT STRAIGHT AHEAD.
YOU'RE ALMOST...
...THERE...
UM...
IGNORE IT, JEAN.

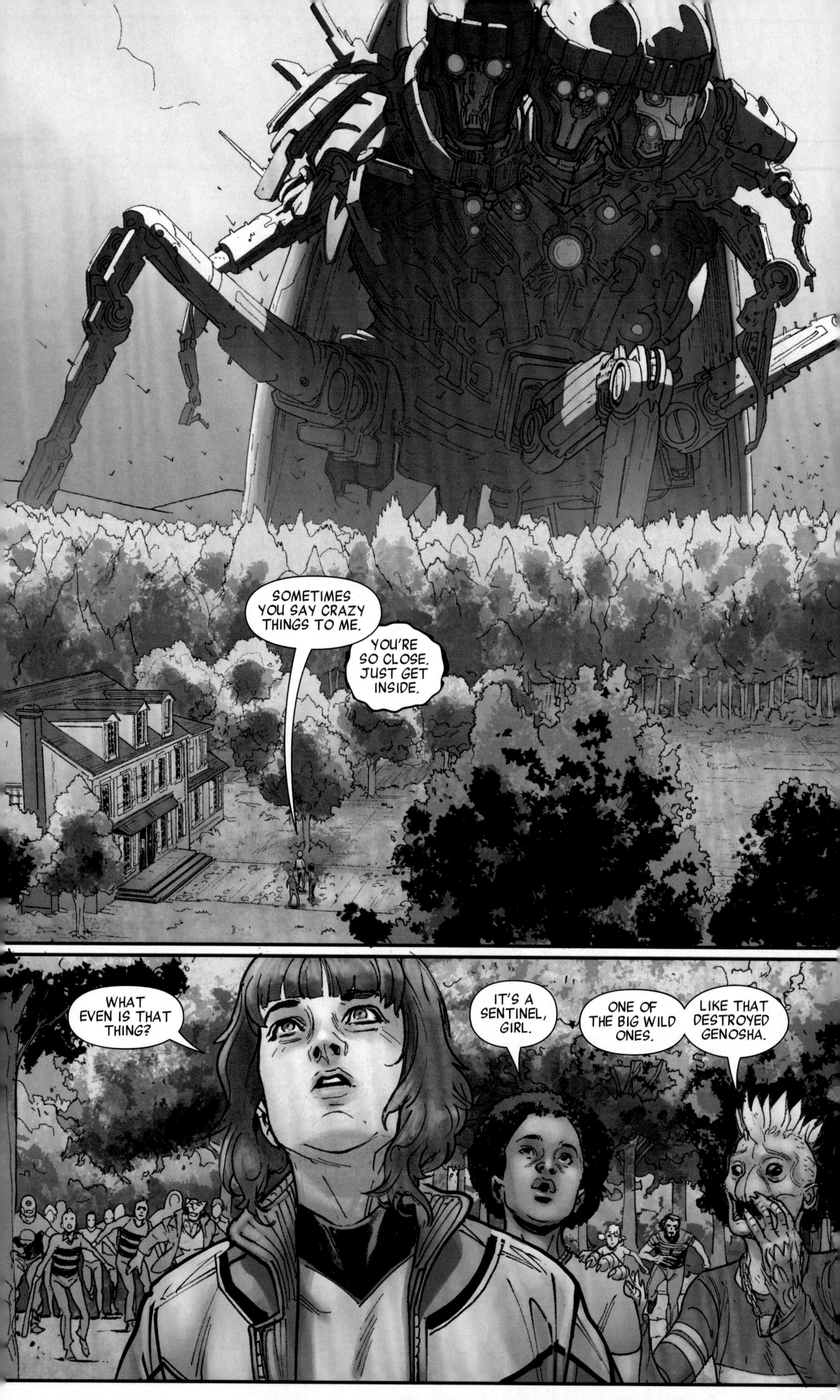
SOMETIMES YOU SAY CRAZY THINGS TO ME.
YOU'RE SO CLOSE. JUST GET INSIDE.
WHAT EVEN IS THAT THING?
IT'S A SENTINEL, GIRL.
ONE OF THE BIG WILD ONES.
LIKE THAT DESTROYED GENOSHA.

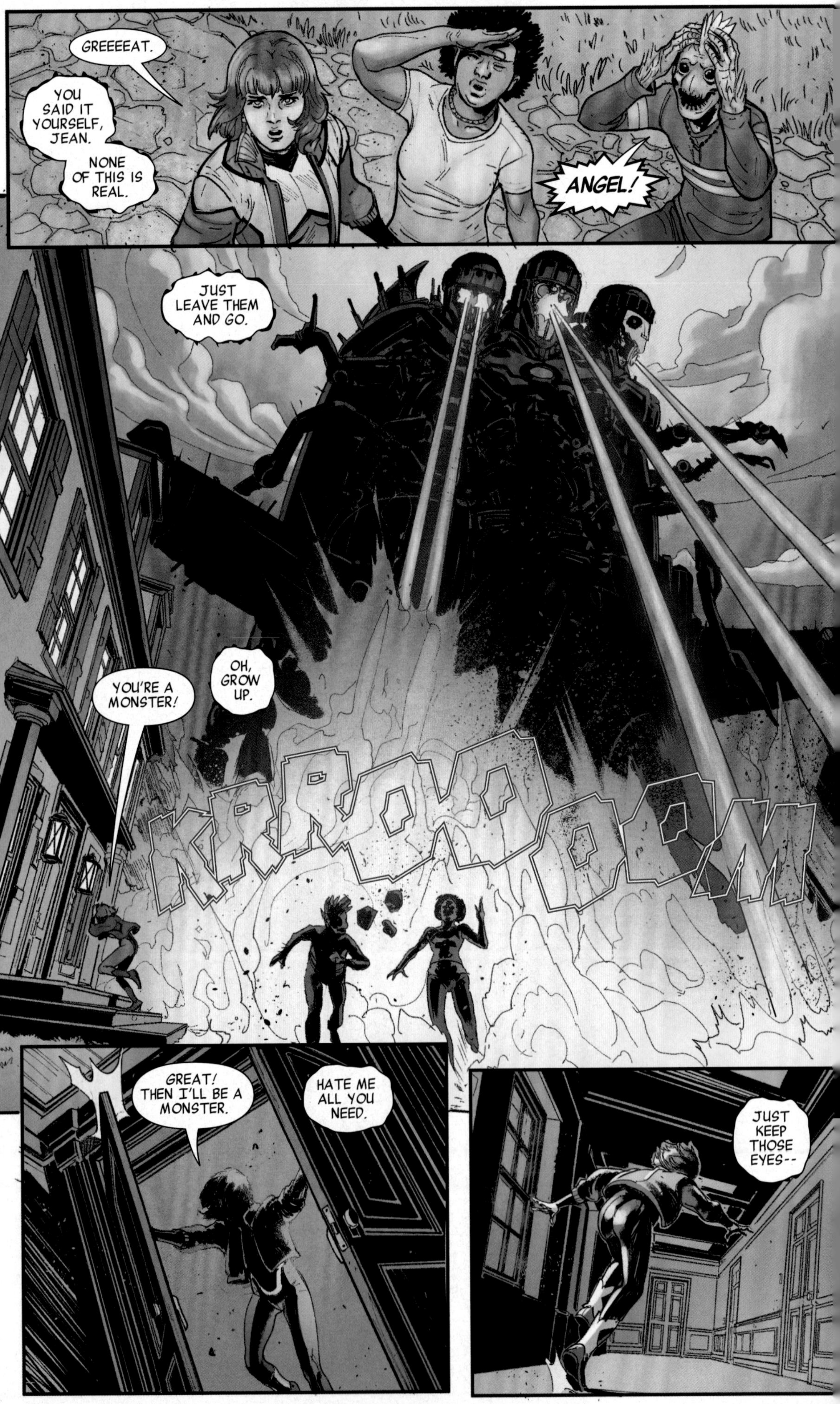
GREEEEAT.
YOU SAID IT YOURSELF, JEAN.
NONE OF THIS IS REAL.
ANGEL!
JUST LEAVE THEM AND GO.
YOU'RE A MONSTER!
OH, GROW UP.
KRROOOOM
GREAT! THEN I'LL BE A MONSTER.
HATE ME ALL YOU NEED.
JUST KEEP THOSE EYES--

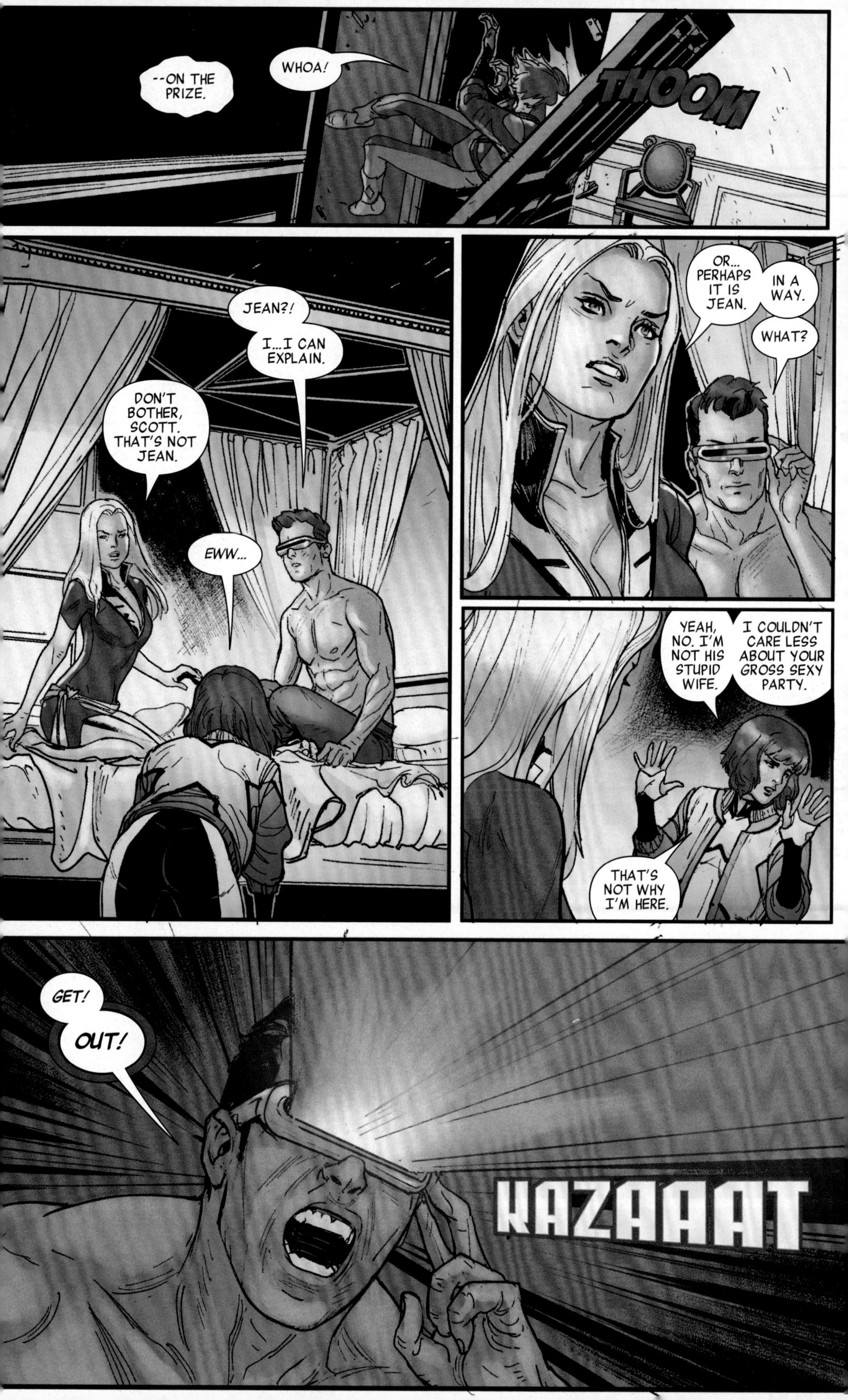
--ON THE PRIZE.
WHOA!
THOOM
JEAN?!
I...I CAN EXPLAIN.
DON'T BOTHER, SCOTT. THAT'S NOT JEAN.
EWW...
OR... PERHAPS IT IS JEAN.
IN A WAY.
WHAT?
YEAH, NO. I'M NOT HIS STUPID WIFE.
I COULDN'T CARE LESS ABOUT YOUR GROSS SEXY PARTY.
THAT'S NOT WHY I'M HERE.
GET!
OUT!
KAZAAAT

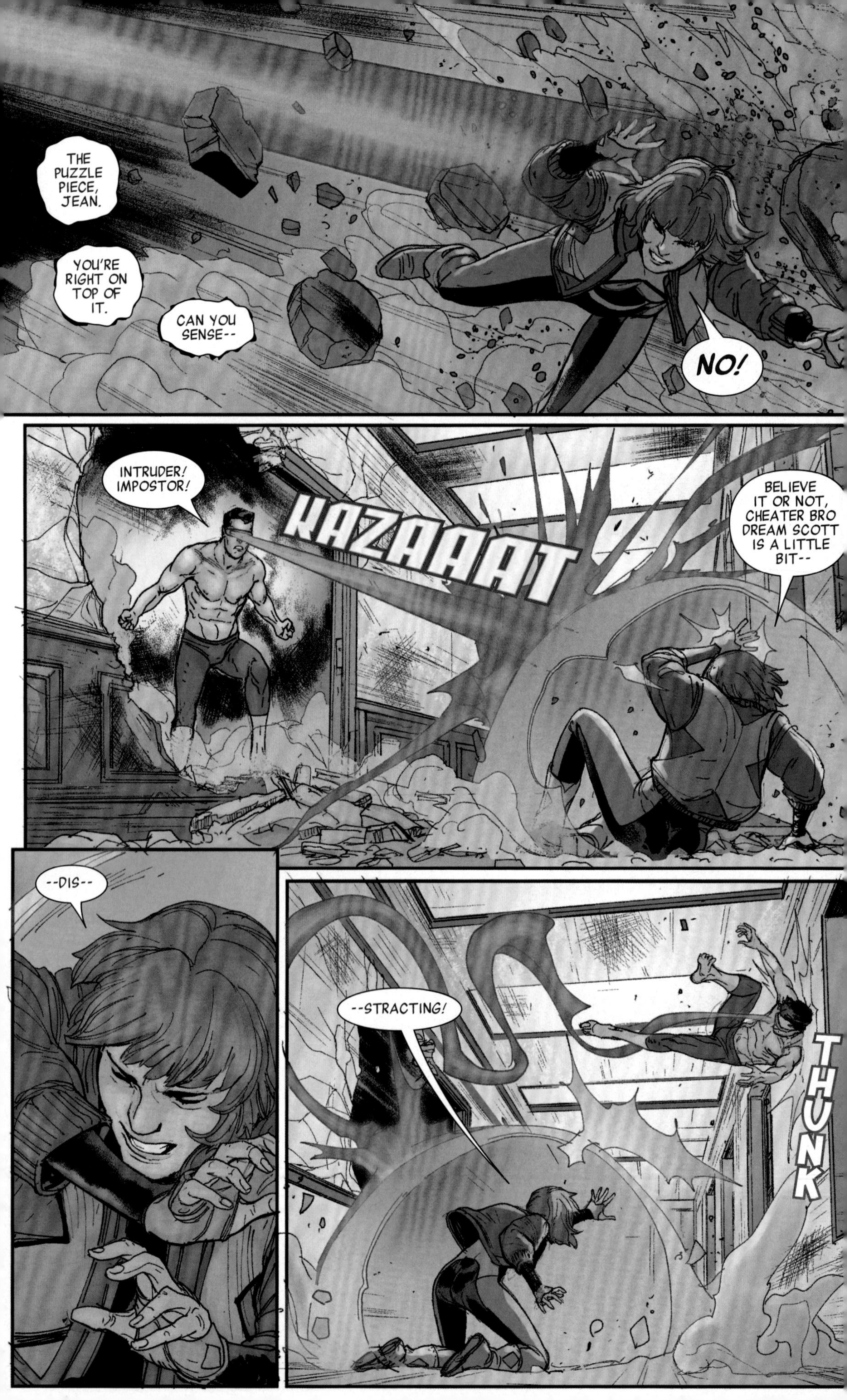

THE PUZZLE PIECE, JEAN.
YOU'RE RIGHT ON TOP OF IT.
CAN YOU SENSE--
NO!
INTRUDER! IMPOSTOR!
KAZAAAT
BELIEVE IT OR NOT, CHEATER BRO DREAM SCOTT IS A LITTLE BIT--
--DIS--
--STRACTING!
THUNK

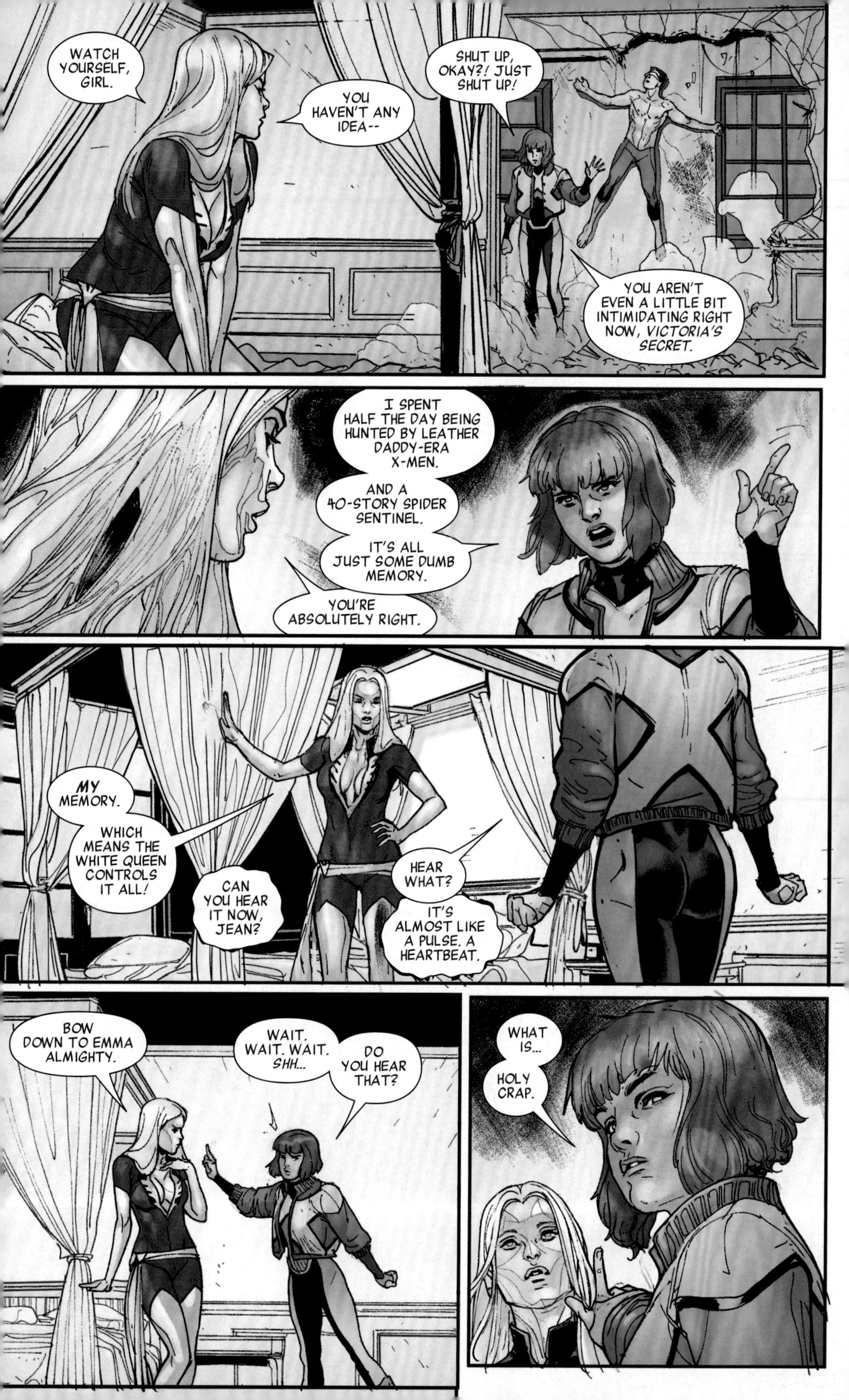
WATCH YOURSELF, GIRL.
YOU HAVEN'T ANY IDEA--
SHUT UP, OKAY?! JUST SHUT UP!
YOU AREN'T EVEN A LITTLE BIT INTIMIDATING RIGHT NOW, VICTORIA'S SECRET.
I SPENT HALF THE DAY BEING HUNTED BY LEATHER DADDY-ERA X-MEN.
AND A 40-STORY SPIDER SENTINEL.
IT'S ALL JUST SOME DUMB MEMORY.
YOU'RE ABSOLUTELY RIGHT.
MY MEMORY.
WHICH MEANS THE WHITE QUEEN CONTROLS IT ALL!
CAN YOU HEAR IT NOW, JEAN?
HEAR WHAT?
IT'S ALMOST LIKE A PULSE. A HEARTBEAT.
BOW DOWN TO EMMA ALMIGHTY.
WAIT. WAIT. WAIT. SHH...
DO YOU HEAR THAT?
WHAT IS...
HOLY CRAP.

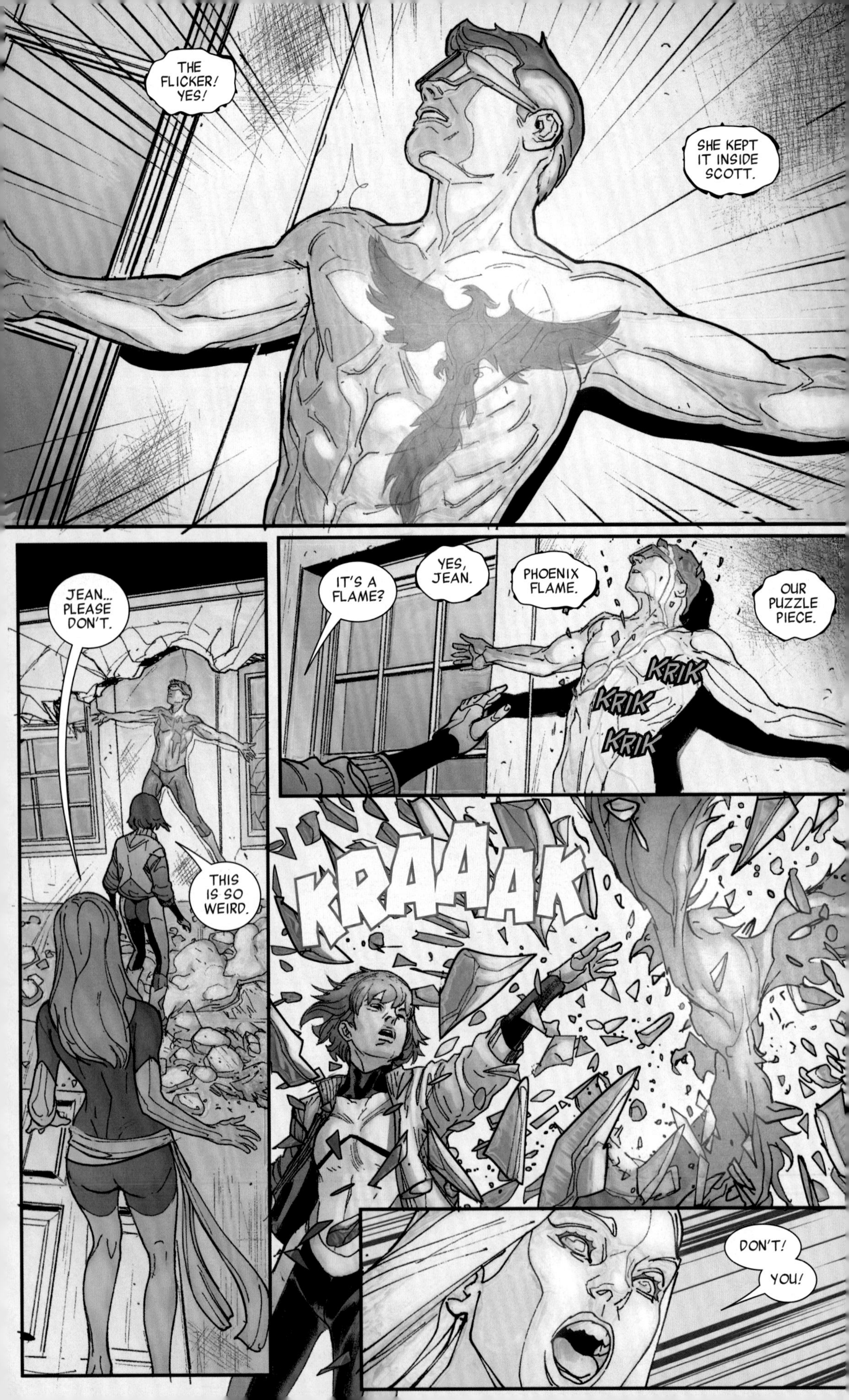
THE FLICKER! YES!
SHE KEPT IT INSIDE SCOTT.
JEAN... PLEASE DON'T.
THIS IS SO WEIRD.
IT'S A FLAME?
YES, JEAN.
PHOENIX FLAME.
OUR PUZZLE PIECE.
KRIK
KRIK
KRIK
KRAAAK
DON'T!
YOU!

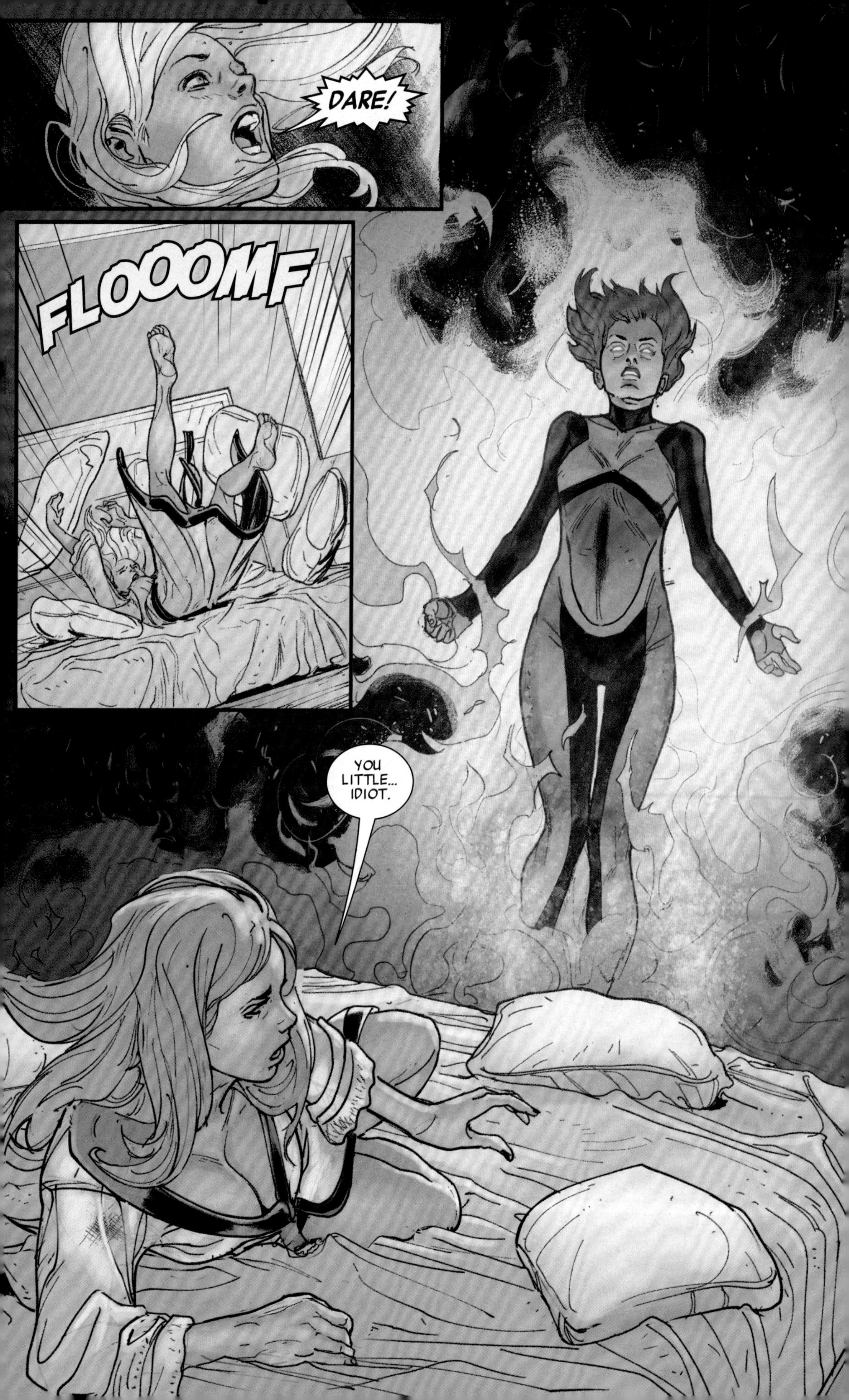
DARE!
FLOOOMF
YOU LITTLE... IDIOT.

9

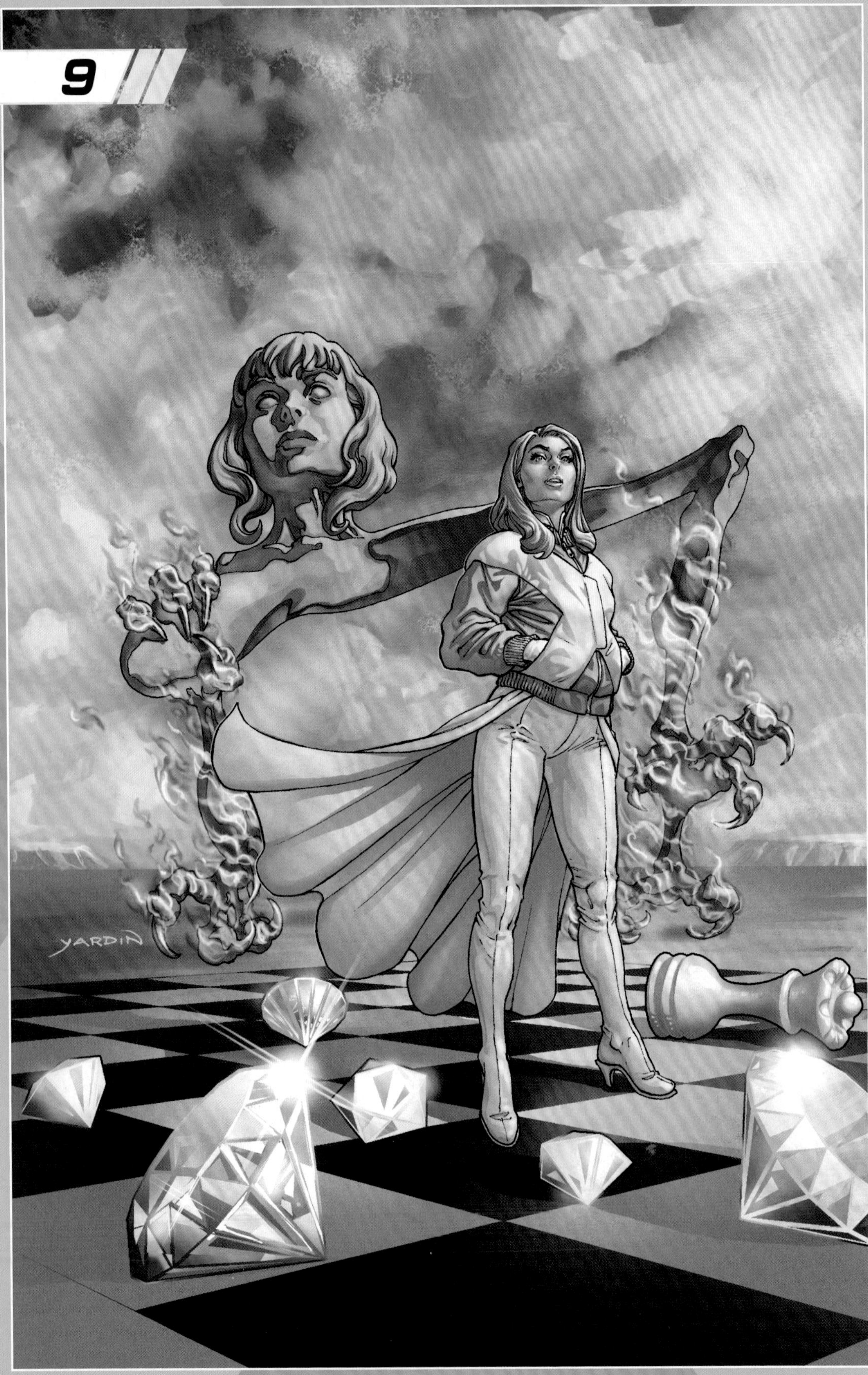
YARDIN

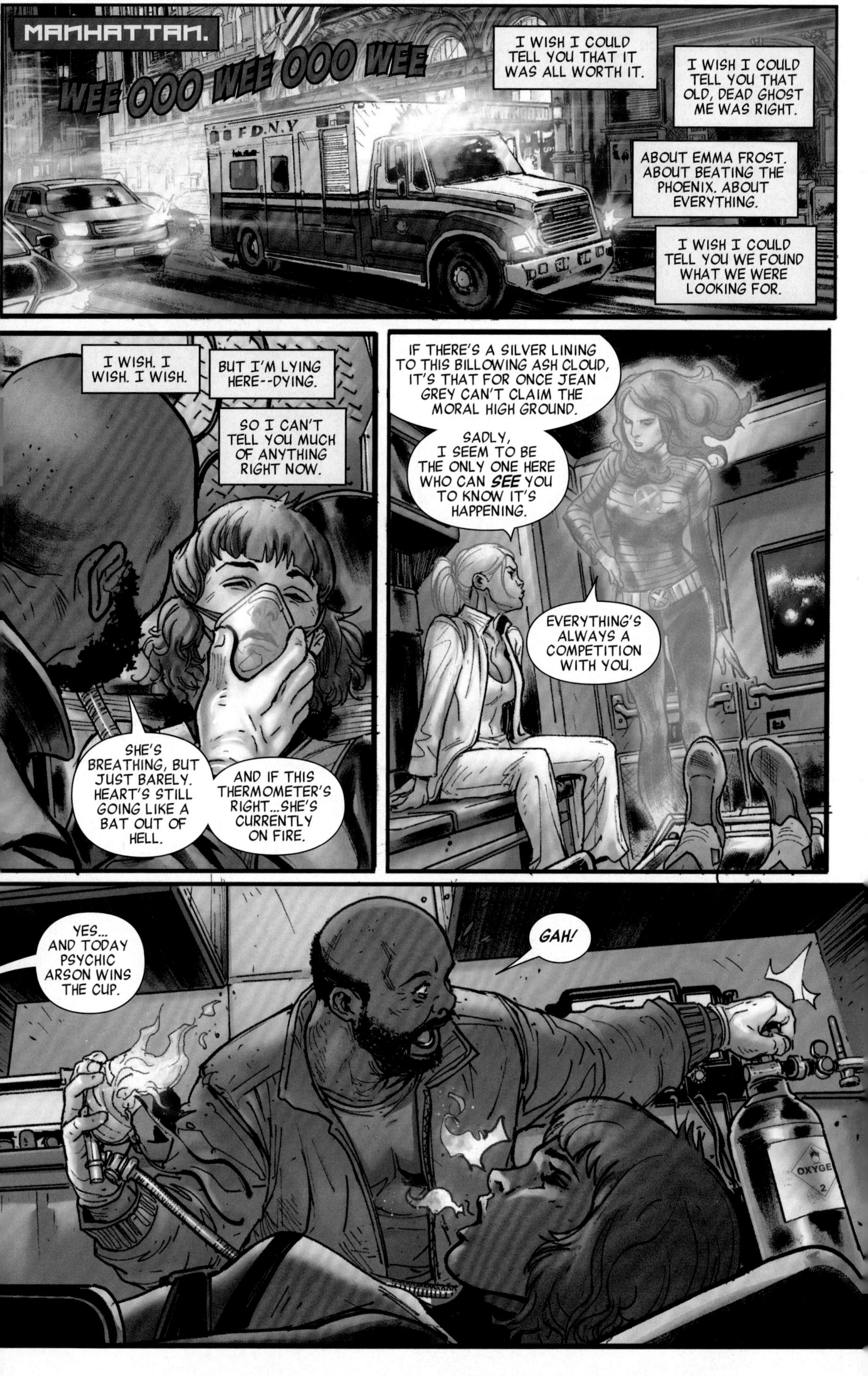
MANHATTAN.
WEE OOO WEE OOO WEE
F.D.N.Y
I WISH I COULD TELL YOU THAT IT WAS ALL WORTH IT.
I WISH I COULD TELL YOU THAT OLD, DEAD GHOST ME WAS RIGHT.
ABOUT EMMA FROST. ABOUT BEATING THE PHOENIX. ABOUT EVERYTHING.
I WISH I COULD TELL YOU WE FOUND WHAT WE WERE LOOKING FOR.
I WISH. I WISH. I WISH.
BUT I'M LYING HERE--DYING.
SO I CAN'T TELL YOU MUCH OF ANYTHING RIGHT NOW.
SHE'S BREATHING, BUT JUST BARELY. HEART'S STILL GOING LIKE A BAT OUT OF HELL.
AND IF THIS THERMOMETER'S RIGHT...SHE'S CURRENTLY ON FIRE.
IF THERE'S A SILVER LINING TO THIS BILLOWING ASH CLOUD, IT'S THAT FOR ONCE JEAN GREY CAN'T CLAIM THE MORAL HIGH GROUND.
SADLY, I SEEM TO BE THE ONLY ONE HERE WHO CAN SEE YOU TO KNOW IT'S HAPPENING.
EVERYTHING'S ALWAYS A COMPETITION WITH YOU.
YES... AND TODAY PSYCHIC ARSON WINS THE CUP.
GAH!
OXYGE
2

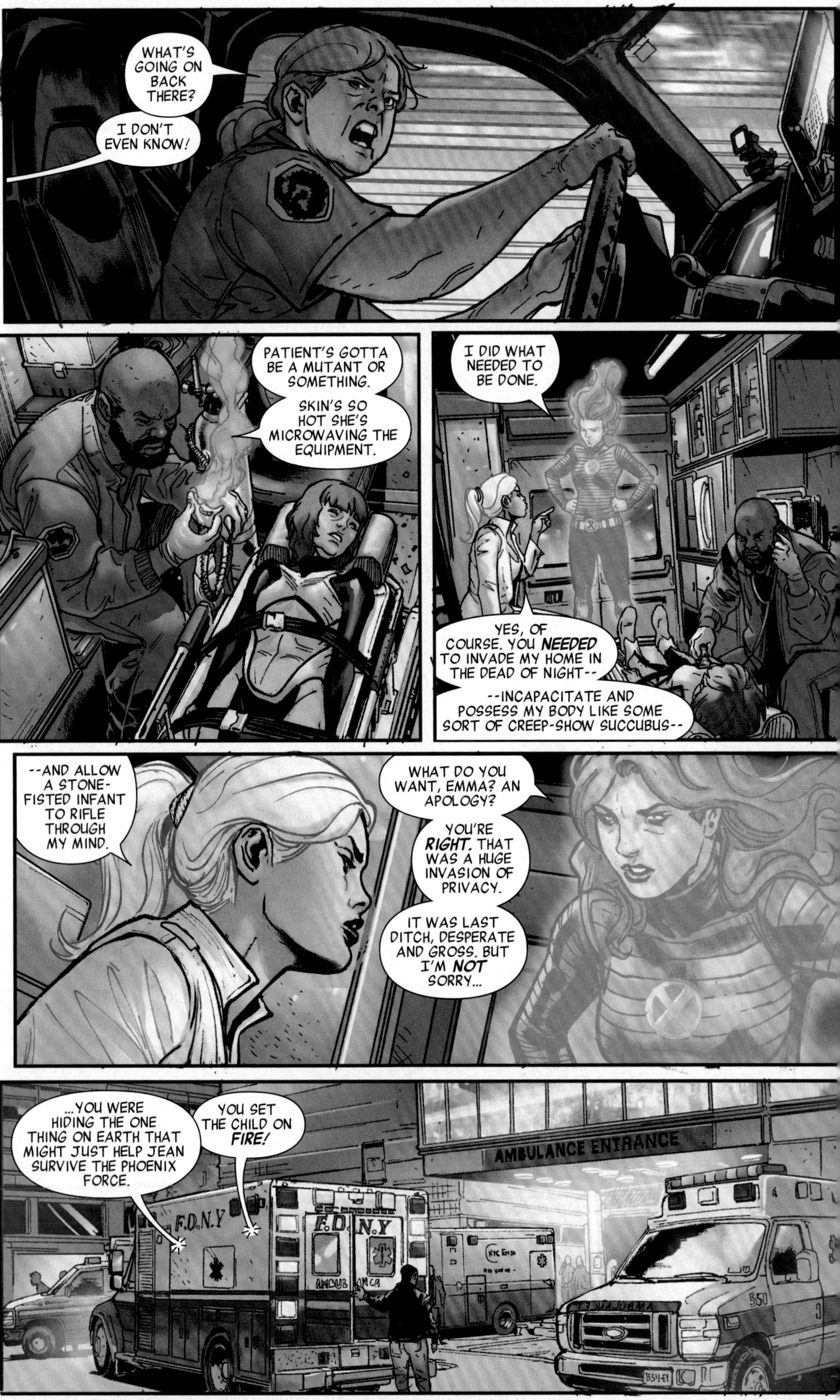
WHAT'S GOING ON BACK THERE?
I DON'T EVEN KNOW!
PATIENT'S GOTTA BE A MUTANT OR SOMETHING.
SKIN'S SO HOT SHE'S MICROWAVING THE EQUIPMENT.
I DID WHAT NEEDED TO BE DONE.
YES, OF COURSE. YOU NEEDED TO INVADE MY HOME IN THE DEAD OF NIGHT--
--INCAPACITATE AND POSSESS MY BODY LIKE SOME SORT OF CREEP-SHOW SUCCUBUS--
--AND ALLOW A STONE-FISTED INFANT TO RIFLE THROUGH MY MIND.
WHAT DO YOU WANT, EMMA? AN APOLOGY?
YOU'RE RIGHT. THAT WAS A HUGE INVASION OF PRIVACY.
IT WAS LAST DITCH, DESPERATE AND GROSS. BUT I'M NOT SORRY...
...YOU WERE HIDING THE ONE THING ON EARTH THAT MIGHT JUST HELP JEAN SURVIVE THE PHOENIX FORCE.
YOU SET THE CHILD ON FIRE!
AMBULANCE ENTRANCE
F.D.N.Y
F.D.N.Y

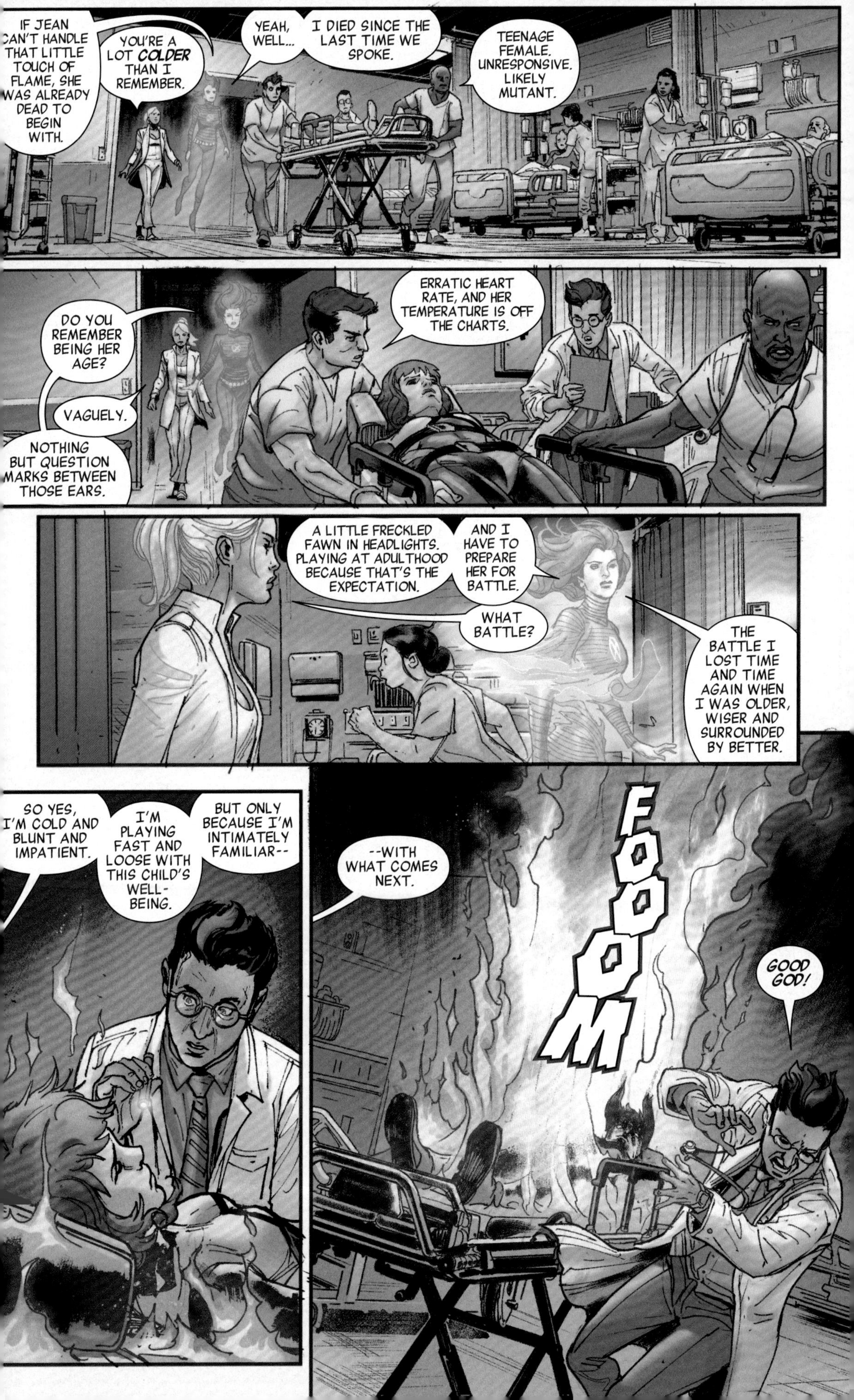
IF JEAN CAN'T HANDLE THAT LITTLE TOUCH OF FLAME, SHE WAS ALREADY DEAD TO BEGIN WITH.
YOU'RE A LOT COLDER THAN I REMEMBER.
YEAH, WELL...
I DIED SINCE THE LAST TIME WE SPOKE.
TEENAGE FEMALE. UNRESPONSIVE. LIKELY MUTANT.
DO YOU REMEMBER BEING HER AGE?
VAGUELY.
NOTHING BUT QUESTION MARKS BETWEEN THOSE EARS.
ERRATIC HEART RATE, AND HER TEMPERATURE IS OFF THE CHARTS.
A LITTLE FRECKLED FAWN IN HEADLIGHTS. PLAYING AT ADULTHOOD BECAUSE THAT'S THE EXPECTATION.
AND I HAVE TO PREPARE HER FOR BATTLE.
WHAT BATTLE?
THE BATTLE I LOST TIME AND TIME AGAIN WHEN I WAS OLDER, WISER AND SURROUNDED BY BETTER.
SO YES, I'M COLD AND BLUNT AND IMPATIENT.
I'M PLAYING FAST AND LOOSE WITH THIS CHILD'S WELL-BEING.
BUT ONLY BECAUSE I'M INTIMATELY FAMILIAR--
--WITH WHAT COMES NEXT.
FOOOM
GOOD GOD!

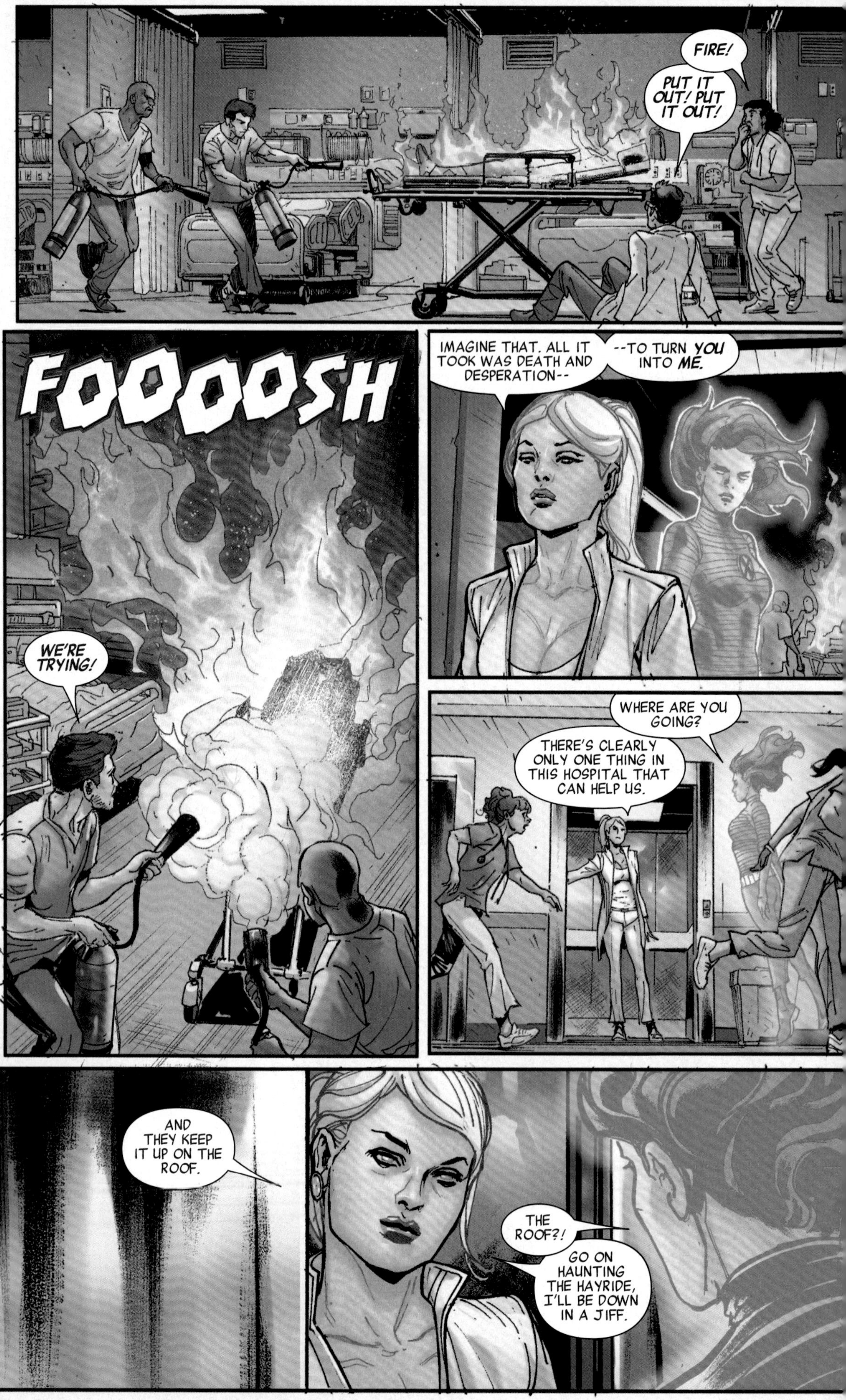
FIRE!
PUT IT OUT! PUT IT OUT!
FOOOOSH
WE'RE TRYING!
IMAGINE THAT. ALL IT TOOK WAS DEATH AND DESPERATION--
--TO TURN YOU INTO ME.
WHERE ARE YOU GOING?
THERE'S CLEARLY ONLY ONE THING IN THIS HOSPITAL THAT CAN HELP US.
AND THEY KEEP IT UP ON THE ROOF.
THE ROOF?!
GO ON HAUNTING THE HAYRIDE, I'LL BE DOWN IN A JIFF.

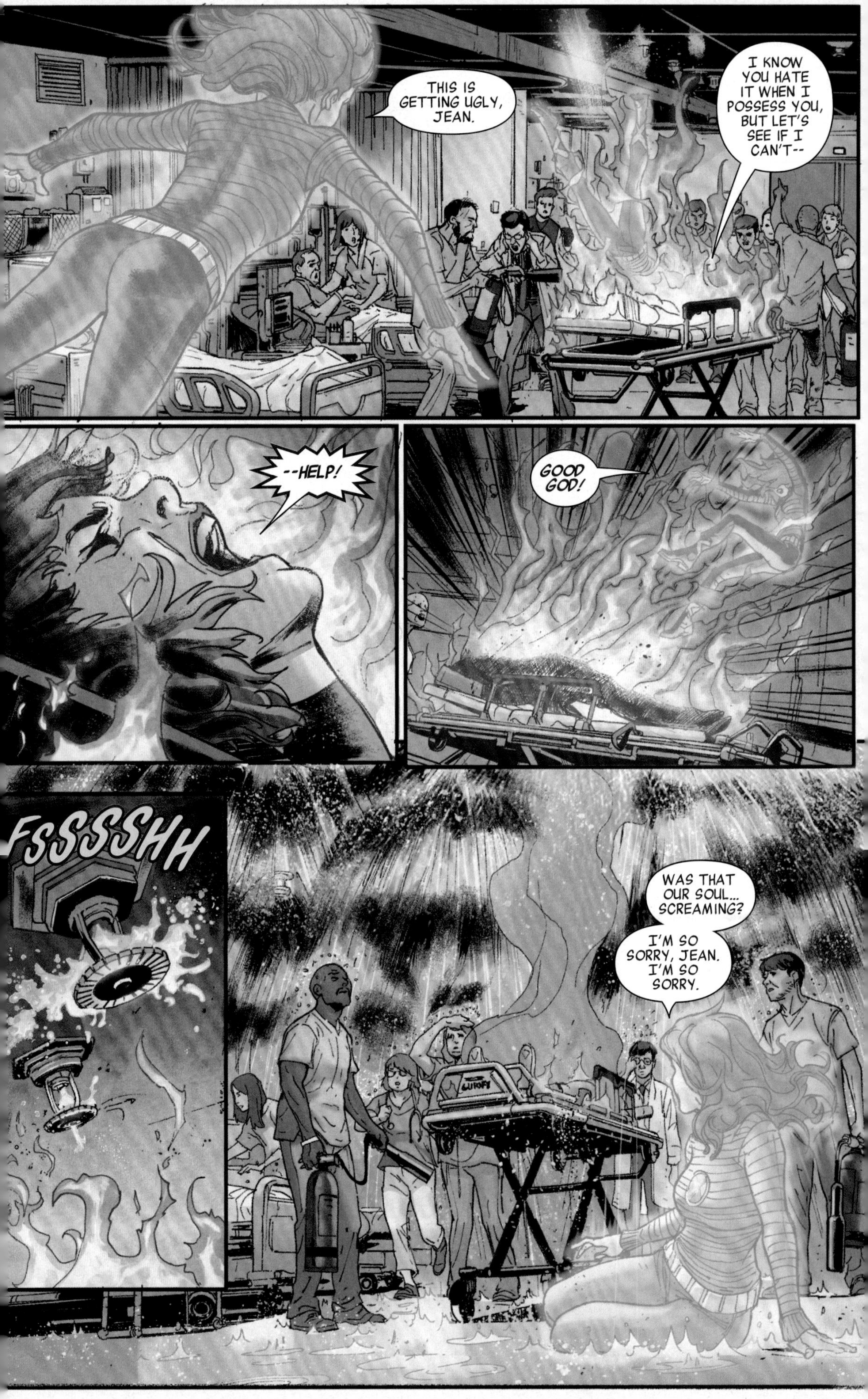
THIS IS GETTING UGLY, JEAN.
I KNOW YOU HATE IT WHEN I POSSESS YOU, BUT LET'S SEE IF I CAN'T--
--HELP!
GOOD GOD!
FSSSSHH
WAS THAT OUR SOUL... SCREAMING?
I'M SO SORRY, JEAN. I'M SO SORRY.

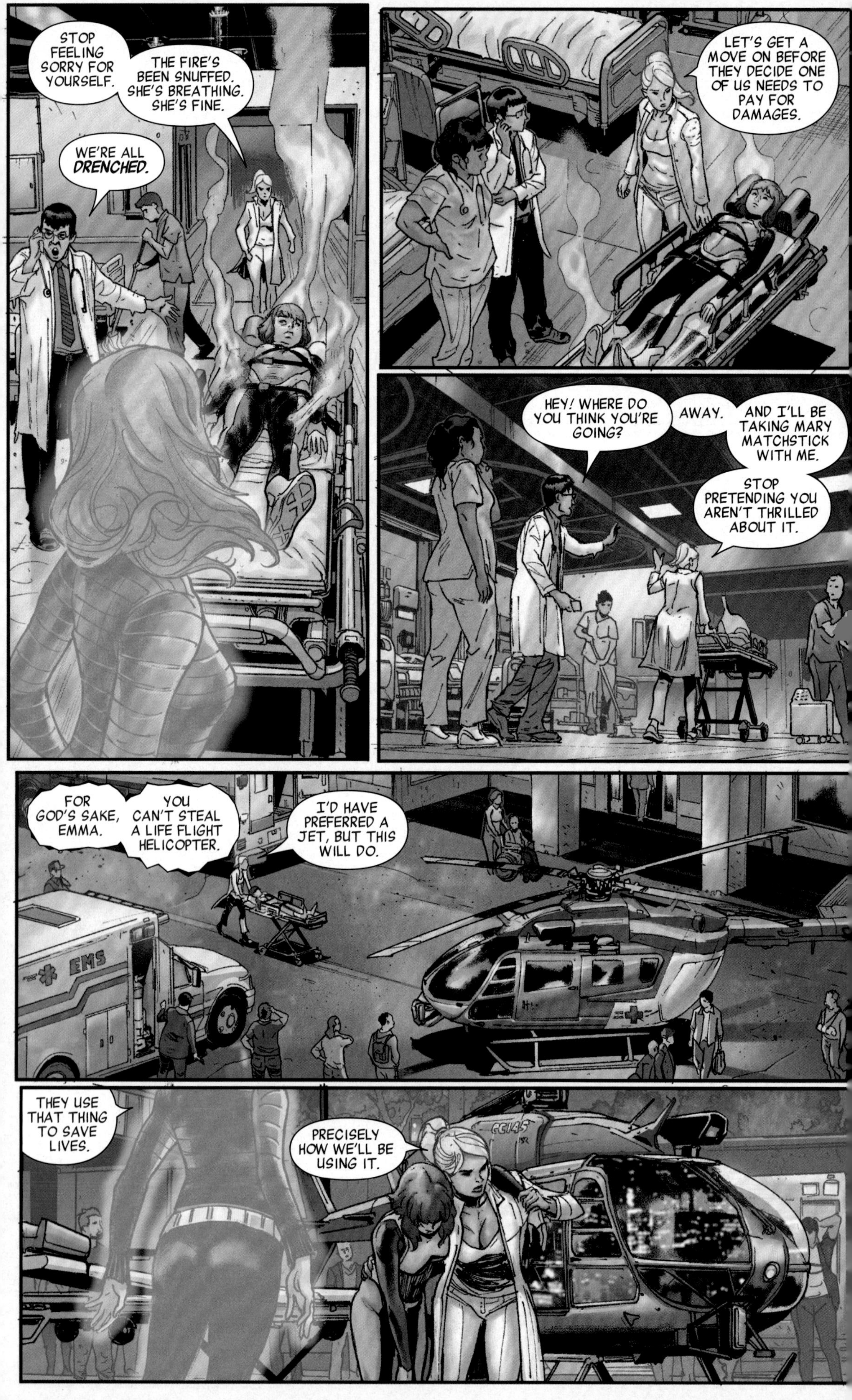
STOP FEELING SORRY FOR YOURSELF.
THE FIRE'S BEEN SNUFFED. SHE'S BREATHING. SHE'S FINE.
WE'RE ALL *DRENCHED.*
LET'S GET A MOVE ON BEFORE THEY DECIDE ONE OF US NEEDS TO PAY FOR DAMAGES.
HEY! WHERE DO YOU THINK YOU'RE GOING?
AWAY.
AND I'LL BE TAKING MARY MATCHSTICK WITH ME.
STOP PRETENDING YOU AREN'T THRILLED ABOUT IT.
FOR GOD'S SAKE, EMMA.
YOU CAN'T STEAL A LIFE FLIGHT HELICOPTER.
I'D HAVE PREFERRED A JET, BUT THIS WILL DO.
EMS
THEY USE THAT THING TO SAVE LIVES.
PRECISELY HOW WE'LL BE USING IT.
EC145

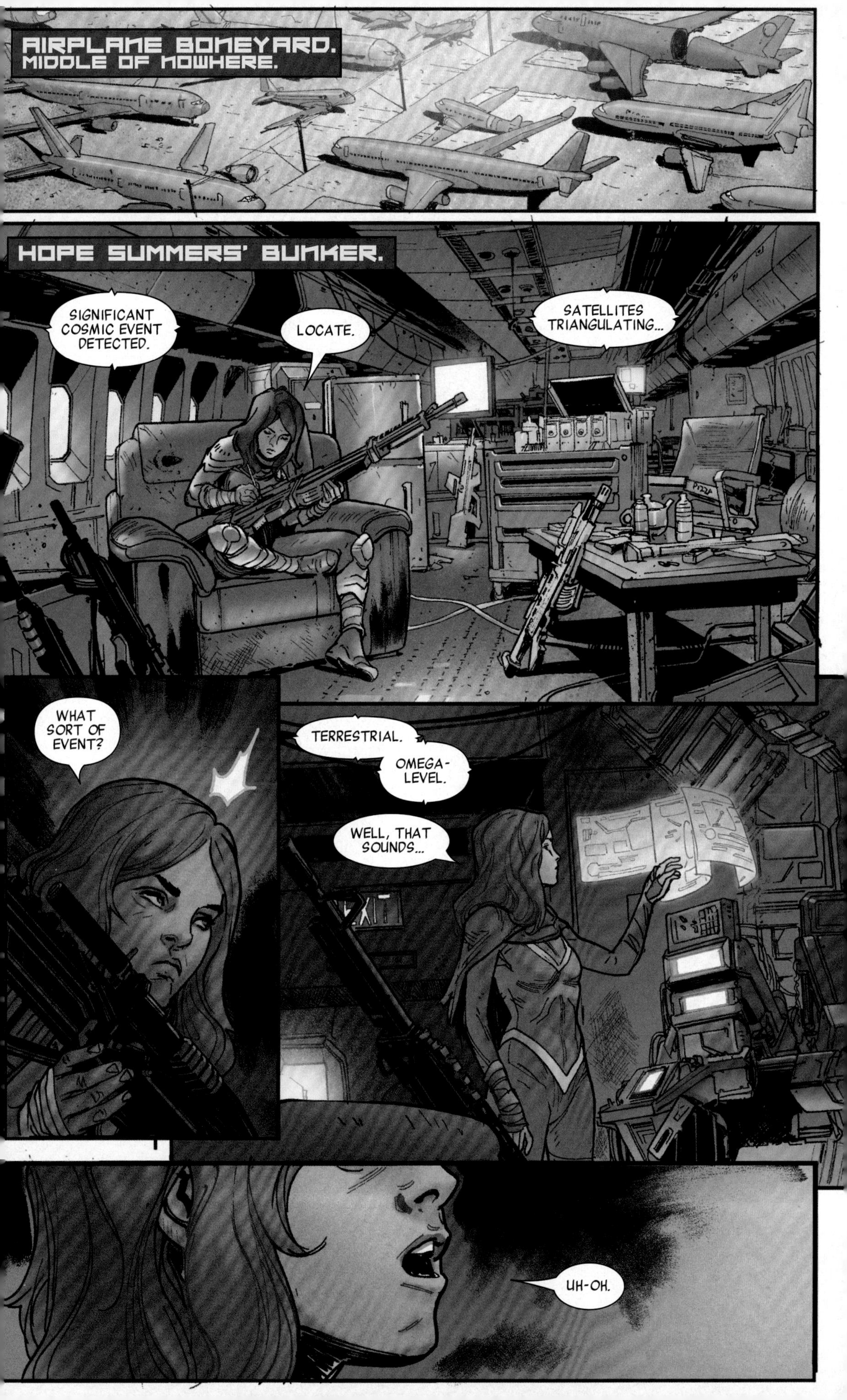
AIRPLANE BONEYARD. MIDDLE OF NOWHERE.
HOPE SUMMERS' BUNKER.
SIGNIFICANT COSMIC EVENT DETECTED.
LOCATE.
SATELLITES TRIANGULATING...
WHAT SORT OF EVENT?
TERRESTRIAL.
OMEGA-LEVEL.
WELL, THAT SOUNDS...
UH-OH.

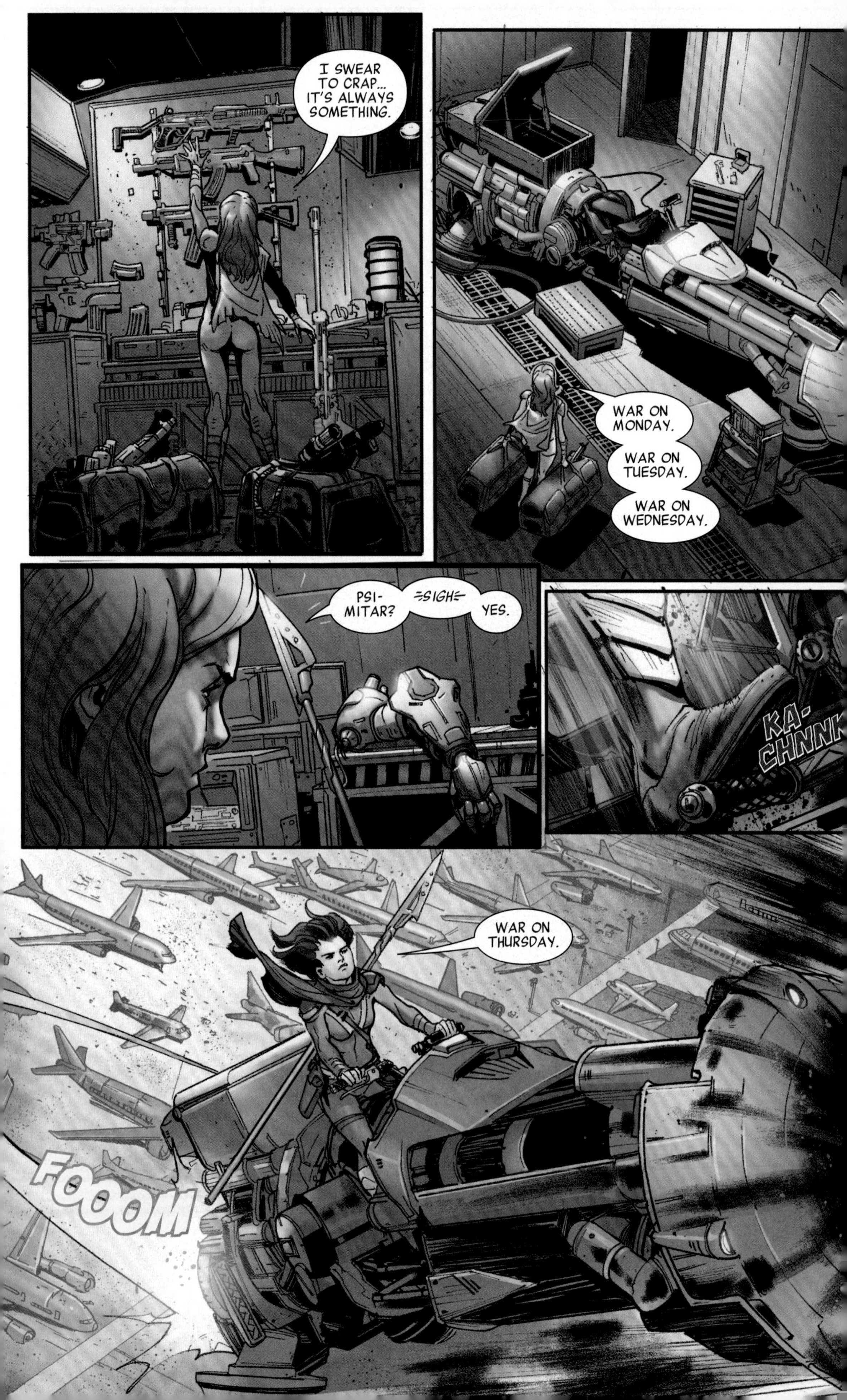
I SWEAR TO CRAP... IT'S ALWAYS SOMETHING.
WAR ON MONDAY.
WAR ON TUESDAY.
WAR ON WEDNESDAY.
PSI-MITAR?
=SIGH=
YES.
KA-CHNNK
WAR ON THURSDAY.
FOOOM

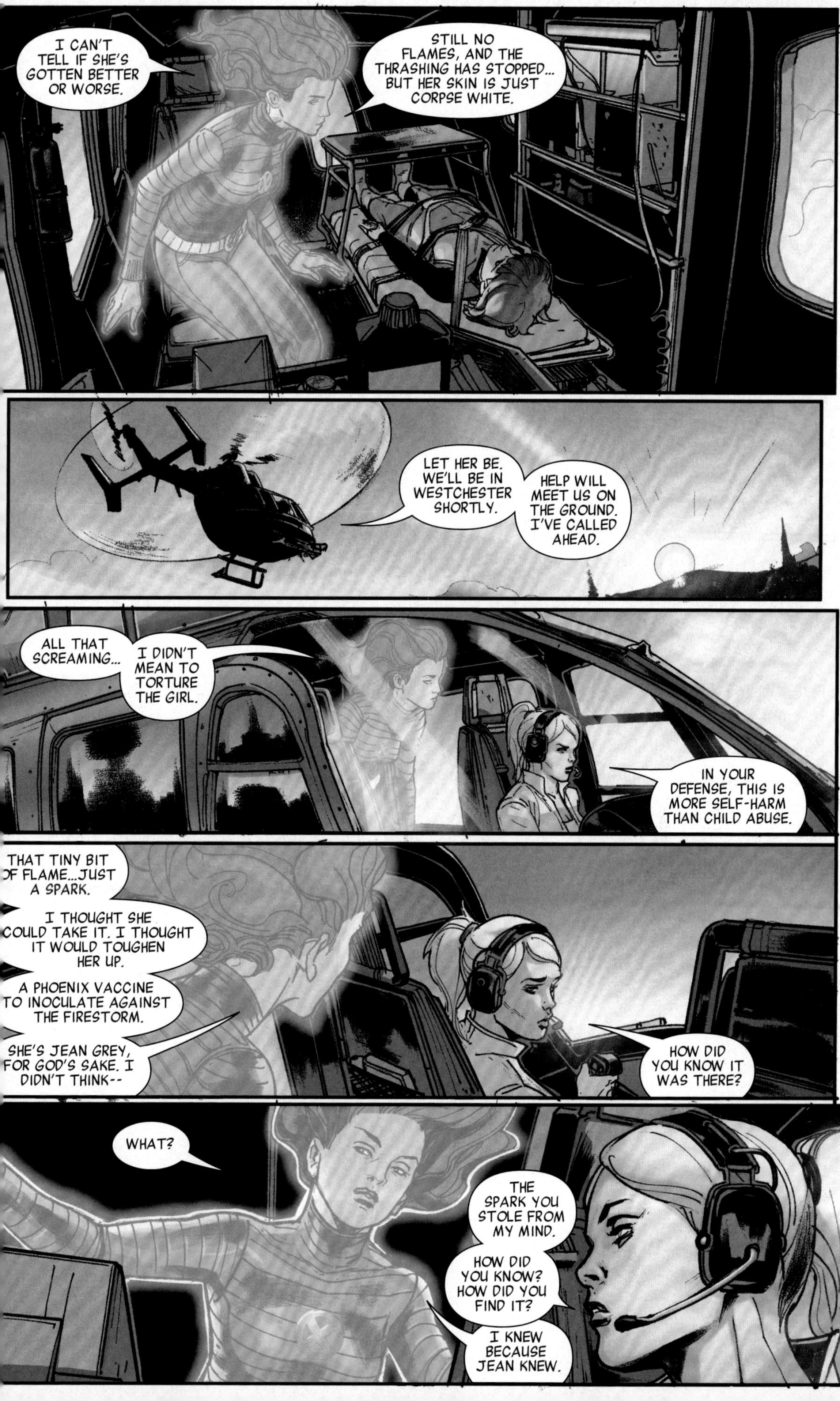
I CAN'T TELL IF SHE'S GOTTEN BETTER OR WORSE.
STILL NO FLAMES, AND THE THRASHING HAS STOPPED... BUT HER SKIN IS JUST CORPSE WHITE.
LET HER BE. WE'LL BE IN WESTCHESTER SHORTLY.
HELP WILL MEET US ON THE GROUND. I'VE CALLED AHEAD.
ALL THAT SCREAMING...
I DIDN'T MEAN TO TORTURE THE GIRL.
IN YOUR DEFENSE, THIS IS MORE SELF-HARM THAN CHILD ABUSE.
THAT TINY BIT OF FLAME...JUST A SPARK.
I THOUGHT SHE COULD TAKE IT. I THOUGHT IT WOULD TOUGHEN HER UP.
A PHOENIX VACCINE TO INOCULATE AGAINST THE FIRESTORM.
SHE'S JEAN GREY, FOR GOD'S SAKE. I DIDN'T THINK--
HOW DID YOU KNOW IT WAS THERE?
WHAT?
THE SPARK YOU STOLE FROM MY MIND.
HOW DID YOU KNOW? HOW DID YOU FIND IT?
I KNEW BECAUSE JEAN KNEW.

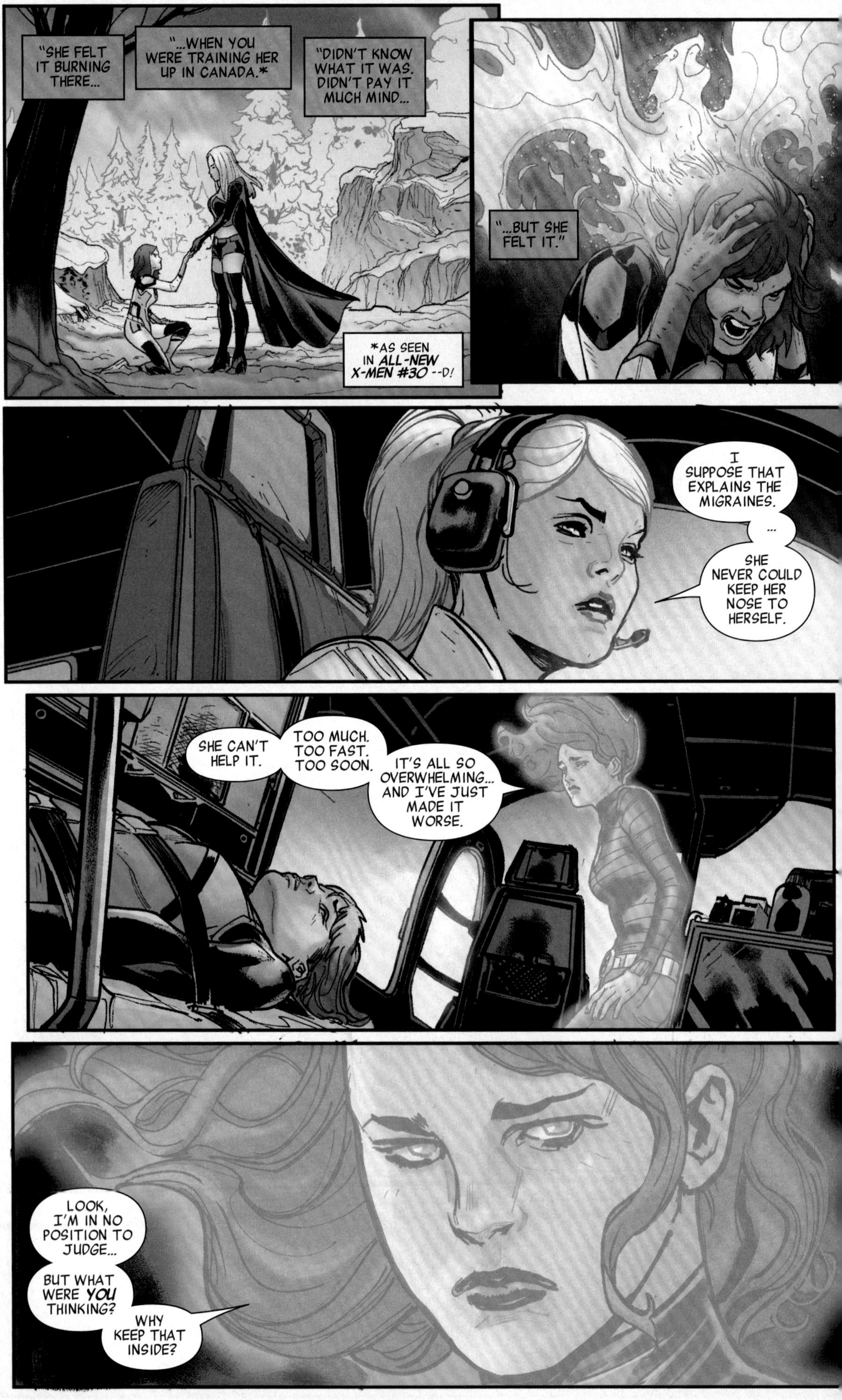
"SHE FELT IT BURNING THERE...
"...WHEN YOU WERE TRAINING HER UP IN CANADA.*
"DIDN'T KNOW WHAT IT WAS. DIDN'T PAY IT MUCH MIND...
*AS SEEN IN ALL-NEW X-MEN #30 --D!
"...BUT SHE FELT IT."
I SUPPOSE THAT EXPLAINS THE MIGRAINES.
...
SHE NEVER COULD KEEP HER NOSE TO HERSELF.
SHE CAN'T HELP IT.
TOO MUCH. TOO FAST. TOO SOON.
IT'S ALL SO OVERWHELMING... AND I'VE JUST MADE IT WORSE.
LOOK, I'M IN NO POSITION TO JUDGE...
BUT WHAT WERE YOU THINKING?
WHY KEEP THAT INSIDE?

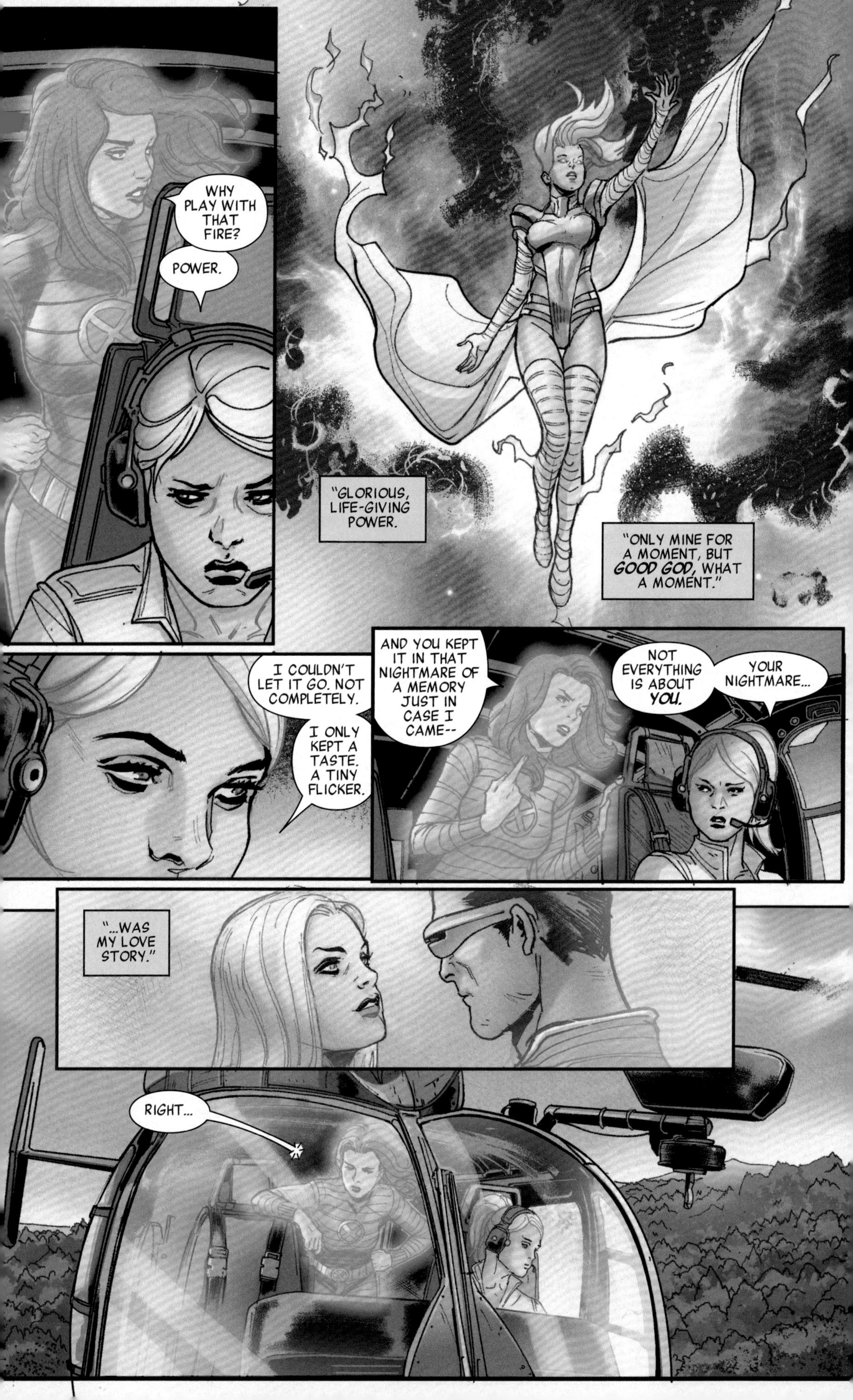
WHY PLAY WITH THAT FIRE?
POWER.
"GLORIOUS, LIFE-GIVING POWER.
"ONLY MINE FOR A MOMENT, BUT GOOD GOD, WHAT A MOMENT."
I COULDN'T LET IT GO. NOT COMPLETELY.
I ONLY KEPT A TASTE. A TINY FLICKER.
AND YOU KEPT IT IN THAT NIGHTMARE OF A MEMORY JUST IN CASE I CAME--
NOT EVERYTHING IS ABOUT YOU.
YOUR NIGHTMARE...
"...WAS MY LOVE STORY."
RIGHT...

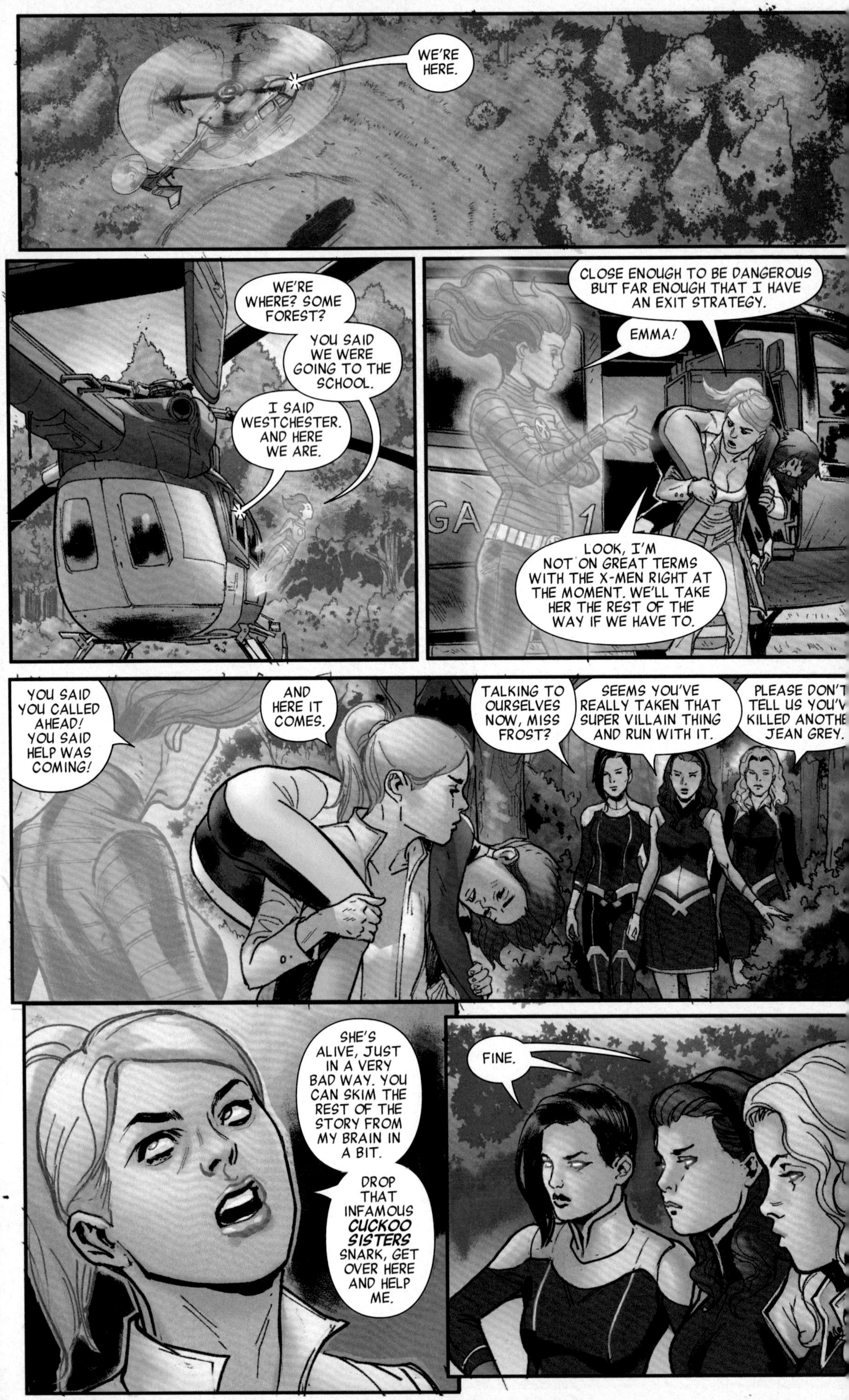
WE'RE HERE.
WE'RE WHERE? SOME FOREST?
YOU SAID WE WERE GOING TO THE SCHOOL.
I SAID WESTCHESTER. AND HERE WE ARE.
CLOSE ENOUGH TO BE DANGEROUS BUT FAR ENOUGH THAT I HAVE AN EXIT STRATEGY.
EMMA!
LOOK, I'M NOT ON GREAT TERMS WITH THE X-MEN RIGHT AT THE MOMENT. WE'LL TAKE HER THE REST OF THE WAY IF WE HAVE TO.
YOU SAID YOU CALLED AHEAD! YOU SAID HELP WAS COMING!
AND HERE IT COMES.
TALKING TO OURSELVES NOW, MISS FROST?
SEEMS YOU'VE REALLY TAKEN THAT SUPER VILLAIN THING AND RUN WITH IT.
PLEASE DON'T TELL US YOU'VE KILLED ANOTHER JEAN GREY.
SHE'S ALIVE, JUST IN A VERY BAD WAY. YOU CAN SKIM THE REST OF THE STORY FROM MY BRAIN IN A BIT.
DROP THAT INFAMOUS CUCKOO SISTERS SNARK, GET OVER HERE AND HELP ME.
FINE.

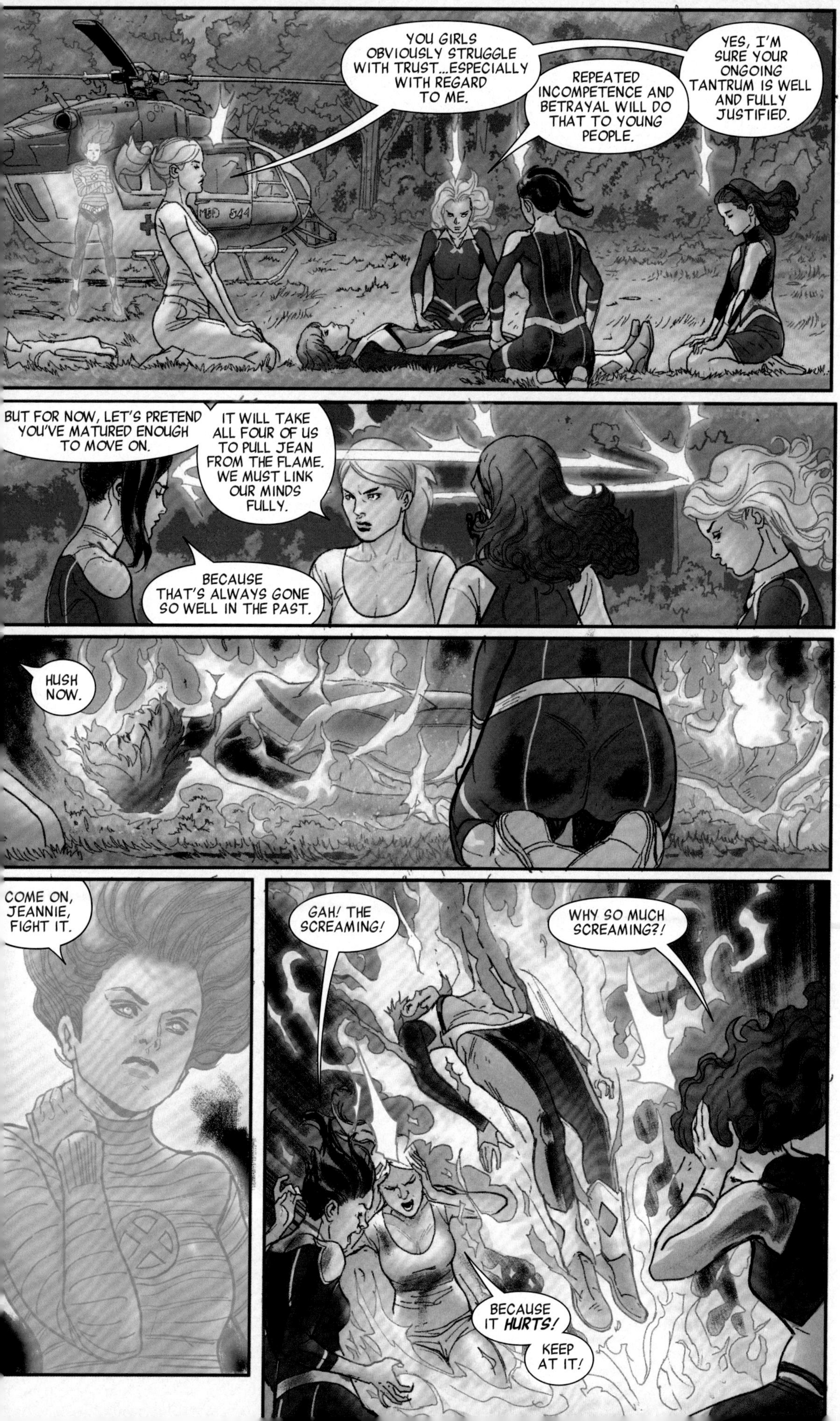
YOU GIRLS OBVIOUSLY STRUGGLE WITH TRUST...ESPECIALLY WITH REGARD TO ME.
REPEATED INCOMPETENCE AND BETRAYAL WILL DO THAT TO YOUNG PEOPLE.
YES, I'M SURE YOUR ONGOING TANTRUM IS WELL AND FULLY JUSTIFIED.
BUT FOR NOW, LET'S PRETEND YOU'VE MATURED ENOUGH TO MOVE ON.
IT WILL TAKE ALL FOUR OF US TO PULL JEAN FROM THE FLAME. WE MUST LINK OUR MINDS FULLY.
BECAUSE THAT'S ALWAYS GONE SO WELL IN THE PAST.
HUSH NOW.
COME ON, JEANNIE, FIGHT IT.
GAH! THE SCREAMING!
WHY SO MUCH SCREAMING?!
BECAUSE IT *HURTS!*
KEEP AT IT!

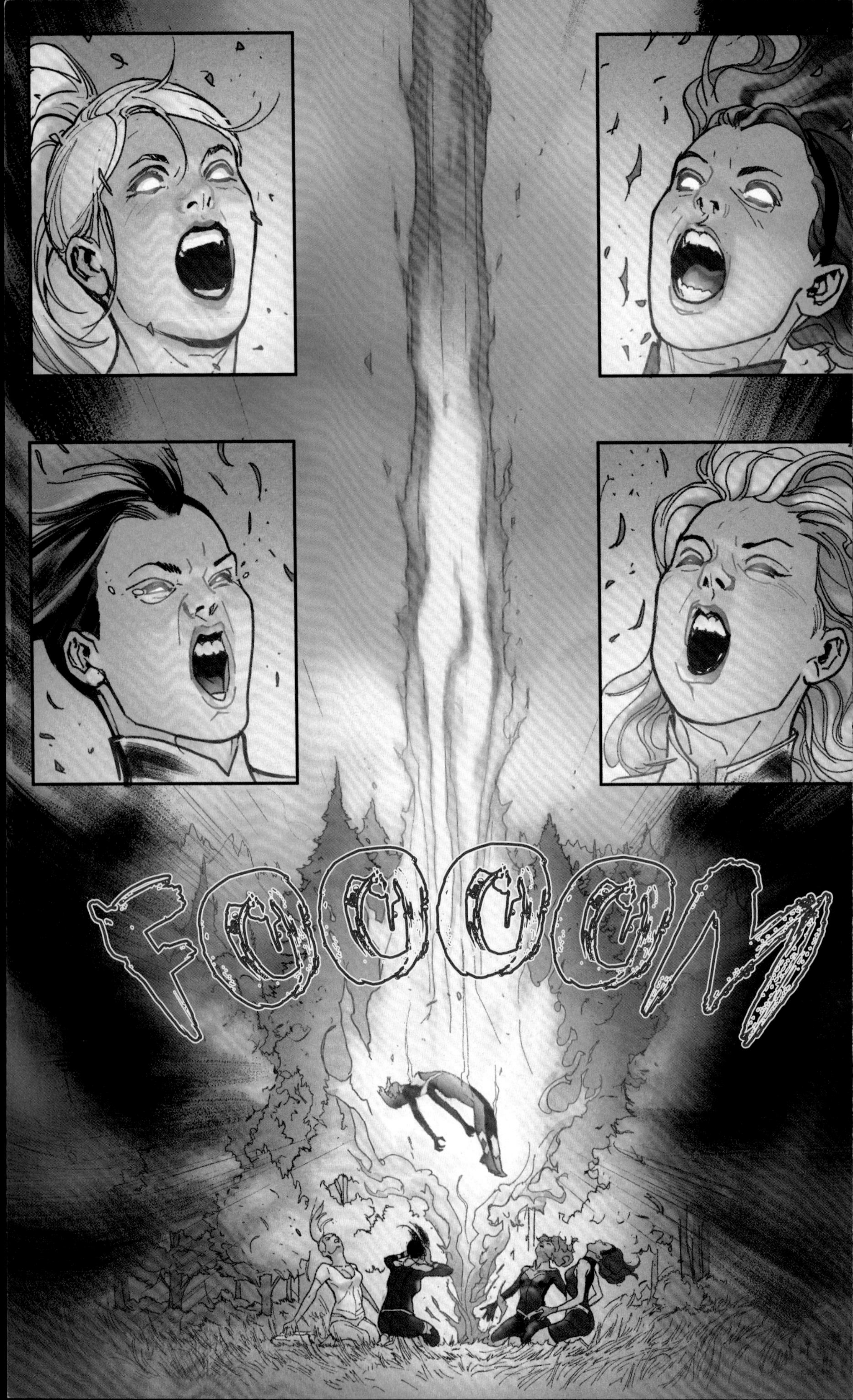
FOOOOM

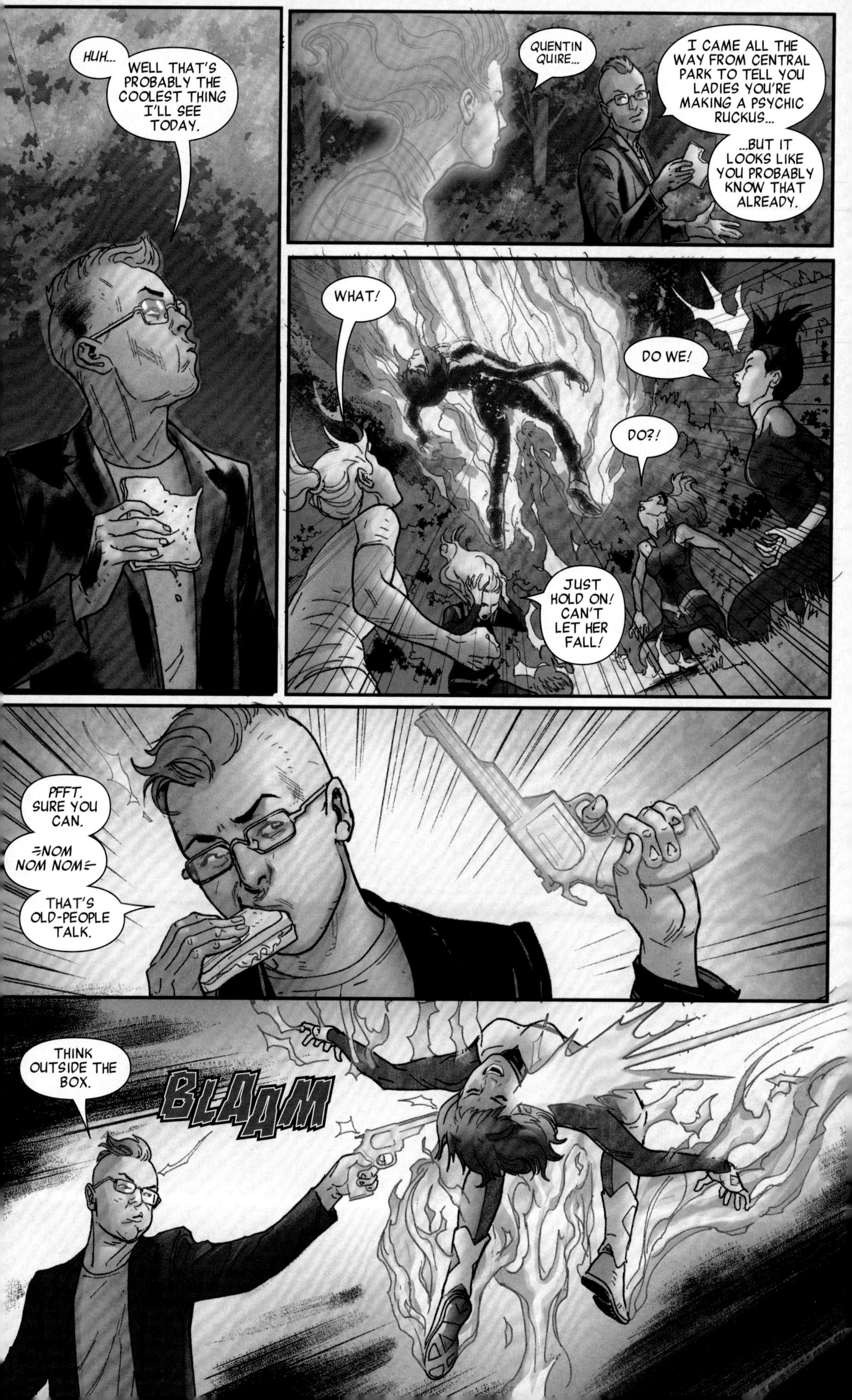
HUH...
WELL THAT'S PROBABLY THE COOLEST THING I'LL SEE TODAY.
QUENTIN QUIRE...
I CAME ALL THE WAY FROM CENTRAL PARK TO TELL YOU LADIES YOU'RE MAKING A PSYCHIC RUCKUS...
...BUT IT LOOKS LIKE YOU PROBABLY KNOW THAT ALREADY.
WHAT!
DO WE!
DO?!
JUST HOLD ON! CAN'T LET HER FALL!
PFFT. SURE YOU CAN.
=NOM NOM NOM=
THAT'S OLD-PEOPLE TALK.
THINK OUTSIDE THE BOX.
BLAAM

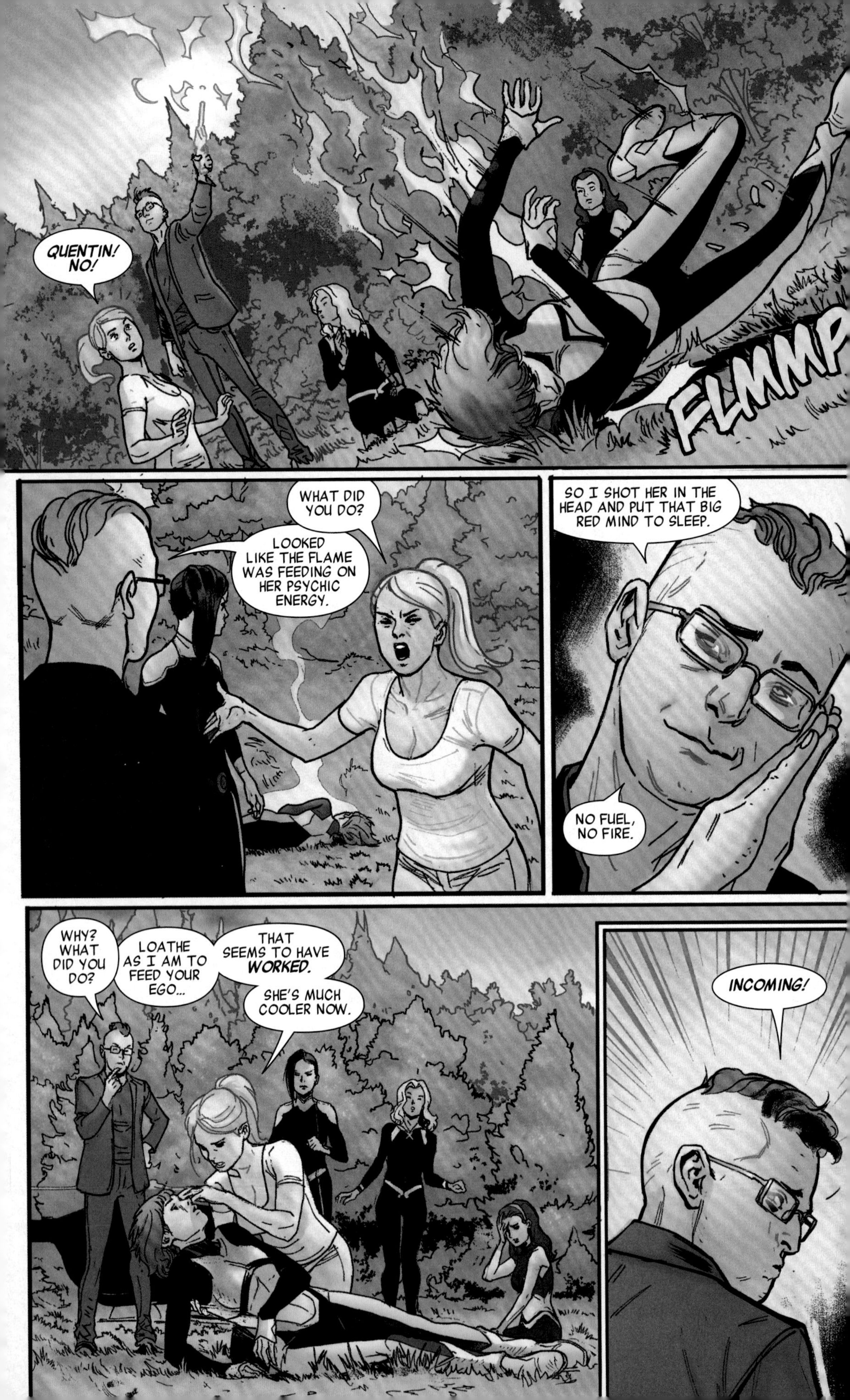

QUENTIN! NO!
FLMMP
WHAT DID YOU DO?
LOOKED LIKE THE FLAME WAS FEEDING ON HER PSYCHIC ENERGY.
SO I SHOT HER IN THE HEAD AND PUT THAT BIG RED MIND TO SLEEP.
NO FUEL, NO FIRE.
WHY? WHAT DID YOU DO?
LOATHE AS I AM TO FEED YOUR EGO...
THAT SEEMS TO HAVE WORKED.
SHE'S MUCH COOLER NOW.
INCOMING!

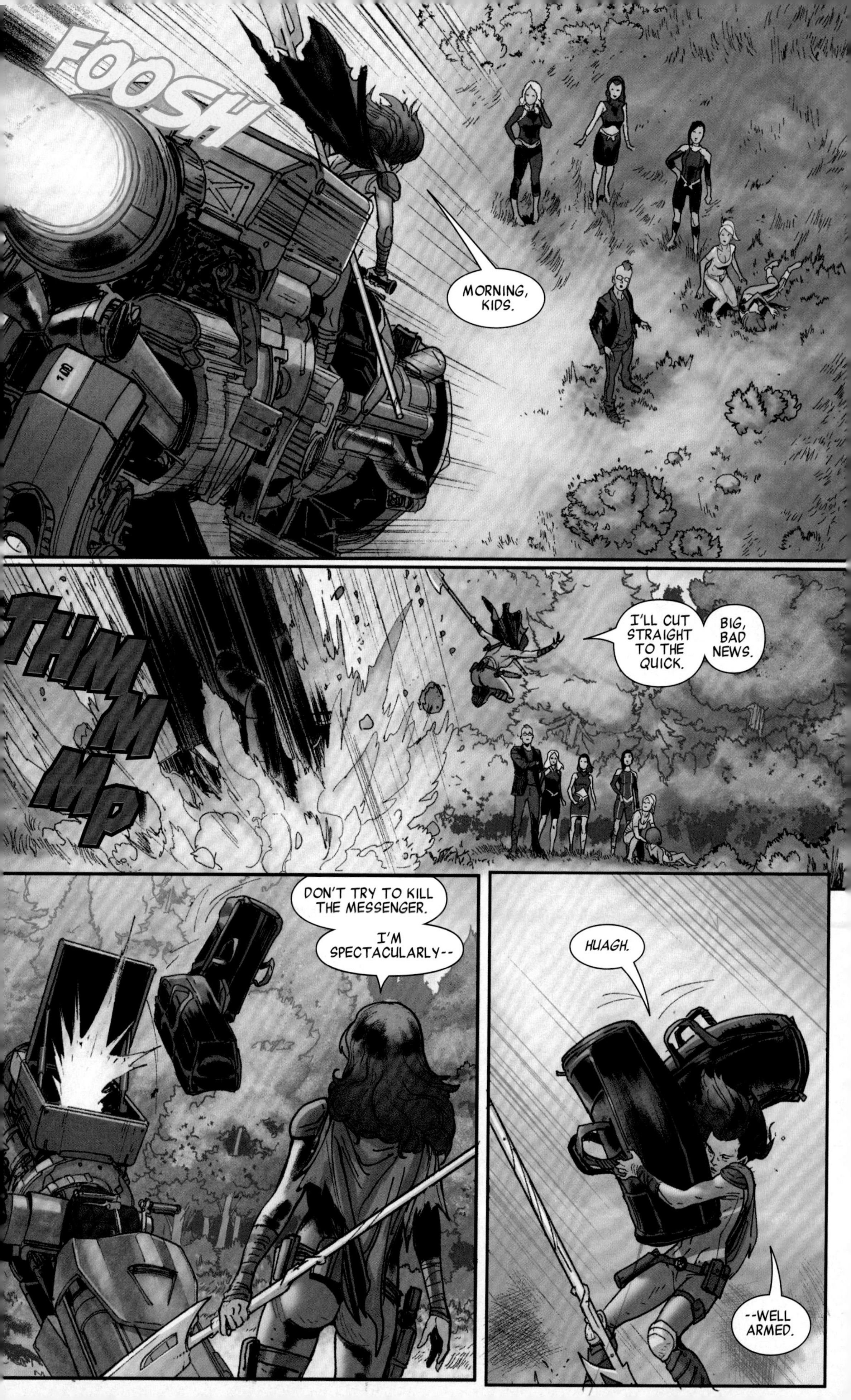
FOOSH
MORNING, KIDS.
THMMMMp
I'LL CUT STRAIGHT TO THE QUICK.
BIG, BAD NEWS.
DON'T TRY TO KILL THE MESSENGER.
I'M SPECTACULARLY--
HUAGH.
--WELL ARMED.

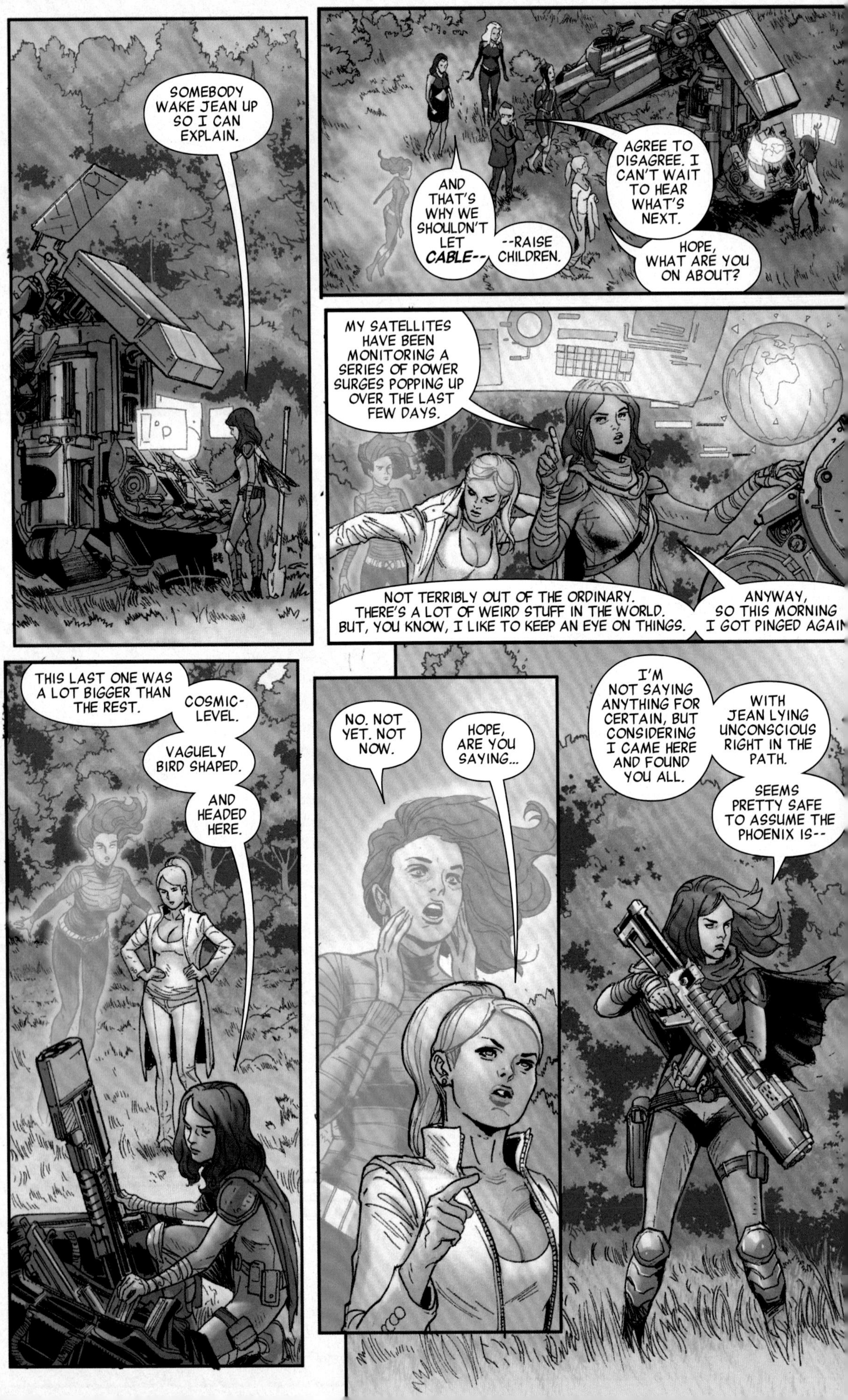
SOMEBODY WAKE JEAN UP SO I CAN EXPLAIN.
AND THAT'S WHY WE SHOULDN'T LET CABLE--
--RAISE CHILDREN.
AGREE TO DISAGREE. I CAN'T WAIT TO HEAR WHAT'S NEXT.
HOPE, WHAT ARE YOU ON ABOUT?
MY SATELLITES HAVE BEEN MONITORING A SERIES OF POWER SURGES POPPING UP OVER THE LAST FEW DAYS.
NOT TERRIBLY OUT OF THE ORDINARY. THERE'S A LOT OF WEIRD STUFF IN THE WORLD. BUT, YOU KNOW, I LIKE TO KEEP AN EYE ON THINGS.
ANYWAY, SO THIS MORNING I GOT PINGED AGAIN
THIS LAST ONE WAS A LOT BIGGER THAN THE REST.
COSMIC-LEVEL.
VAGUELY BIRD SHAPED.
AND HEADED HERE.
NO. NOT YET. NOT NOW.
HOPE, ARE YOU SAYING...
I'M NOT SAYING ANYTHING FOR CERTAIN, BUT CONSIDERING I CAME HERE AND FOUND YOU ALL.
WITH JEAN LYING UNCONSCIOUS RIGHT IN THE PATH.
SEEMS PRETTY SAFE TO ASSUME THE PHOENIX IS--

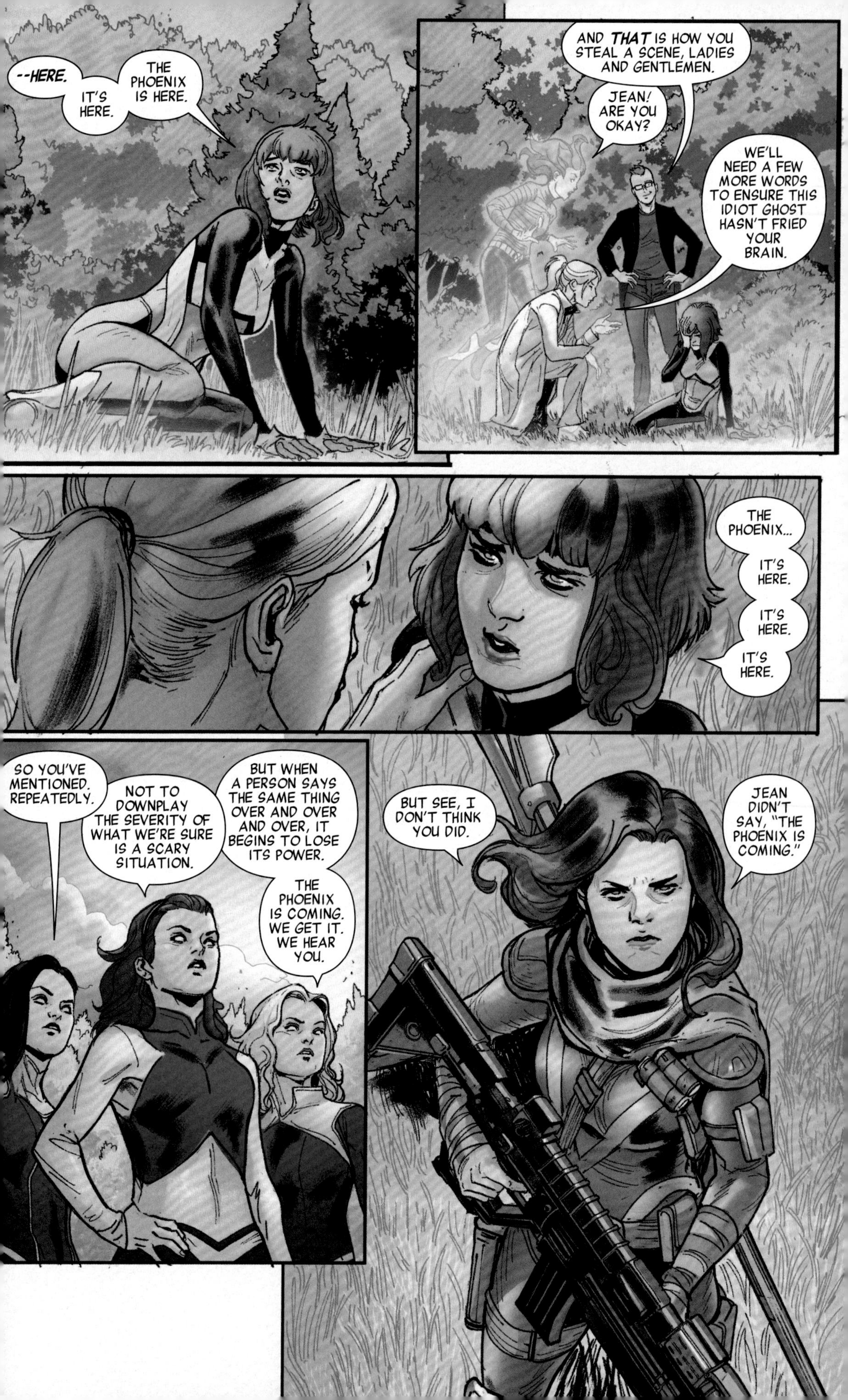
--HERE.
IT'S HERE.
THE PHOENIX IS HERE.
AND THAT IS HOW YOU STEAL A SCENE, LADIES AND GENTLEMEN.
JEAN! ARE YOU OKAY?
WE'LL NEED A FEW MORE WORDS TO ENSURE THIS IDIOT GHOST HASN'T FRIED YOUR BRAIN.
THE PHOENIX...
IT'S HERE.
IT'S HERE.
IT'S HERE.
SO YOU'VE MENTIONED. REPEATEDLY.
NOT TO DOWNPLAY THE SEVERITY OF WHAT WE'RE SURE IS A SCARY SITUATION.
BUT WHEN A PERSON SAYS THE SAME THING OVER AND OVER AND OVER, IT BEGINS TO LOSE ITS POWER.
THE PHOENIX IS COMING. WE GET IT. WE HEAR YOU.
BUT SEE, I DON'T THINK YOU DID.
JEAN DIDN'T SAY, "THE PHOENIX IS COMING."

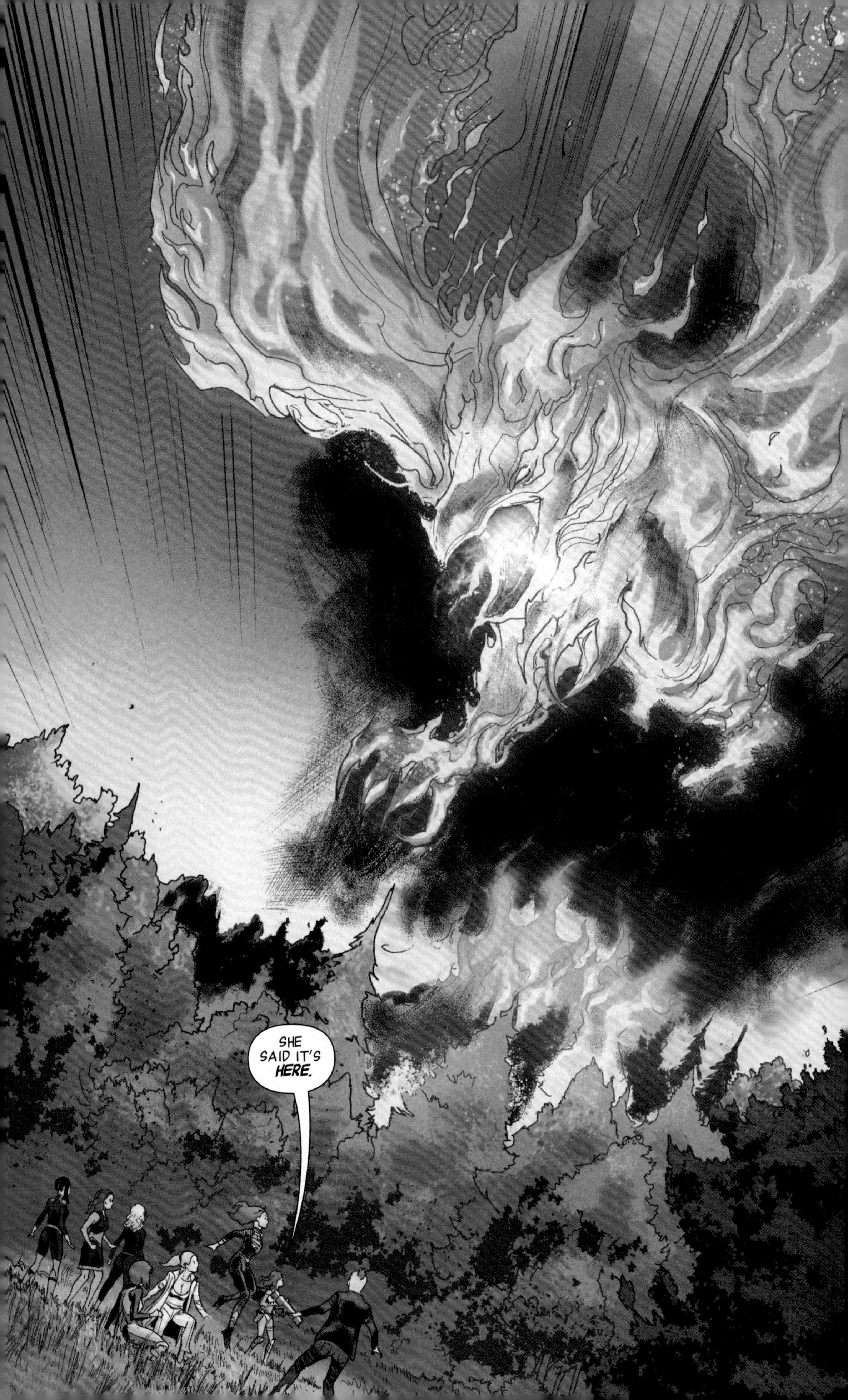
SHE SAID IT'S **HERE.**

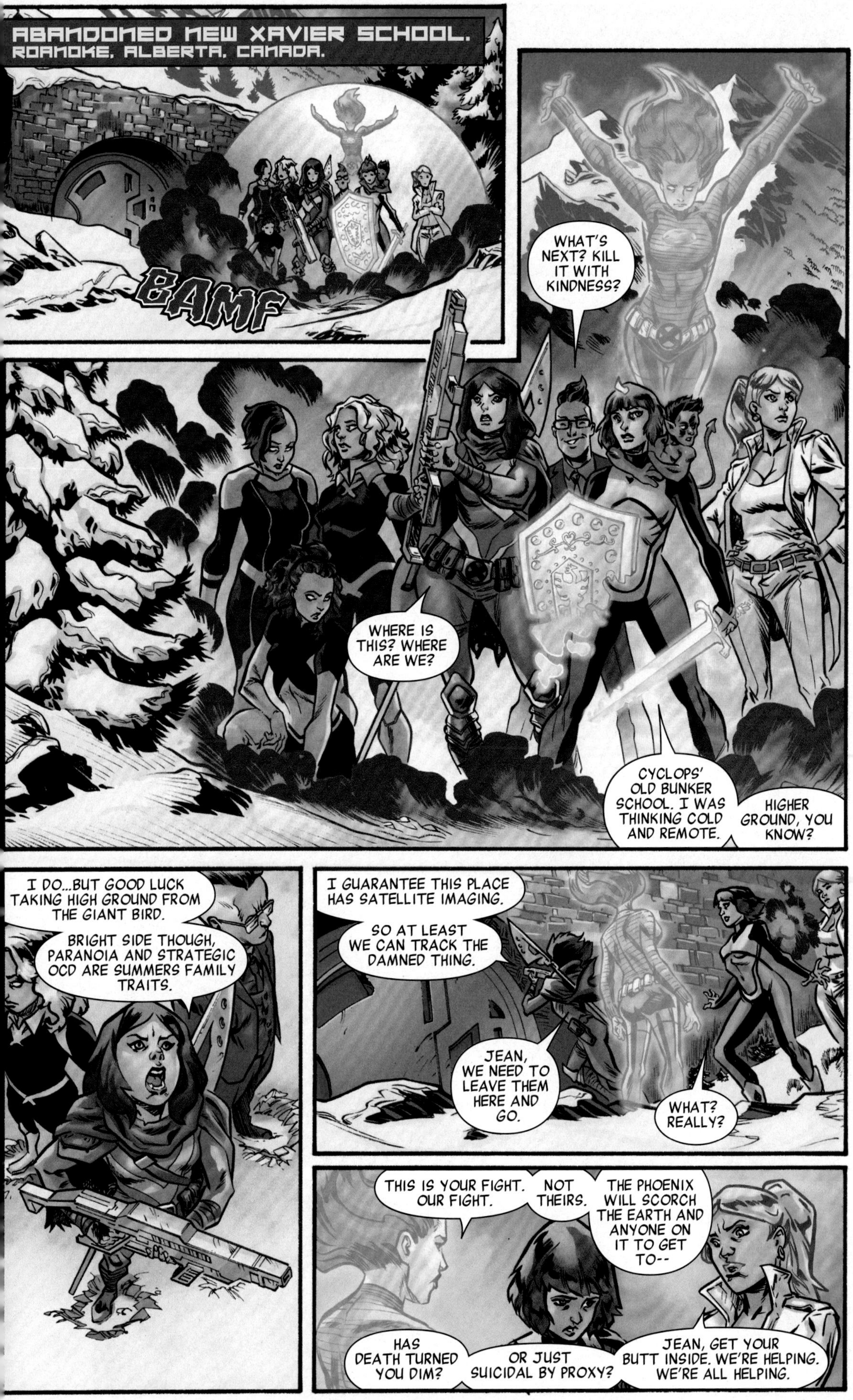
ABANDONED NEW XAVIER SCHOOL.
ROANOKE, ALBERTA, CANADA.
BAMF
WHAT'S NEXT? KILL IT WITH KINDNESS?
WHERE IS THIS? WHERE ARE WE?
CYCLOPS' OLD BUNKER SCHOOL. I WAS THINKING COLD AND REMOTE.
HIGHER GROUND, YOU KNOW?
I DO...BUT GOOD LUCK TAKING HIGH GROUND FROM THE GIANT BIRD.
BRIGHT SIDE THOUGH, PARANOIA AND STRATEGIC OCD ARE SUMMERS FAMILY TRAITS.
I GUARANTEE THIS PLACE HAS SATELLITE IMAGING.
SO AT LEAST WE CAN TRACK THE DAMNED THING.
JEAN, WE NEED TO LEAVE THEM HERE AND GO.
WHAT? REALLY?
THIS IS YOUR FIGHT. OUR FIGHT.
NOT THEIRS.
THE PHOENIX WILL SCORCH THE EARTH AND ANYONE ON IT TO GET TO--
HAS DEATH TURNED YOU DIM?
OR JUST SUICIDAL BY PROXY?
JEAN, GET YOUR BUTT INSIDE. WE'RE HELPING. WE'RE ALL HELPING.

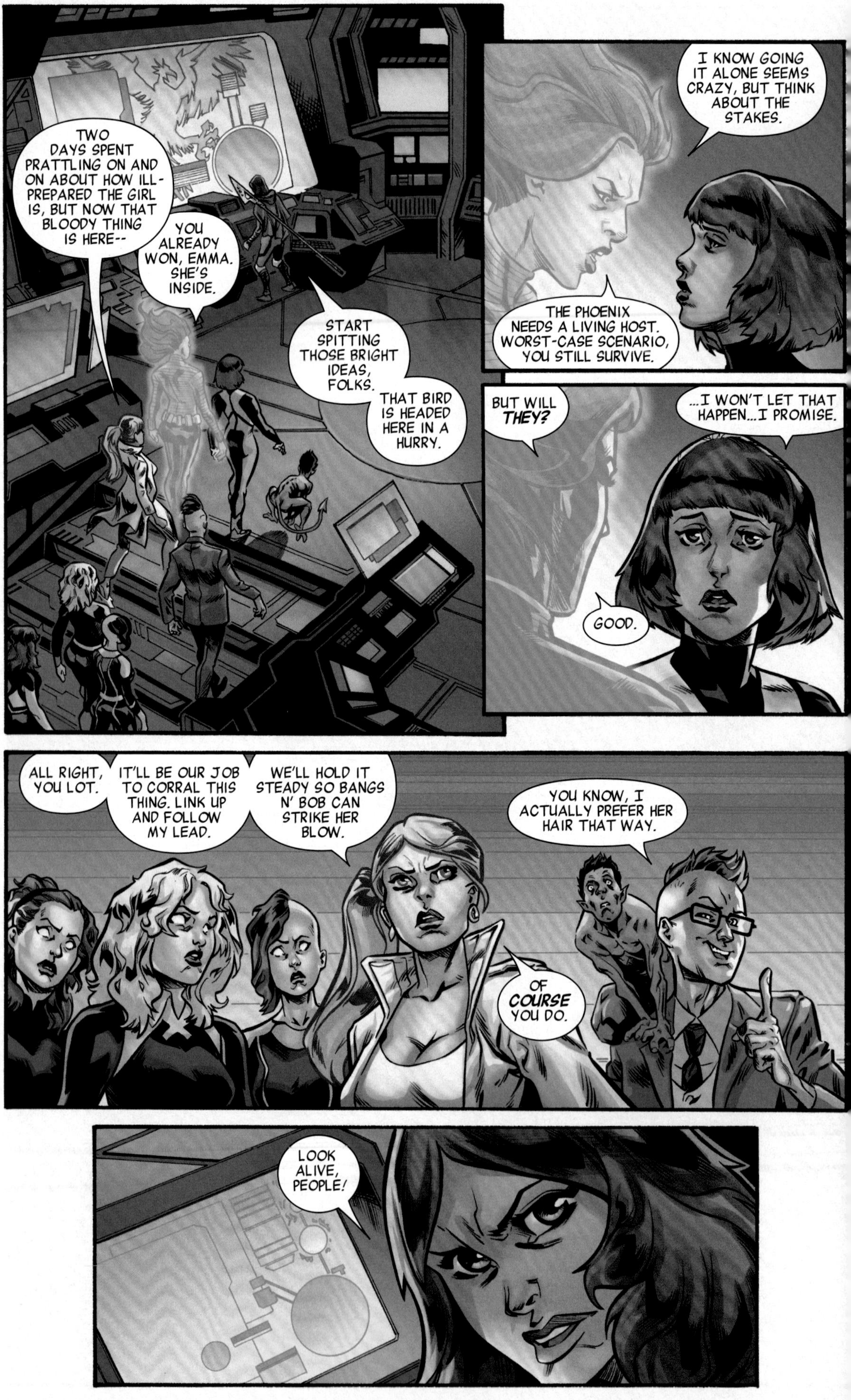
TWO DAYS SPENT PRATTLING ON AND ON ABOUT HOW ILL-PREPARED THE GIRL IS, BUT NOW THAT BLOODY THING IS HERE--
YOU ALREADY WON, EMMA. SHE'S INSIDE.
START SPITTING THOSE BRIGHT IDEAS, FOLKS.
THAT BIRD IS HEADED HERE IN A HURRY.
I KNOW GOING IT ALONE SEEMS CRAZY, BUT THINK ABOUT THE STAKES.
THE PHOENIX NEEDS A LIVING HOST. WORST-CASE SCENARIO, YOU STILL SURVIVE.
BUT WILL *THEY?*
...I WON'T LET THAT HAPPEN...I PROMISE.
GOOD.
ALL RIGHT, YOU LOT.
IT'LL BE OUR JOB TO CORRAL THIS THING. LINK UP AND FOLLOW MY LEAD.
WE'LL HOLD IT STEADY SO BANGS N' BOB CAN STRIKE HER BLOW.
YOU KNOW, I ACTUALLY PREFER HER HAIR THAT WAY.
OF *COURSE* YOU DO.
LOOK ALIVE, PEOPLE!

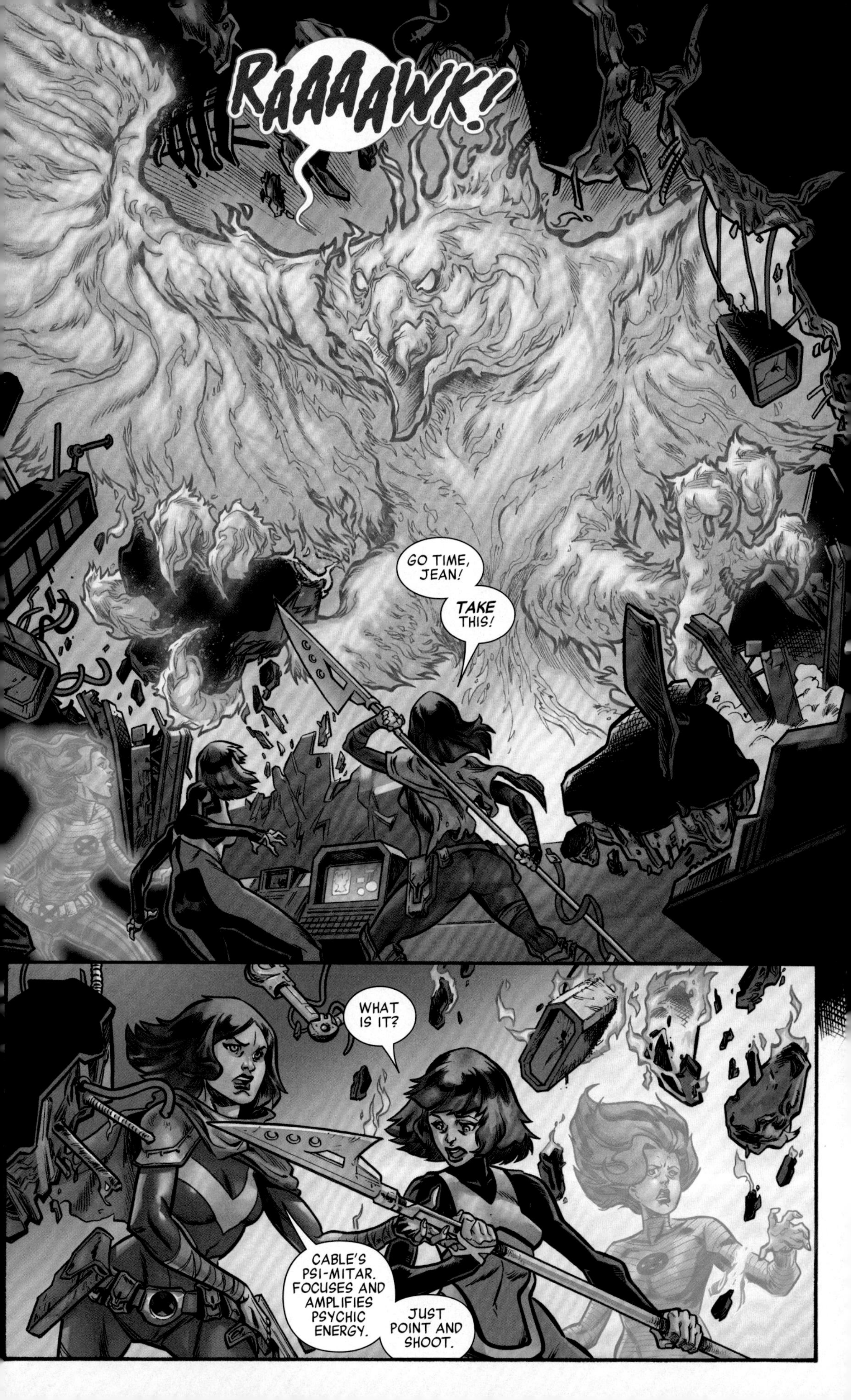
RAAAAWK!
GO TIME, JEAN!
TAKE THIS!
WHAT IS IT?
CABLE'S PSI-MITAR. FOCUSES AND AMPLIFIES PSYCHIC ENERGY.
JUST POINT AND SHOOT.

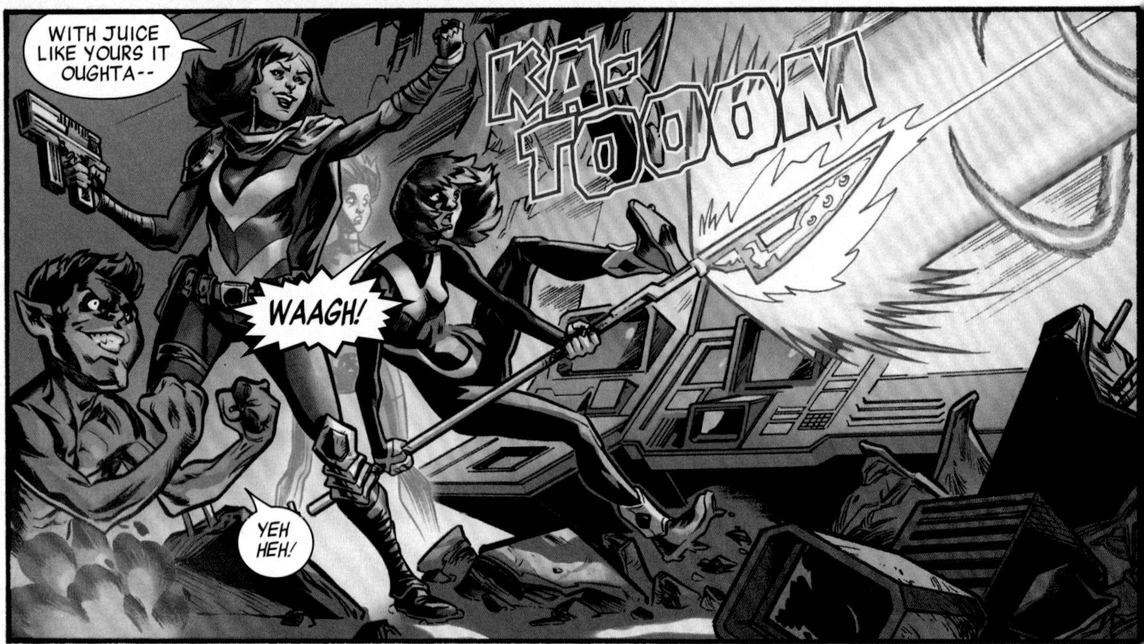
WITH JUICE LIKE YOURS IT OUGHTA--
KA-TOOOOM
WAAGH!
YEH HEH!

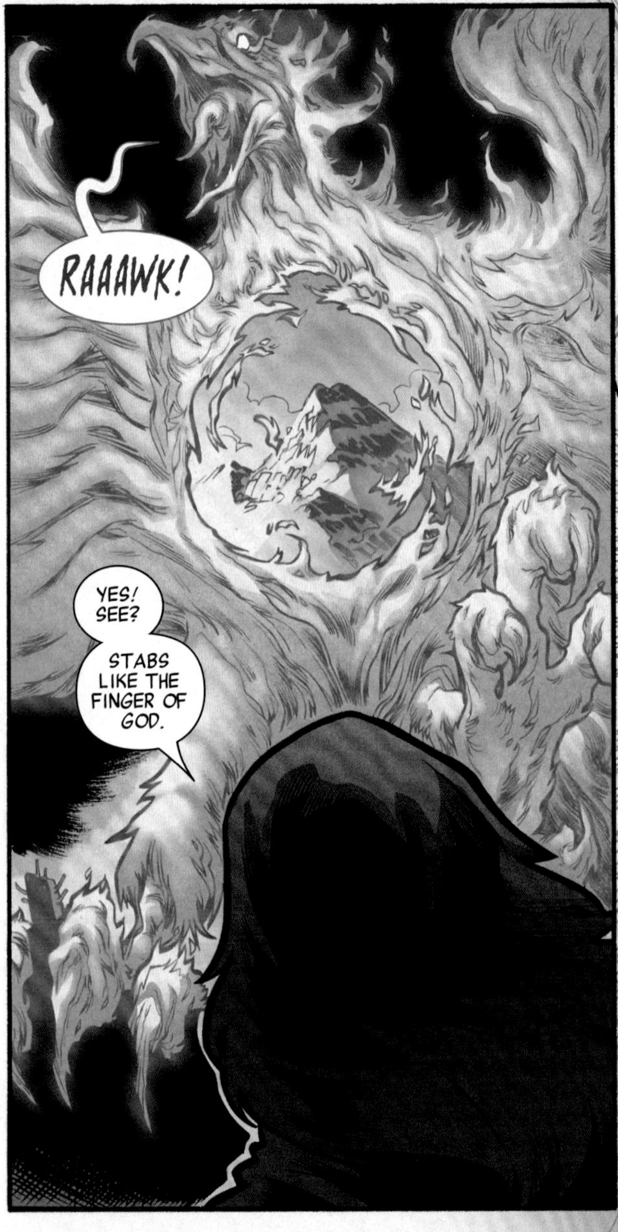
RAAAWK!
YES! SEE?
STABS LIKE THE FINGER OF GOD.

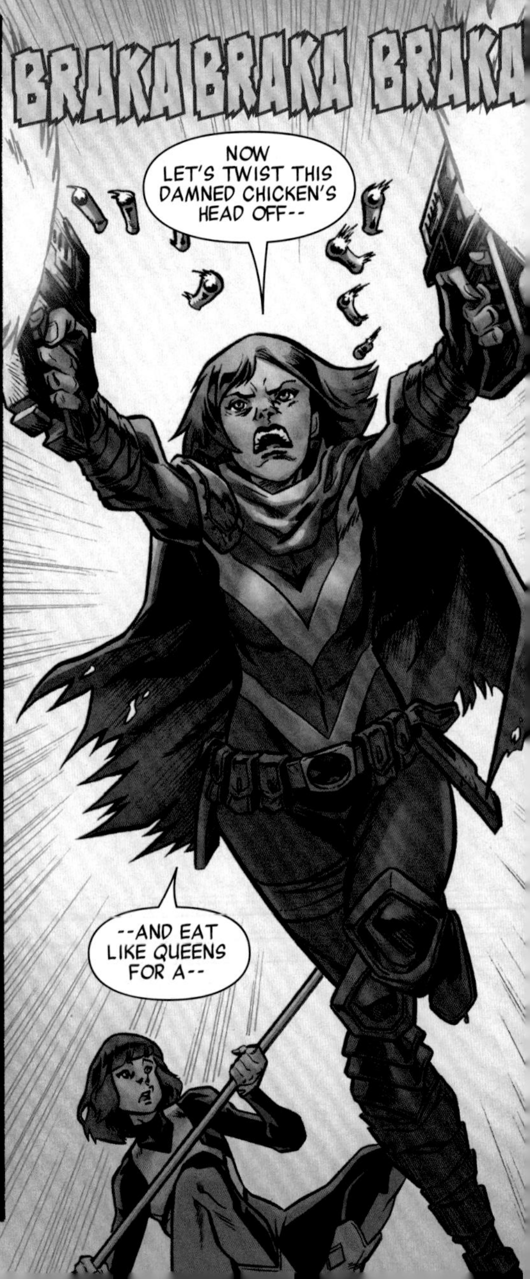
BRAKA BRAKA BRAKA
NOW LET'S TWIST THIS DAMNED CHICKEN'S HEAD OFF--
--AND EAT LIKE QUEENS FOR A--

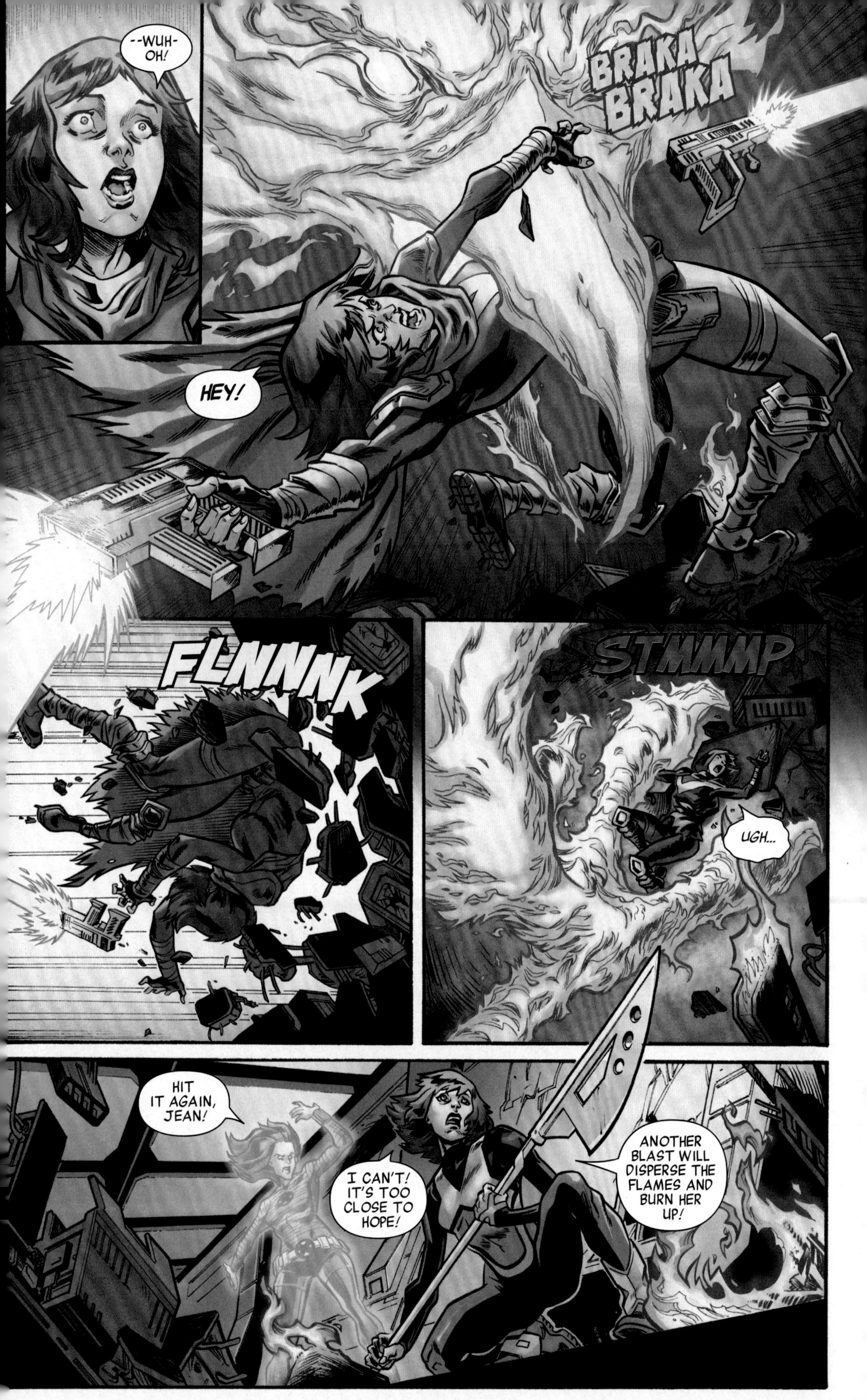
--WUH-OH!
BRAKA BRAKA
HEY!
FLNNNNK
STMMMMP
UGH...
HIT IT AGAIN, JEAN!
I CAN'T! IT'S TOO CLOSE TO HOPE!
ANOTHER BLAST WILL DISPERSE THE FLAMES AND BURN HER UP!

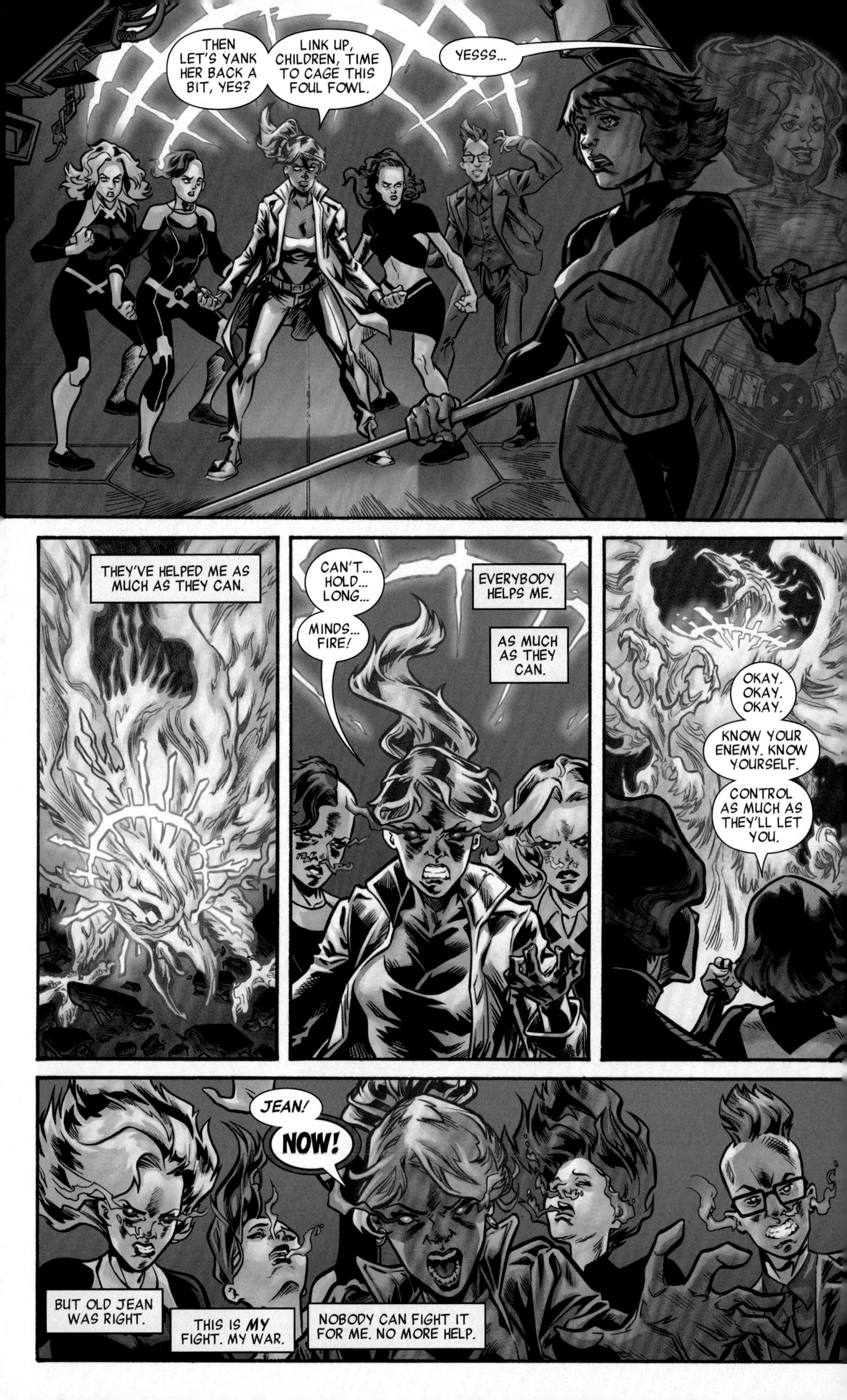

THEN LET'S YANK HER BACK A BIT, YES?
LINK UP, CHILDREN, TIME TO CAGE THIS FOUL FOWL.
YESSS...
THEY'VE HELPED ME AS MUCH AS THEY CAN.
CAN'T... HOLD... LONG...
MINDS... FIRE!
EVERYBODY HELPS ME.
AS MUCH AS THEY CAN.
OKAY. OKAY. OKAY.
KNOW YOUR ENEMY. KNOW YOURSELF.
CONTROL AS MUCH AS THEY'LL LET YOU.
JEAN!
NOW!
BUT OLD JEAN WAS RIGHT.
THIS IS MY FIGHT. MY WAR.
NOBODY CAN FIGHT IT FOR ME. NO MORE HELP.

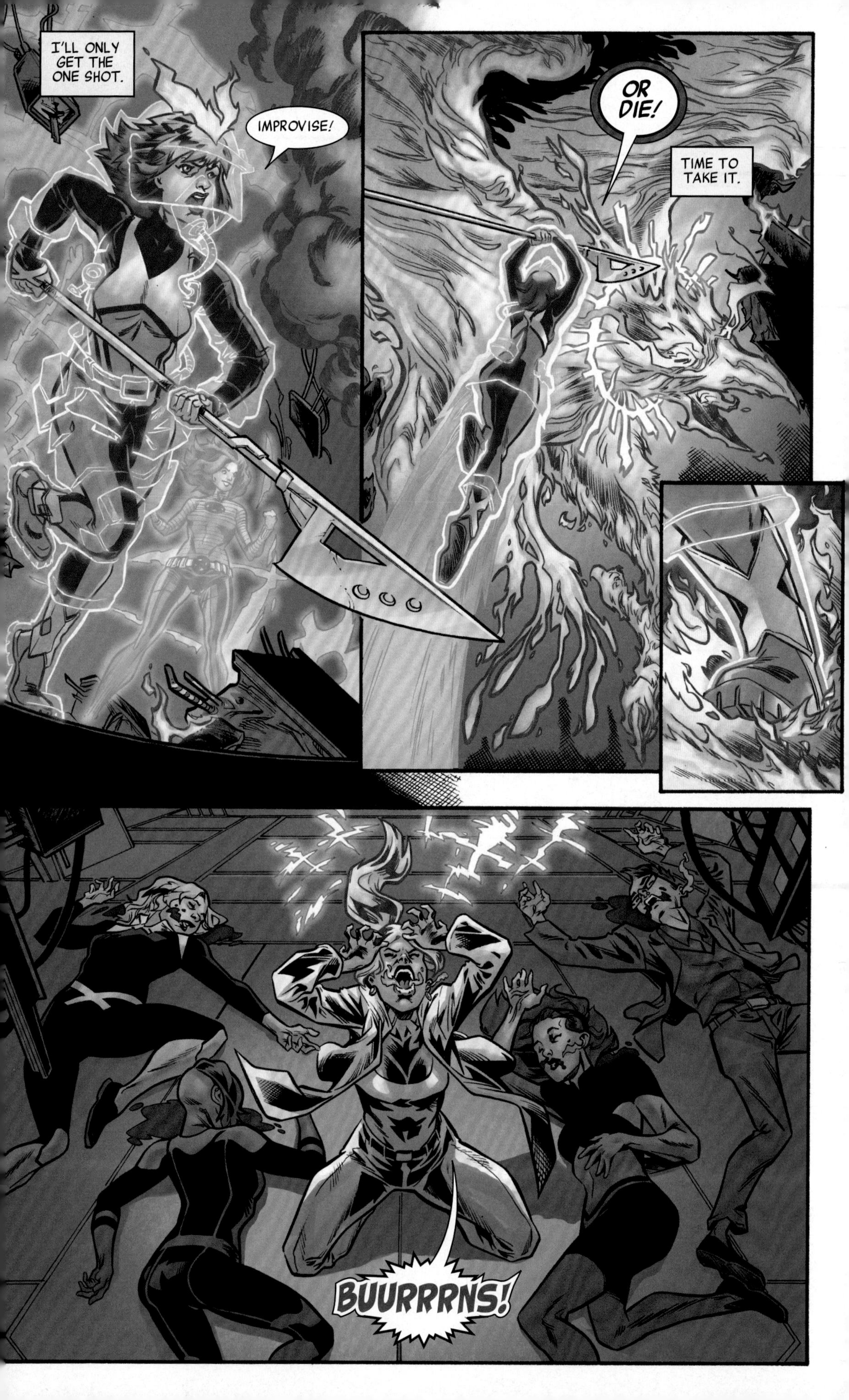
I'LL ONLY GET THE ONE SHOT.
IMPROVISE!
OR DIE!
TIME TO TAKE IT.
BUURRRNS!

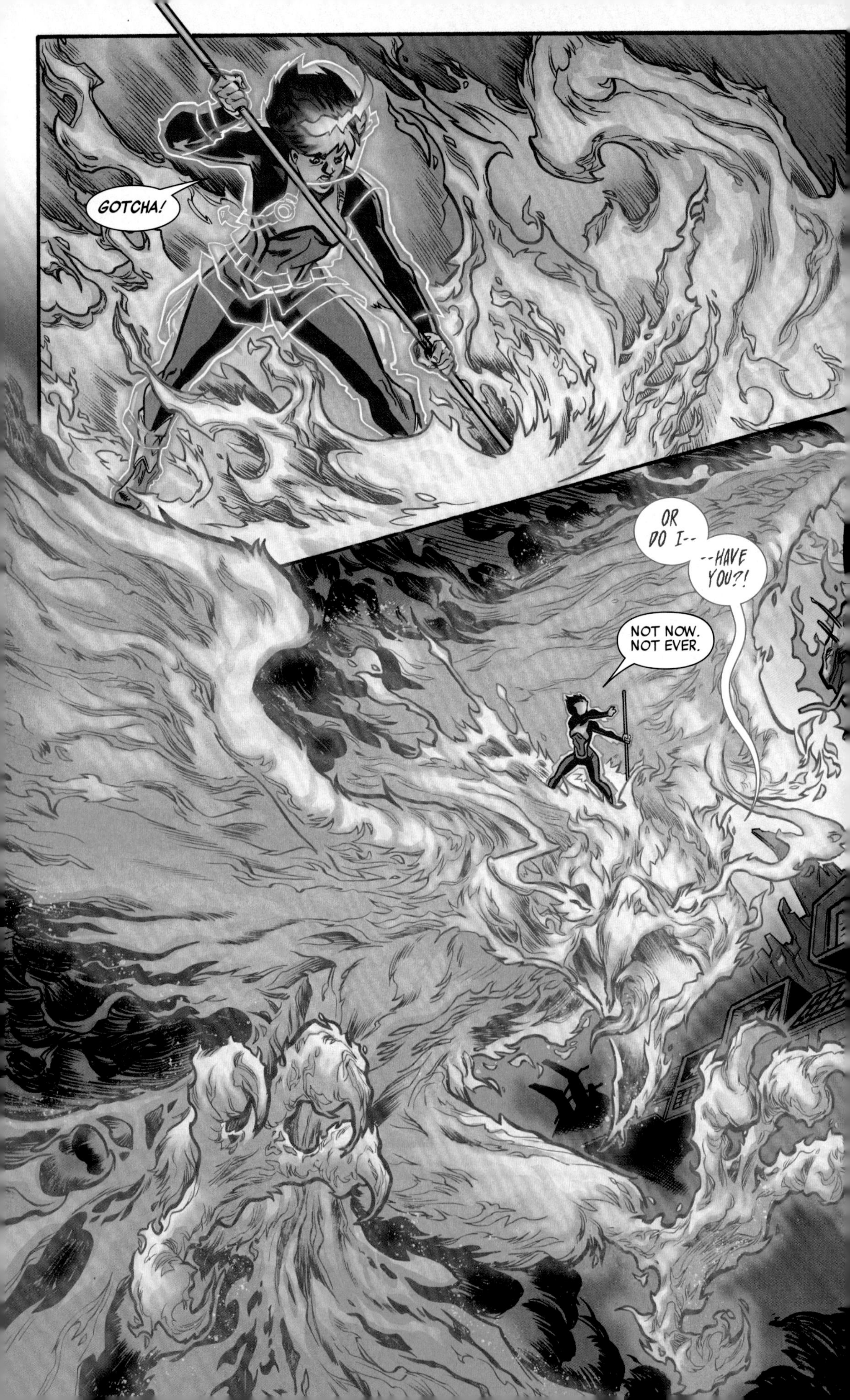
GOTCHA!
OR DO I--
--HAVE YOU?!
NOT NOW. NOT EVER.

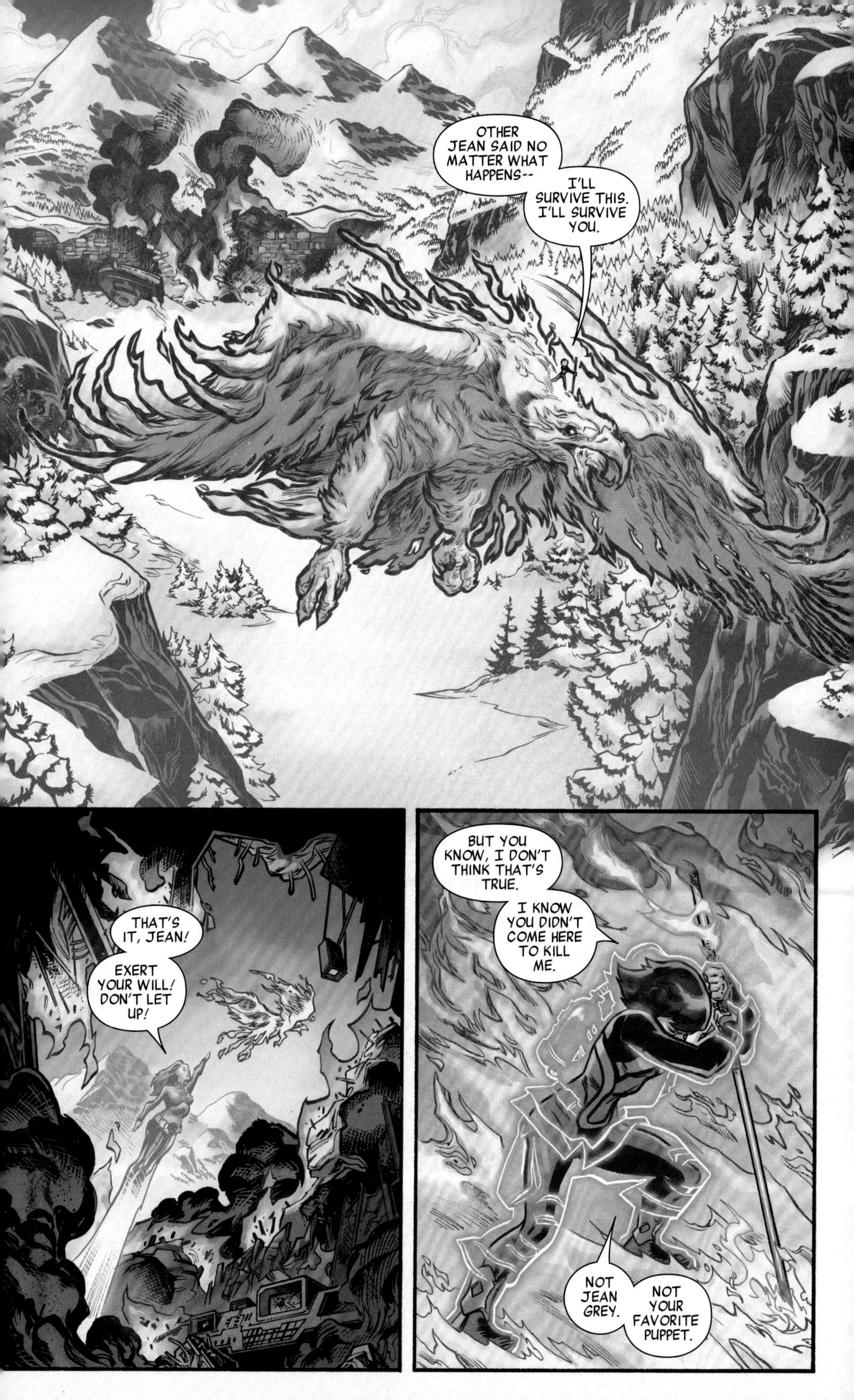
OTHER JEAN SAID NO MATTER WHAT HAPPENS--
I'LL SURVIVE THIS. I'LL SURVIVE YOU.
THAT'S IT, JEAN!
EXERT YOUR WILL! DON'T LET UP!
BUT YOU KNOW, I DON'T THINK THAT'S TRUE.
I KNOW YOU DIDN'T COME HERE TO KILL ME.
NOT JEAN GREY.
NOT YOUR FAVORITE PUPPET.

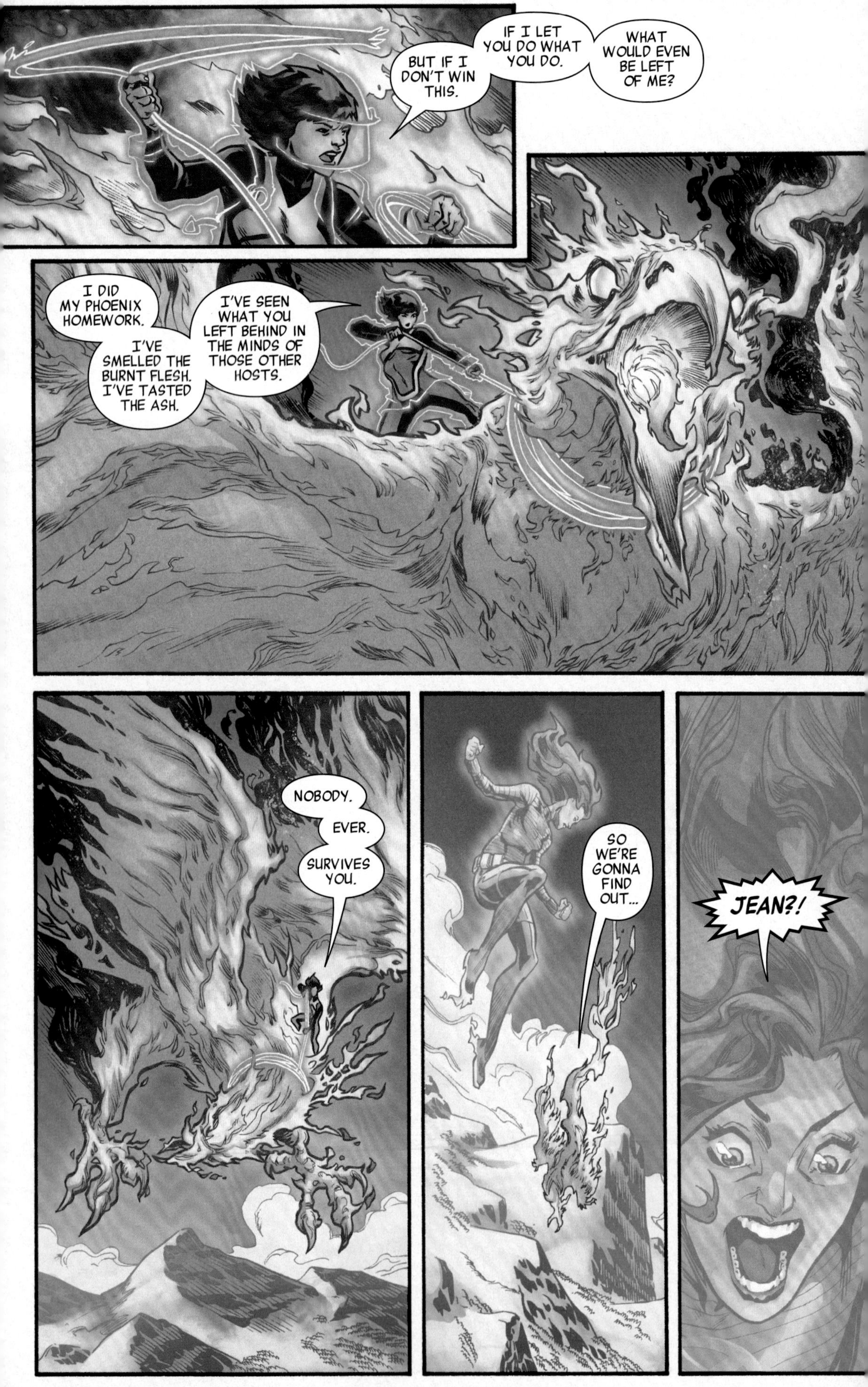
BUT IF I DON'T WIN THIS.
IF I LET YOU DO WHAT YOU DO.
WHAT WOULD EVEN BE LEFT OF ME?
I DID MY PHOENIX HOMEWORK.
I'VE SMELLED THE BURNT FLESH. I'VE TASTED THE ASH.
I'VE SEEN WHAT YOU LEFT BEHIND IN THE MINDS OF THOSE OTHER HOSTS.
NOBODY.
EVER.
SURVIVES YOU.
SO WE'RE GONNA FIND OUT...
JEAN?!

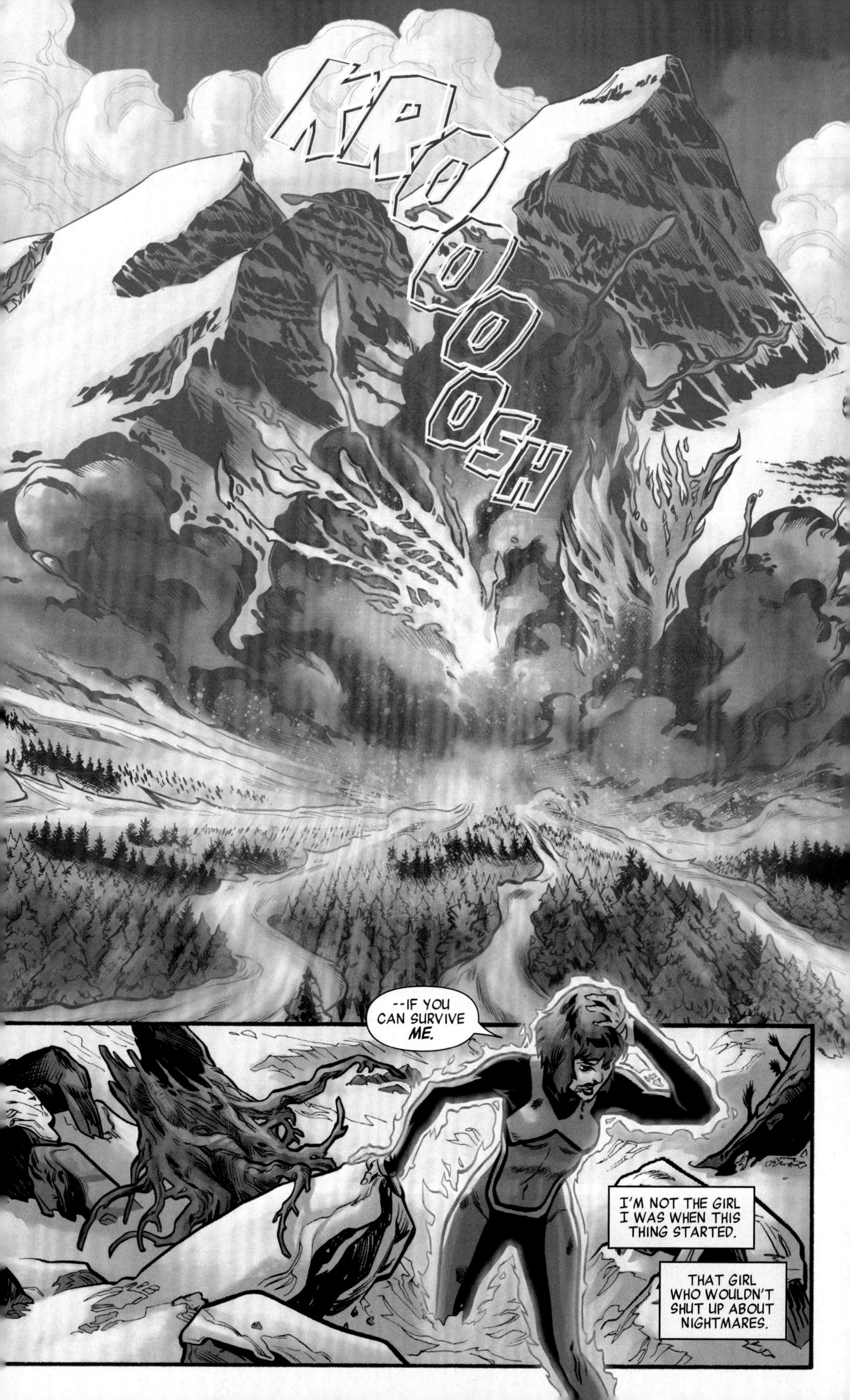
KROOOOOSH
--IF YOU CAN SURVIVE *ME.*
I'M NOT THE GIRL I WAS WHEN THIS THING STARTED.
THAT GIRL WHO WOULDN'T SHUT UP ABOUT NIGHTMARES.

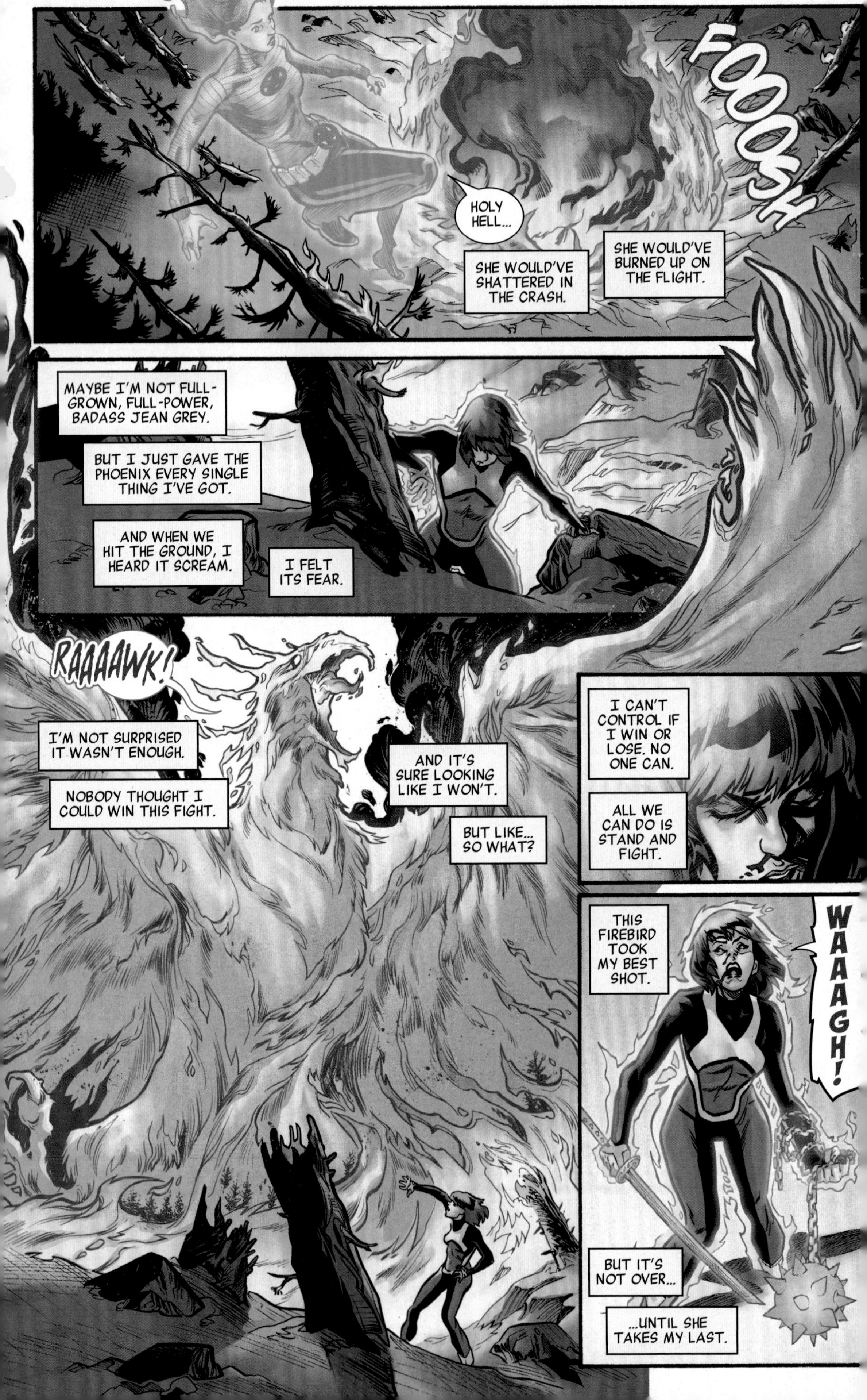
FOOOSH
HOLY HELL...
SHE WOULD'VE SHATTERED IN THE CRASH.
SHE WOULD'VE BURNED UP ON THE FLIGHT.
MAYBE I'M NOT FULL-GROWN, FULL-POWER, BADASS JEAN GREY.
BUT I JUST GAVE THE PHOENIX EVERY SINGLE THING I'VE GOT.
AND WHEN WE HIT THE GROUND, I HEARD IT SCREAM.
I FELT ITS FEAR.
RAAAAWK!
I'M NOT SURPRISED IT WASN'T ENOUGH.
NOBODY THOUGHT I COULD WIN THIS FIGHT.
AND IT'S SURE LOOKING LIKE I WON'T.
BUT LIKE... SO WHAT?
I CAN'T CONTROL IF I WIN OR LOSE. NO ONE CAN.
ALL WE CAN DO IS STAND AND FIGHT.
THIS FIREBIRD TOOK MY BEST SHOT.
WAAAGH!
BUT IT'S NOT OVER...
...UNTIL SHE TAKES MY LAST.

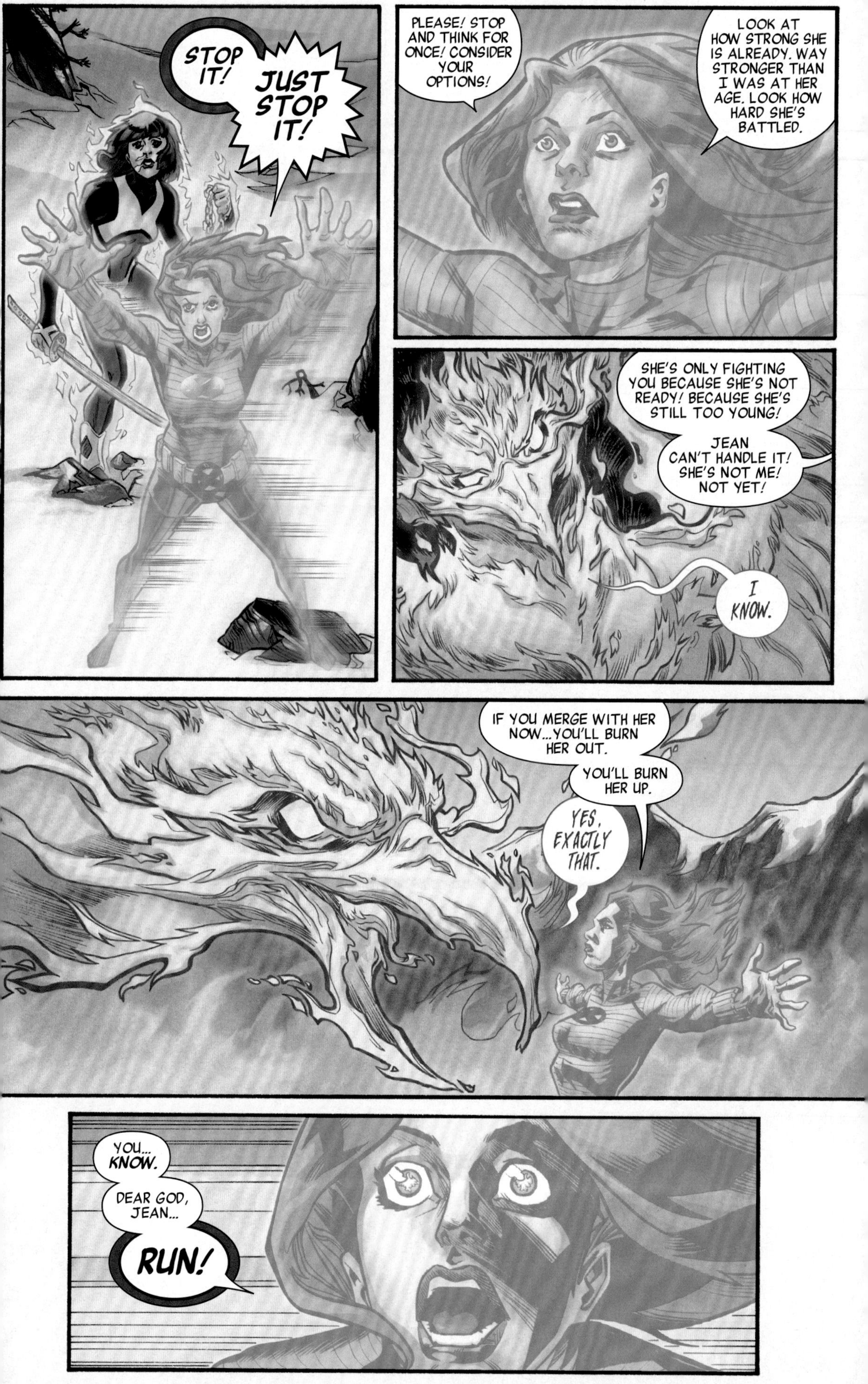
STOP IT!
JUST STOP IT!
PLEASE! STOP AND THINK FOR ONCE! CONSIDER YOUR OPTIONS!
LOOK AT HOW STRONG SHE IS ALREADY. WAY STRONGER THAN I WAS AT HER AGE. LOOK HOW HARD SHE'S BATTLED.
SHE'S ONLY FIGHTING YOU BECAUSE SHE'S NOT READY! BECAUSE SHE'S STILL TOO YOUNG!
JEAN CAN'T HANDLE IT! SHE'S NOT ME! NOT YET!
I KNOW.
IF YOU MERGE WITH HER NOW...YOU'LL BURN HER OUT.
YOU'LL BURN HER UP.
YES, EXACTLY THAT.
YOU... KNOW.
DEAR GOD, JEAN...
RUN!

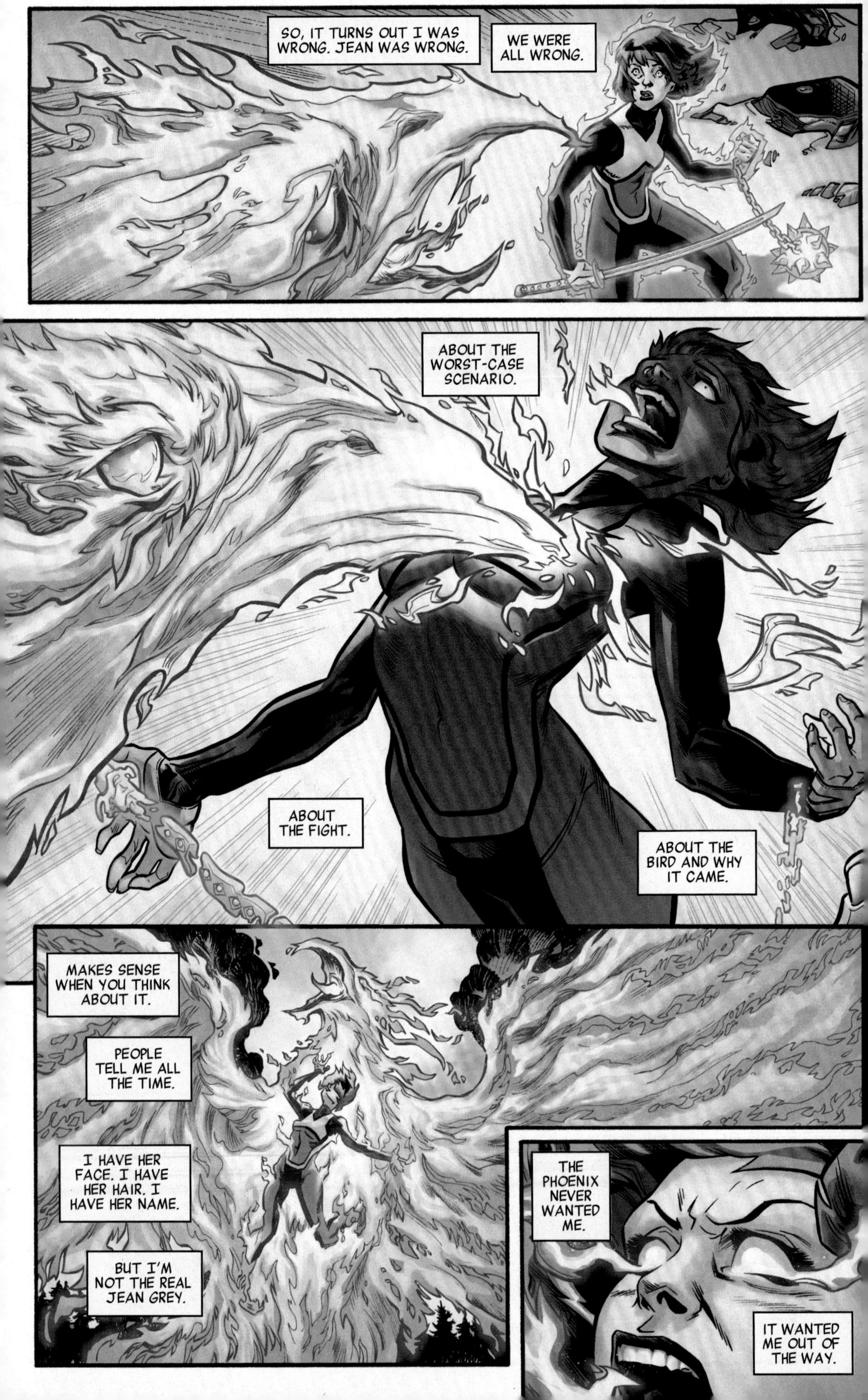
SO, IT TURNS OUT I WAS WRONG. JEAN WAS WRONG.
WE WERE ALL WRONG.
ABOUT THE WORST-CASE SCENARIO.
ABOUT THE FIGHT.
ABOUT THE BIRD AND WHY IT CAME.
MAKES SENSE WHEN YOU THINK ABOUT IT.
PEOPLE TELL ME ALL THE TIME.
I HAVE HER FACE. I HAVE HER HAIR. I HAVE HER NAME.
BUT I'M NOT THE REAL JEAN GREY.
THE PHOENIX NEVER WANTED ME.
IT WANTED ME OUT OF THE WAY.

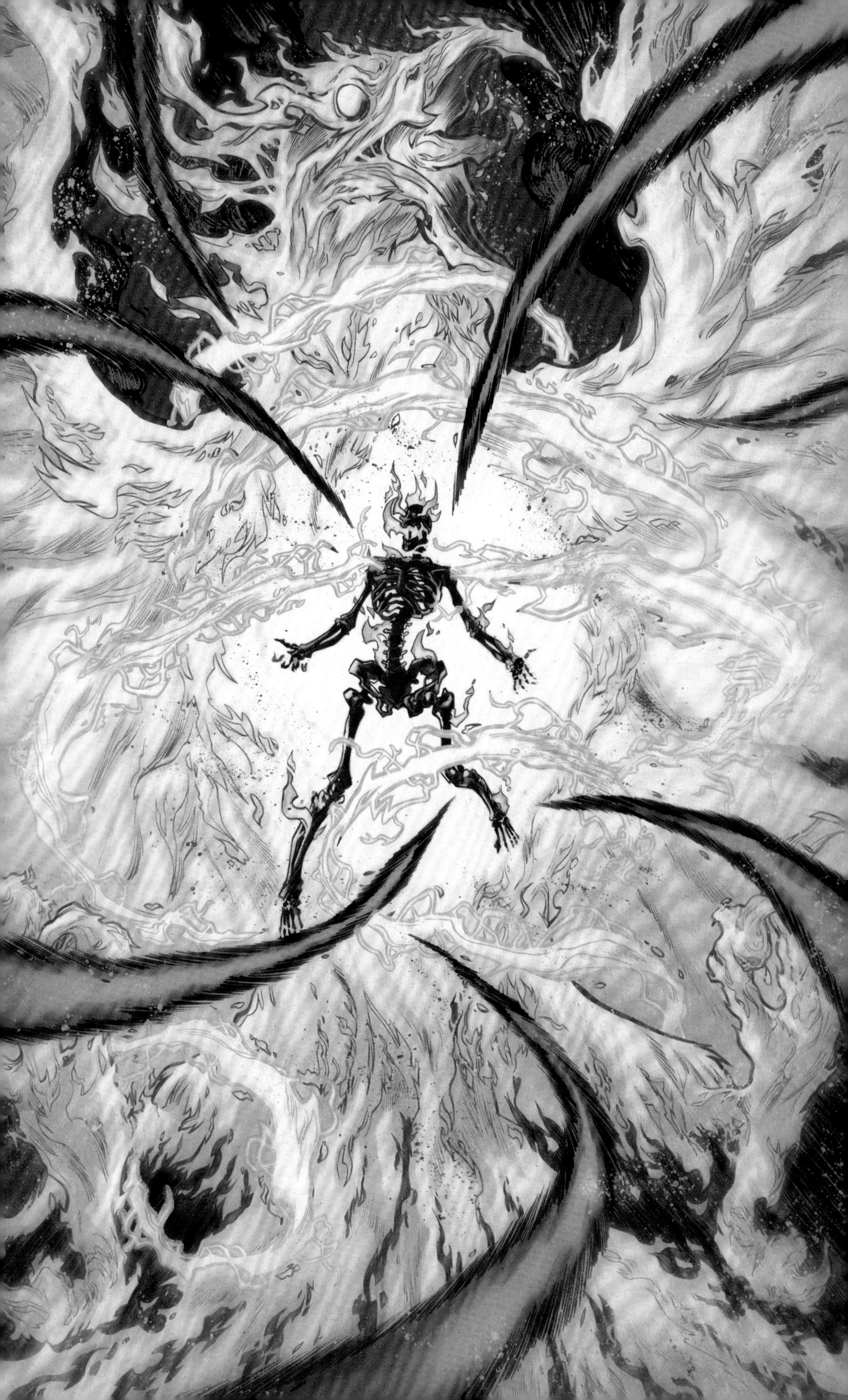

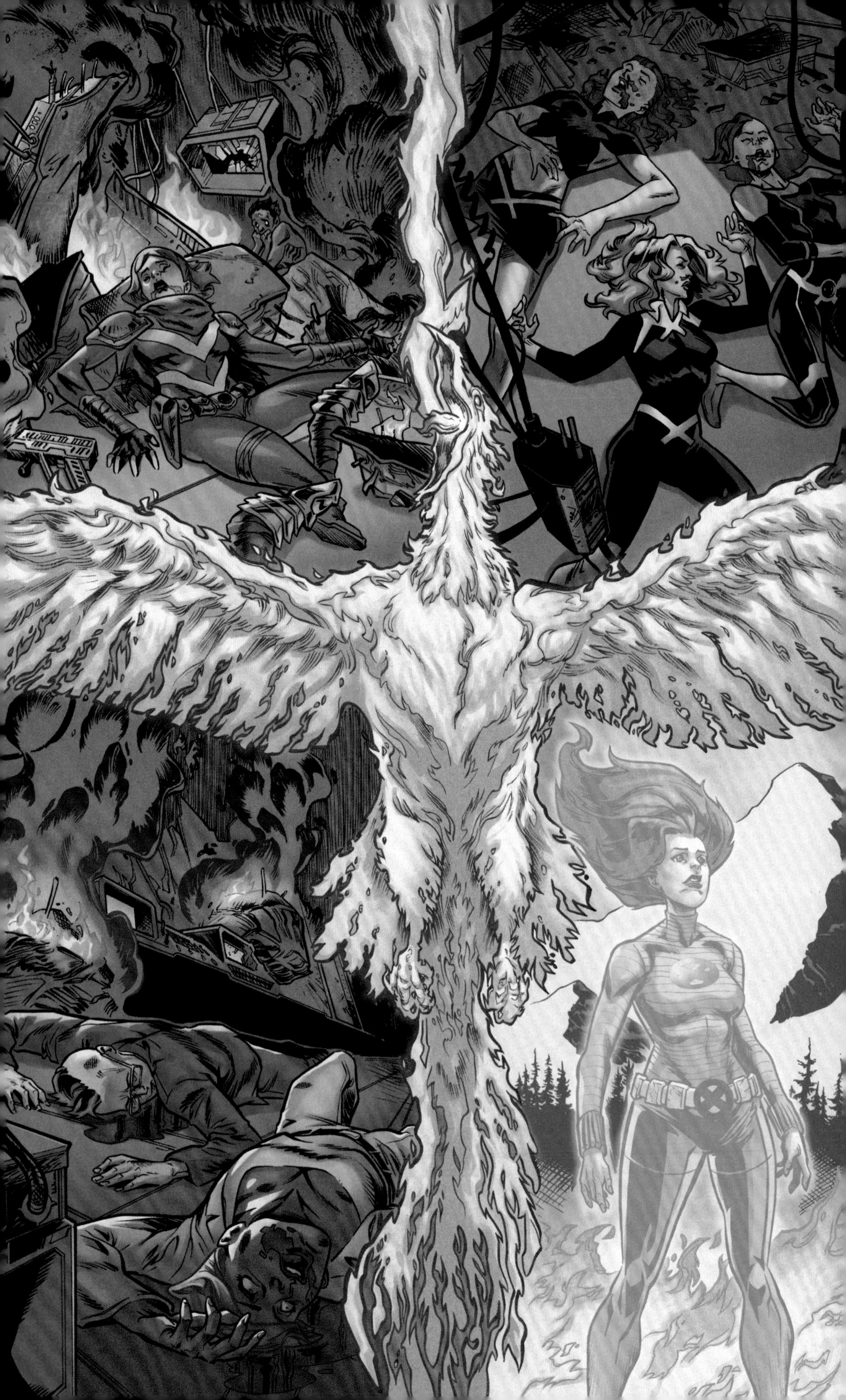

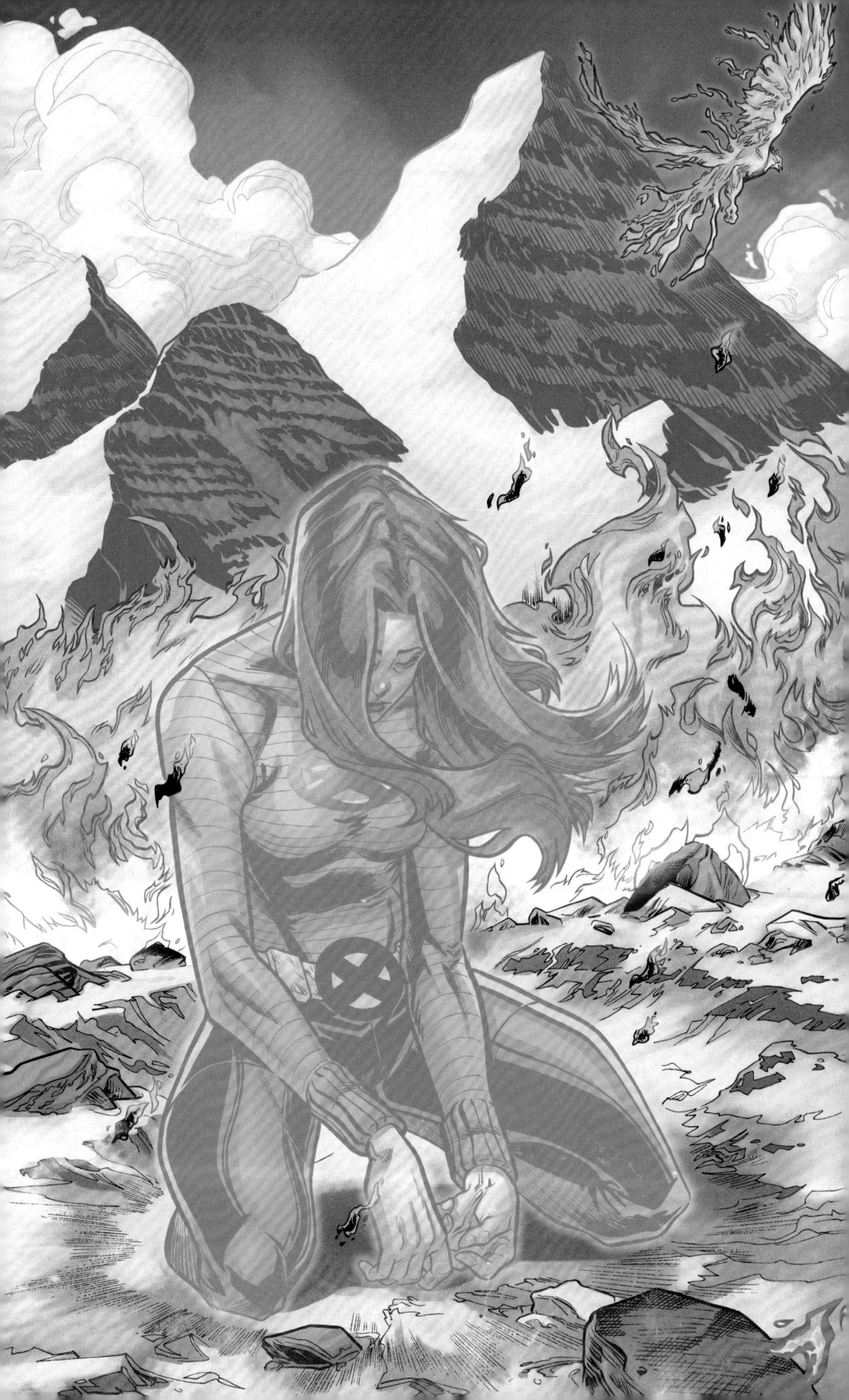

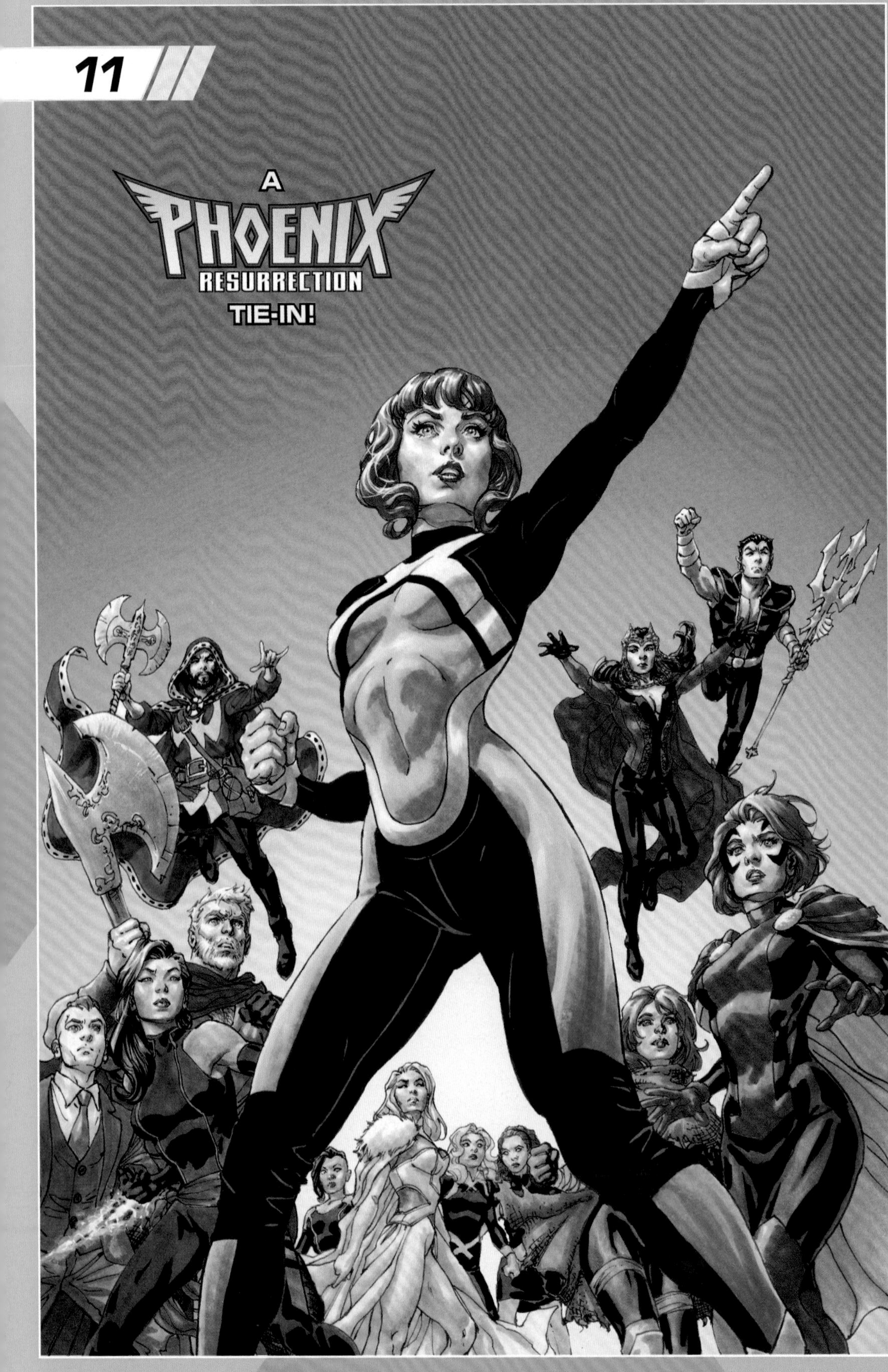
11
A PHOENIX RESURRECTION TIE-IN!

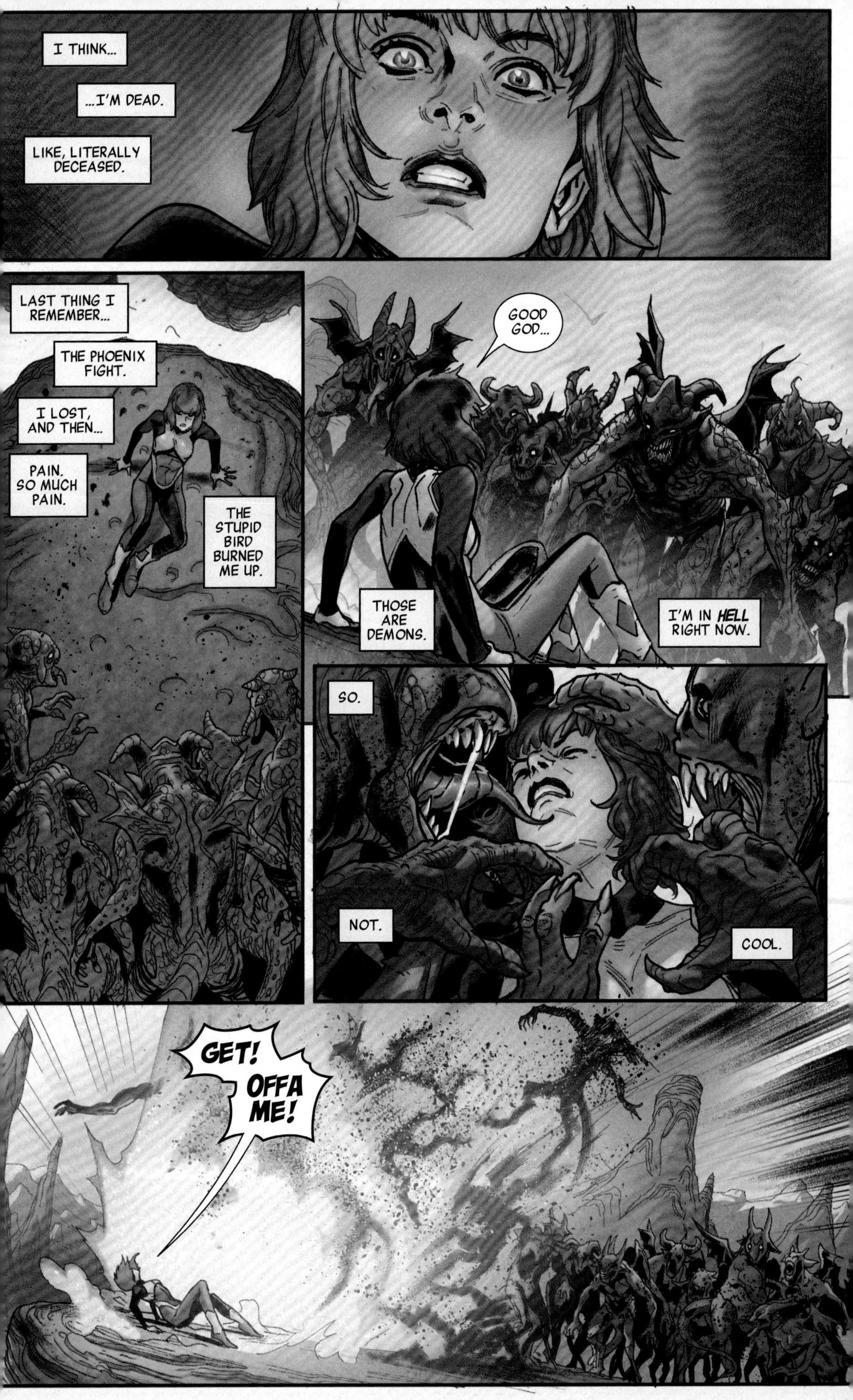
I THINK...
...I'M DEAD.
LIKE, LITERALLY DECEASED.
LAST THING I REMEMBER...
THE PHOENIX FIGHT.
I LOST, AND THEN...
PAIN. SO MUCH PAIN.
THE STUPID BIRD BURNED ME UP.
GOOD GOD...
THOSE ARE DEMONS.
I'M IN HELL RIGHT NOW.
SO.
NOT.
COOL.
GET! OFFA ME!

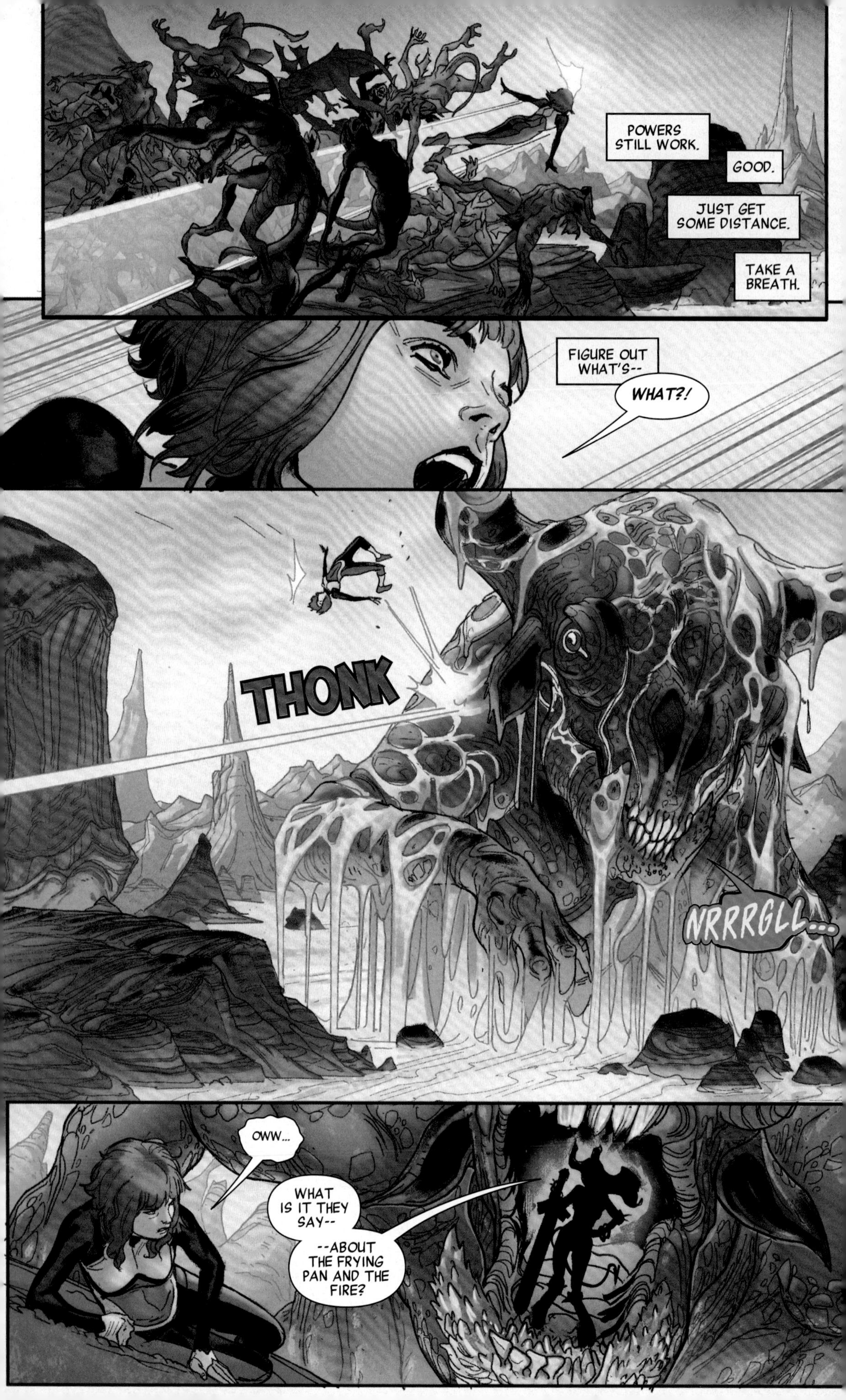
POWERS STILL WORK.
GOOD.
JUST GET SOME DISTANCE.
TAKE A BREATH.
FIGURE OUT WHAT'S--
WHAT?!
THONK
NRRRGLL...
OWW...
WHAT IS IT THEY SAY--
--ABOUT THE FRYING PAN AND THE FIRE?

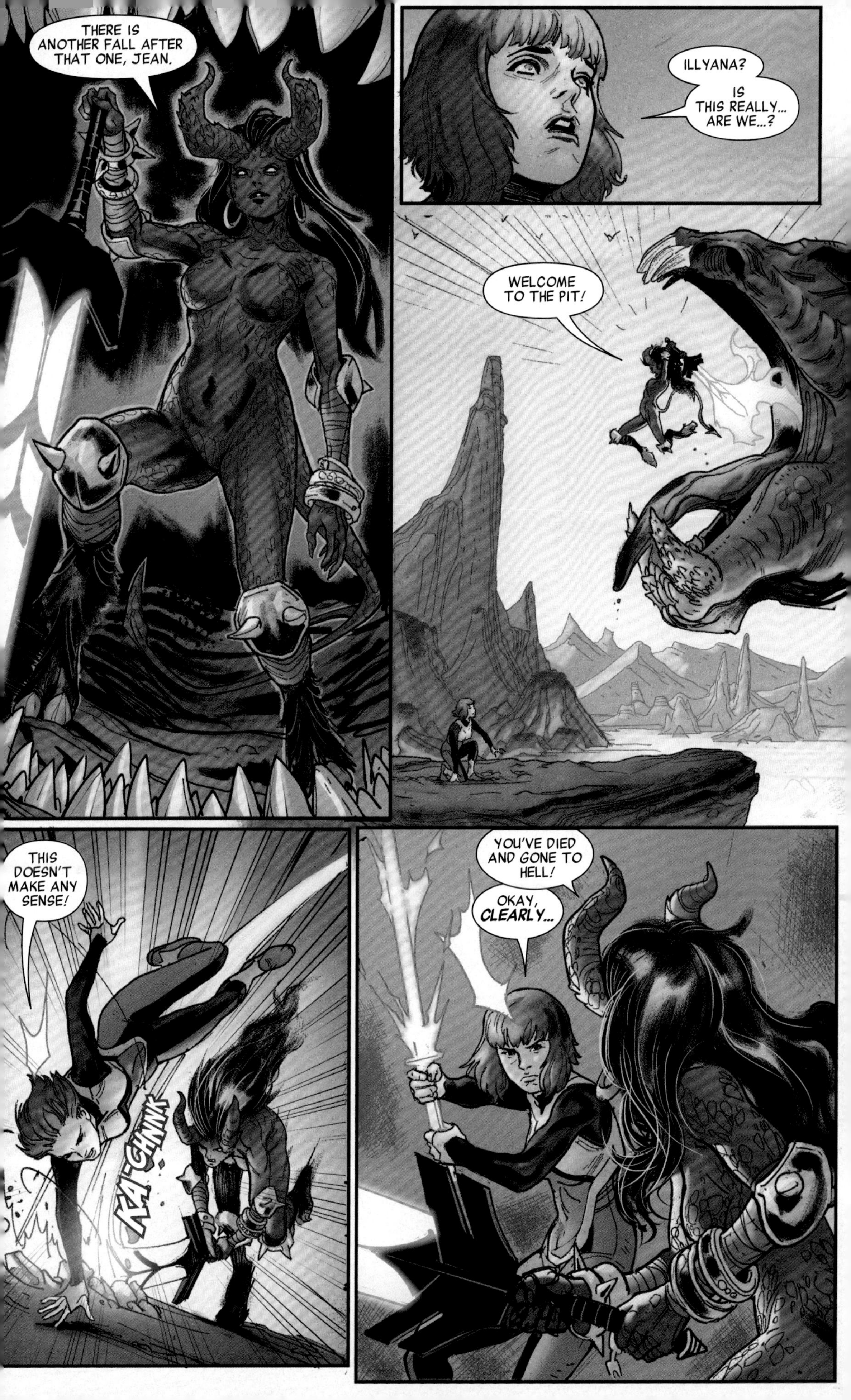
THERE IS ANOTHER FALL AFTER THAT ONE, JEAN.
ILLYANA?
IS THIS REALLY... ARE WE...?
WELCOME TO THE PIT!
THIS DOESN'T MAKE ANY SENSE!
KA-CHNNK
YOU'VE DIED AND GONE TO HELL!
OKAY, CLEARLY...

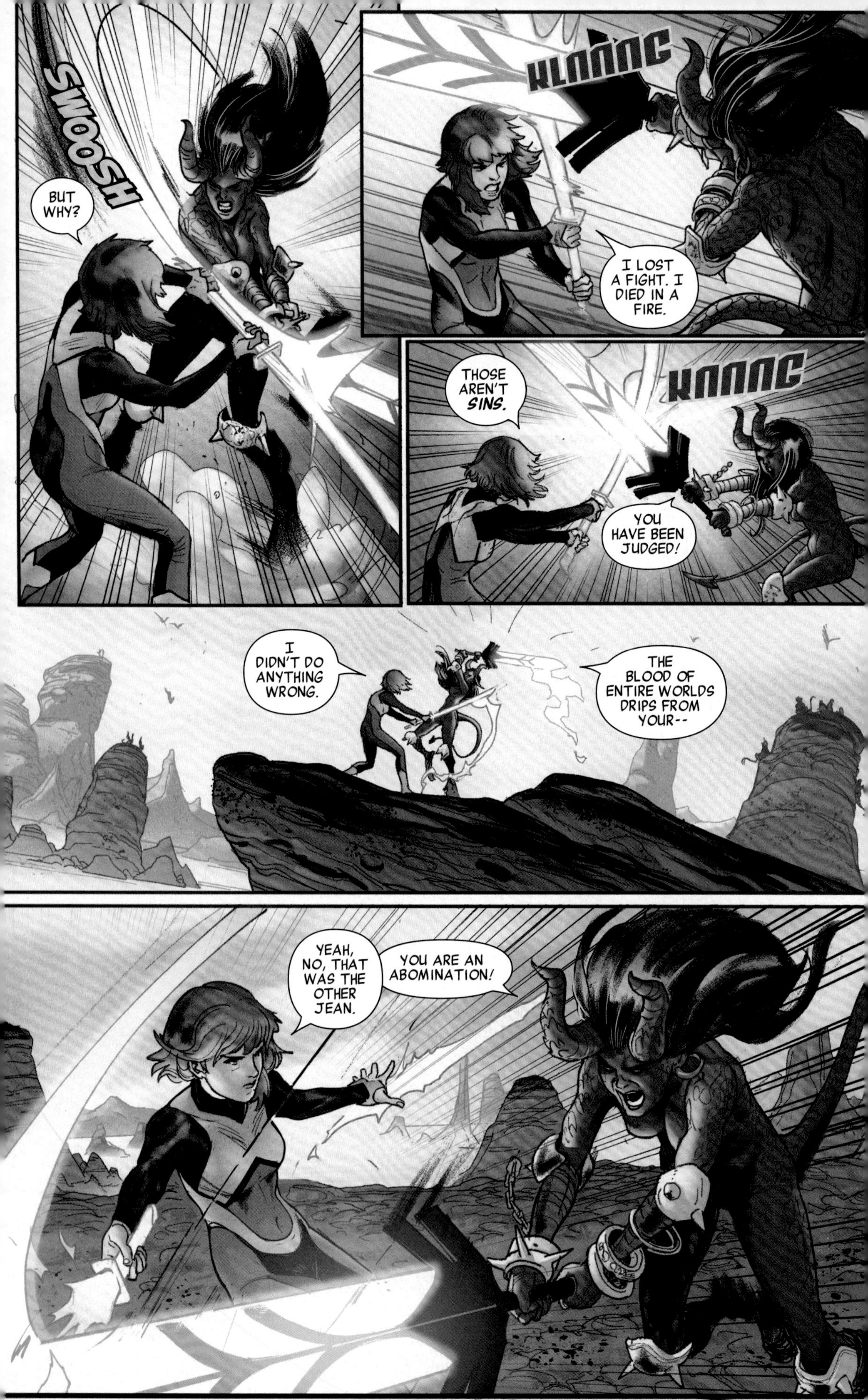
SWOOSH
BUT WHY?
KLAANNG
I LOST A FIGHT. I DIED IN A FIRE.
THOSE AREN'T *SINS.*
KANNNG
YOU HAVE BEEN JUDGED!
I DIDN'T DO ANYTHING WRONG.
THE BLOOD OF ENTIRE WORLDS DRIPS FROM YOUR--
YEAH, NO, THAT WAS THE OTHER JEAN.
YOU ARE AN ABOMINATION!

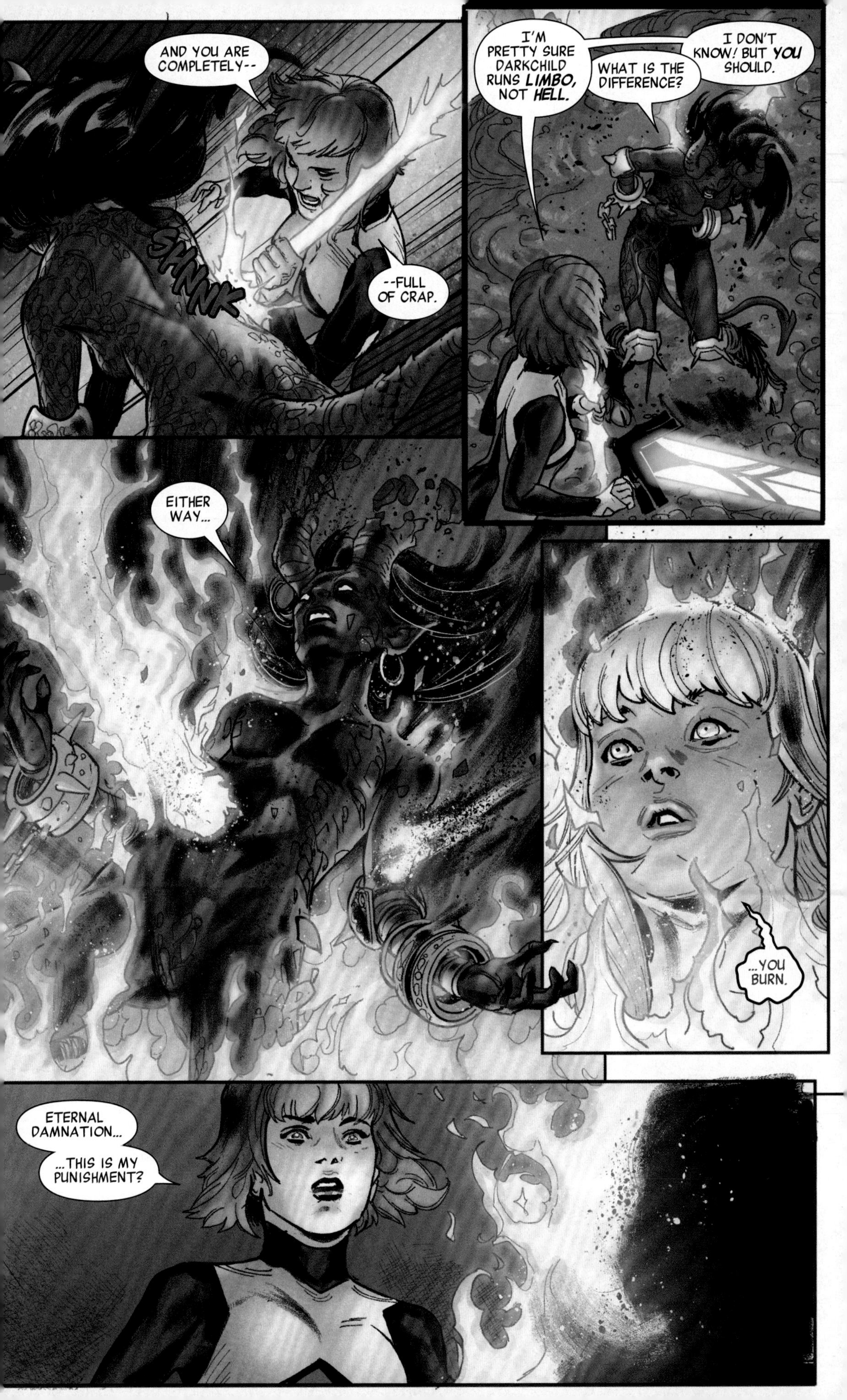
AND YOU ARE COMPLETELY--
SHHNNK
--FULL OF CRAP.
I'M PRETTY SURE DARKCHILD RUNS LIMBO, NOT HELL.
WHAT IS THE DIFFERENCE?
I DON'T KNOW! BUT YOU SHOULD.
EITHER WAY...
...YOU BURN.
ETERNAL DAMNATION...
...THIS IS MY PUNISHMENT?

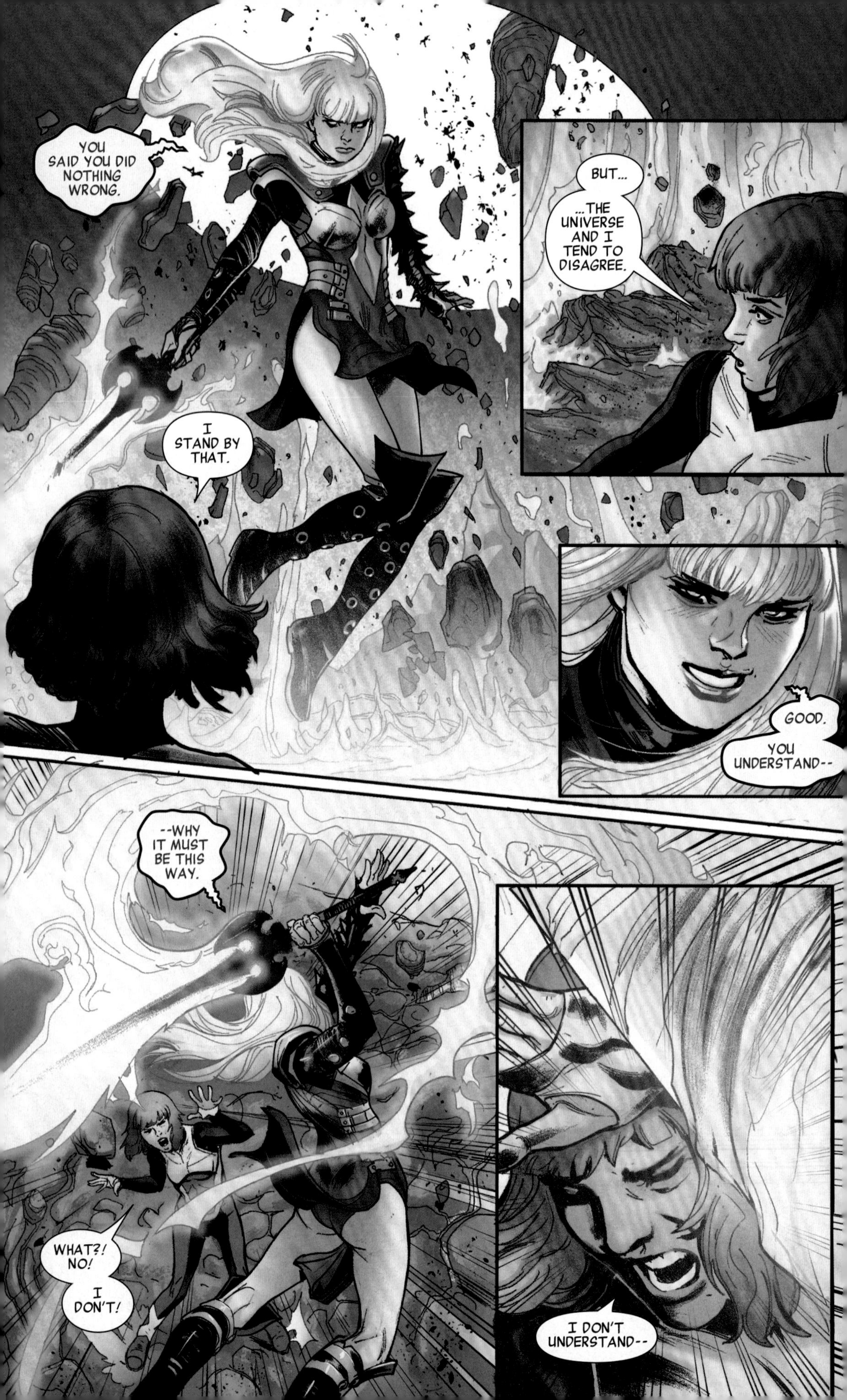
YOU SAID YOU DID NOTHING WRONG.
I STAND BY THAT.
BUT...
...THE UNIVERSE AND I TEND TO DISAGREE.
GOOD.
YOU UNDERSTAND--
--WHY IT MUST BE THIS WAY.
WHAT?! NO!
I DON'T!
I DON'T UNDERSTAND--

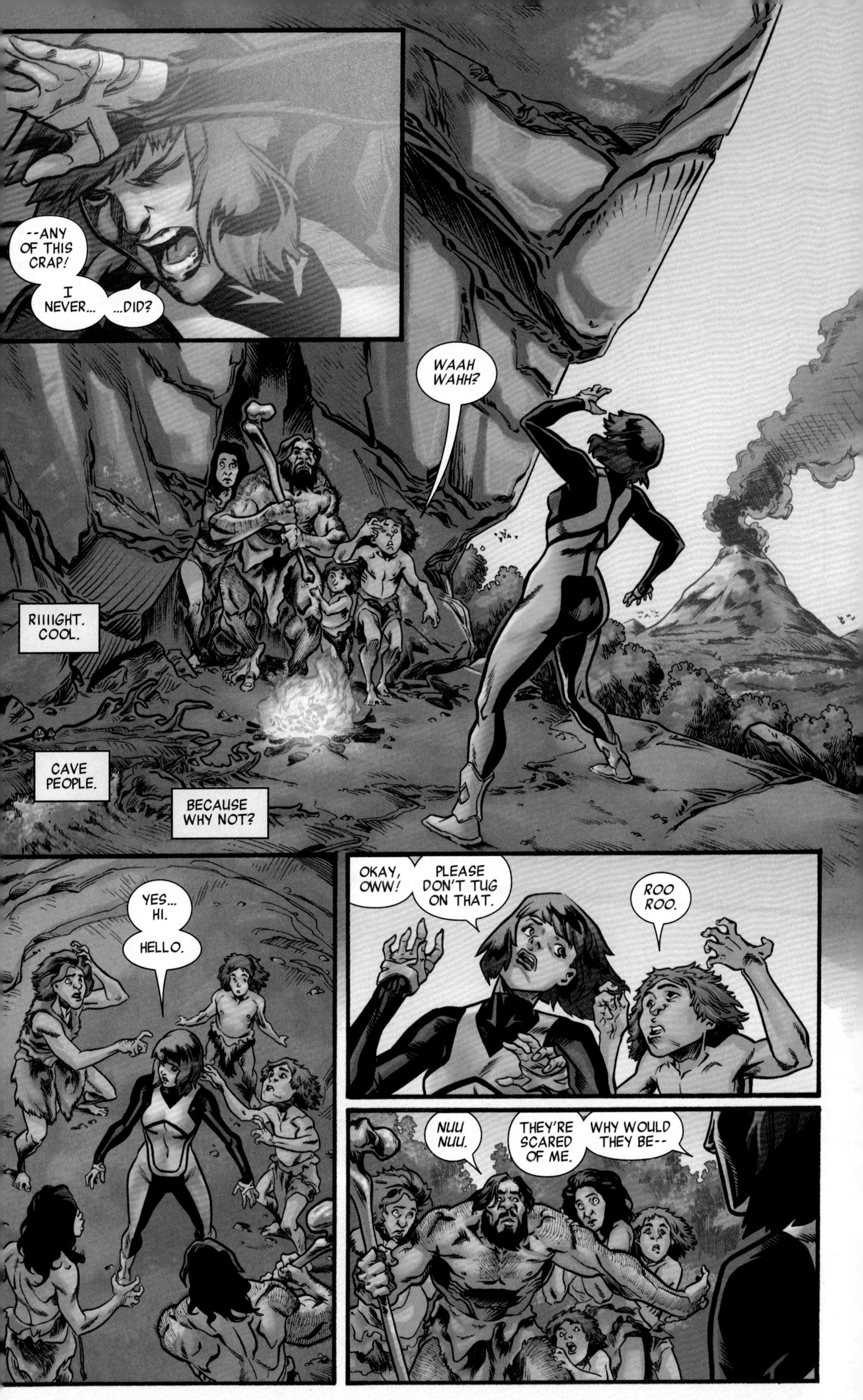
--ANY OF THIS CRAP!
I NEVER...
...DID?
WAAH WAHH?
RIIIIGHT. COOL.
CAVE PEOPLE.
BECAUSE WHY NOT?
YES... HI.
HELLO.
OKAY, OWW!
PLEASE DON'T TUG ON THAT.
ROO ROO.
NUU NUU.
THEY'RE SCARED OF ME.
WHY WOULD THEY BE--

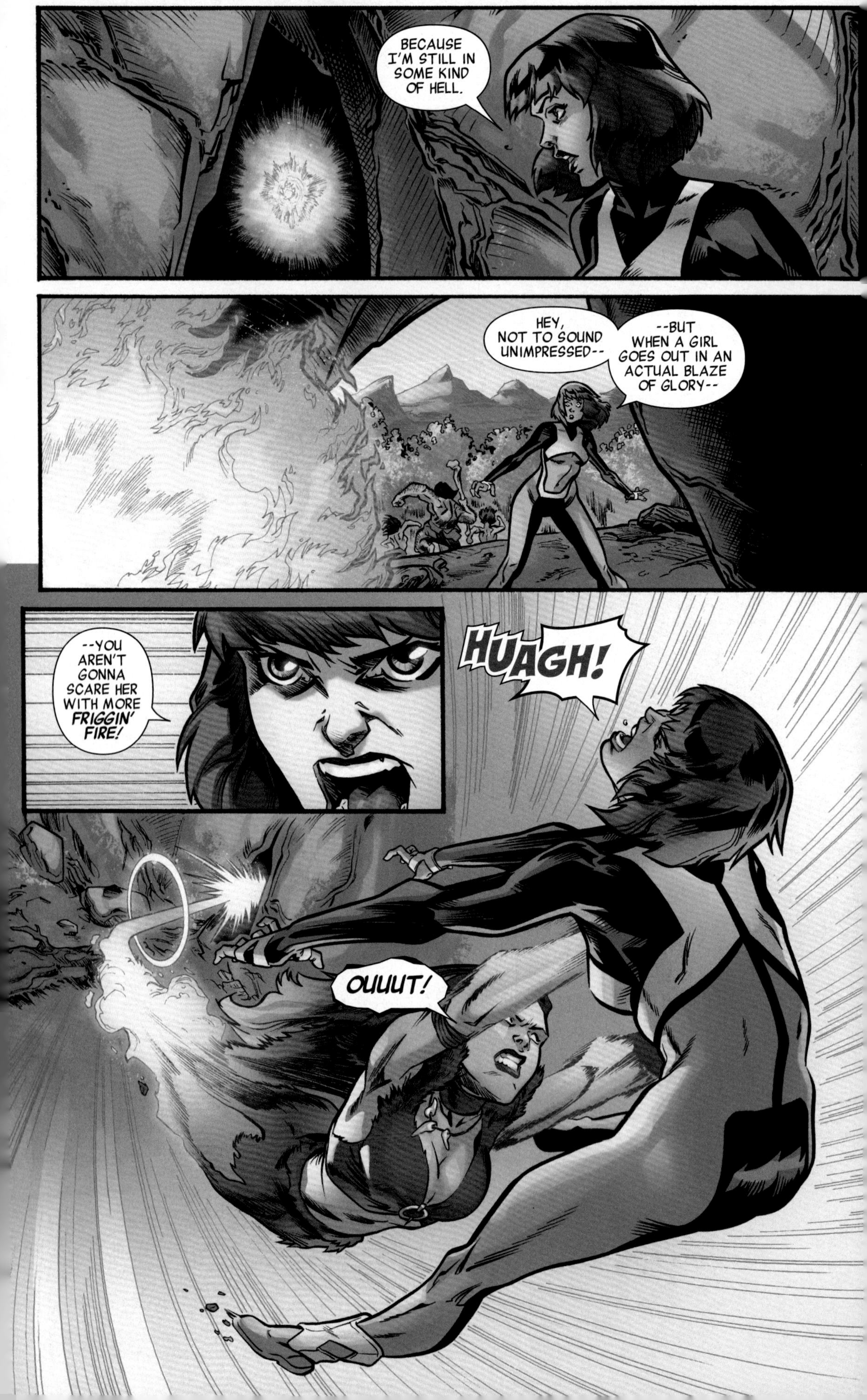
BECAUSE I'M STILL IN SOME KIND OF HELL.
HEY, NOT TO SOUND UNIMPRESSED--
--BUT WHEN A GIRL GOES OUT IN AN ACTUAL BLAZE OF GLORY--
--YOU AREN'T GONNA SCARE HER WITH MORE FRIGGIN' FIRE!
HUAGH!
OUUUT!

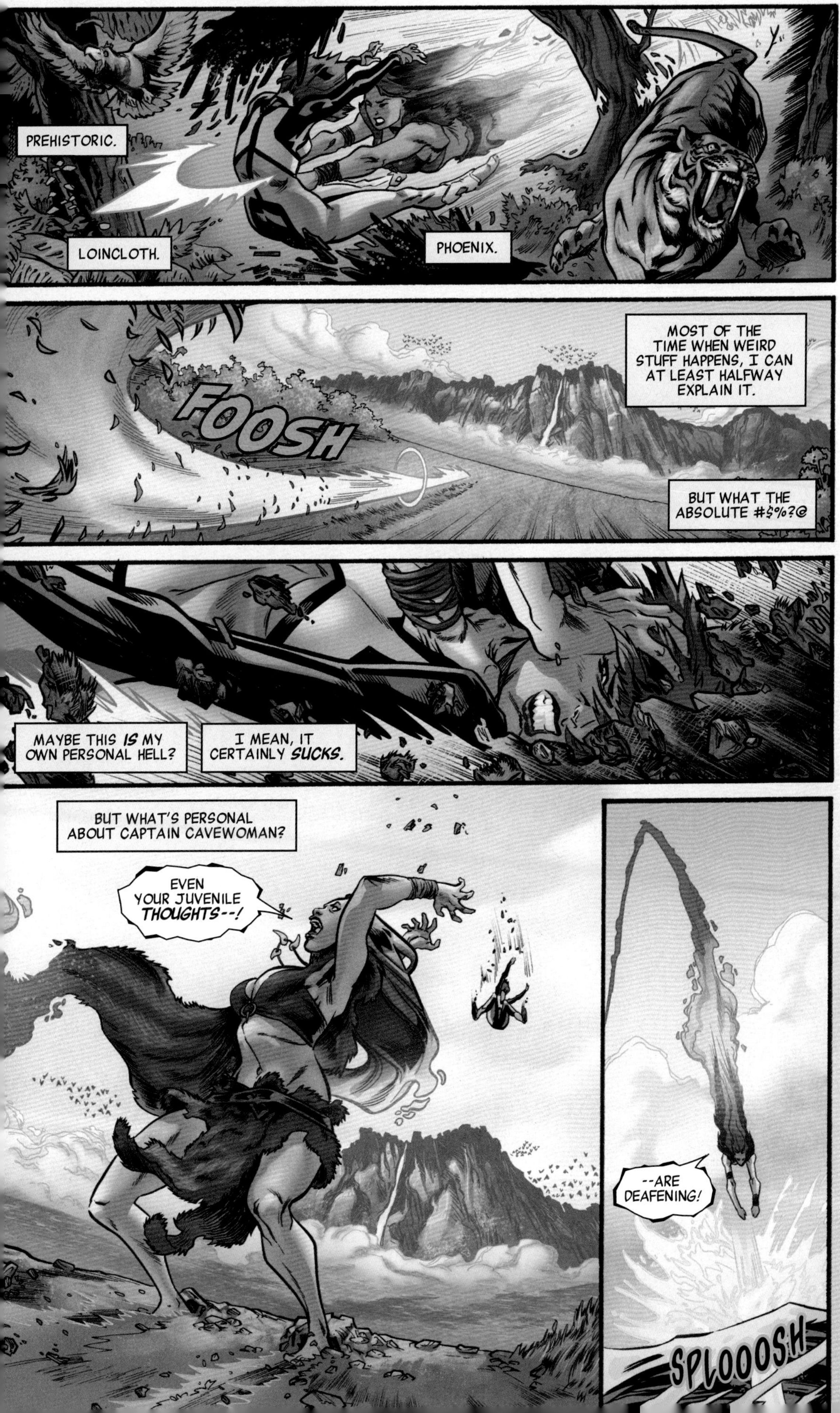

PREHISTORIC.
LOINCLOTH.
PHOENIX.
FOOSH
MOST OF THE TIME WHEN WEIRD STUFF HAPPENS, I CAN AT LEAST HALFWAY EXPLAIN IT.
BUT WHAT THE ABSOLUTE #$%?@
MAYBE THIS IS MY OWN PERSONAL HELL?
I MEAN, IT CERTAINLY SUCKS.
BUT WHAT'S PERSONAL ABOUT CAPTAIN CAVEWOMAN?
EVEN YOUR JUVENILE THOUGHTS--!
--ARE DEAFENING!
SPLOOOSH

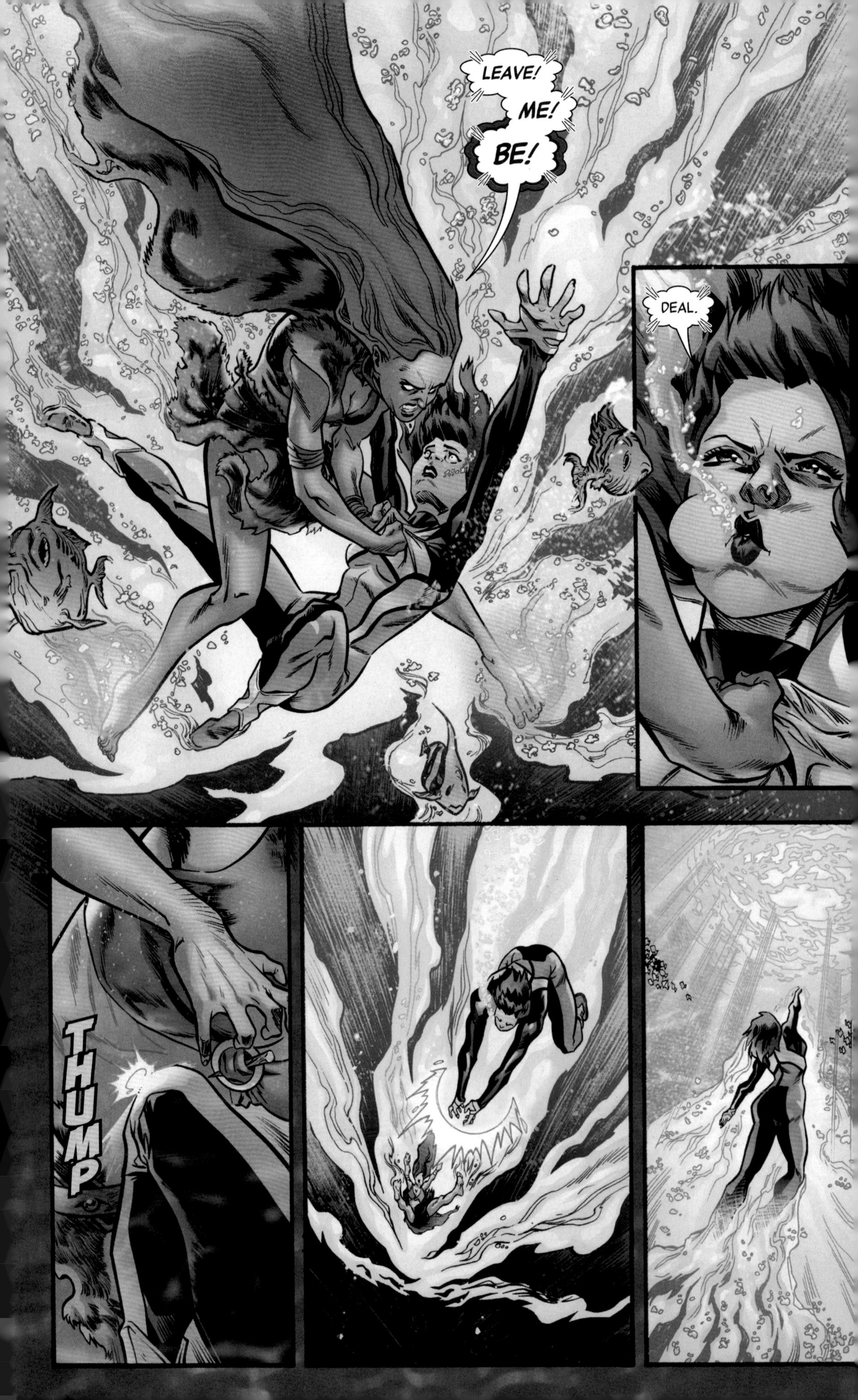
LEAVE!
ME!
BE!
DEAL.
THUMP

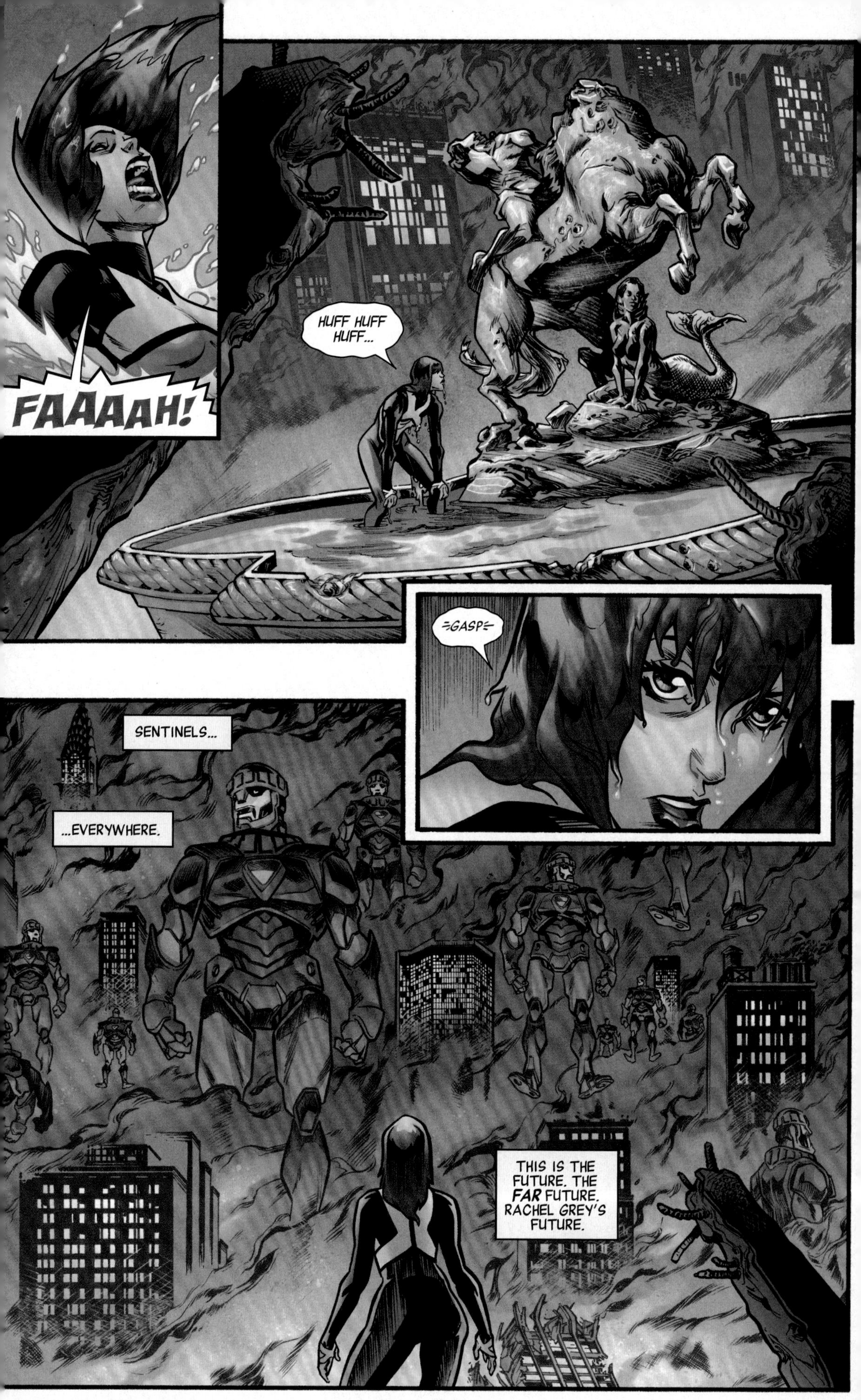
FAAAAH!
HUFF HUFF HUFF...
GASP
SENTINELS...
...EVERYWHERE.
THIS IS THE FUTURE. THE FAR FUTURE. RACHEL GREY'S FUTURE.

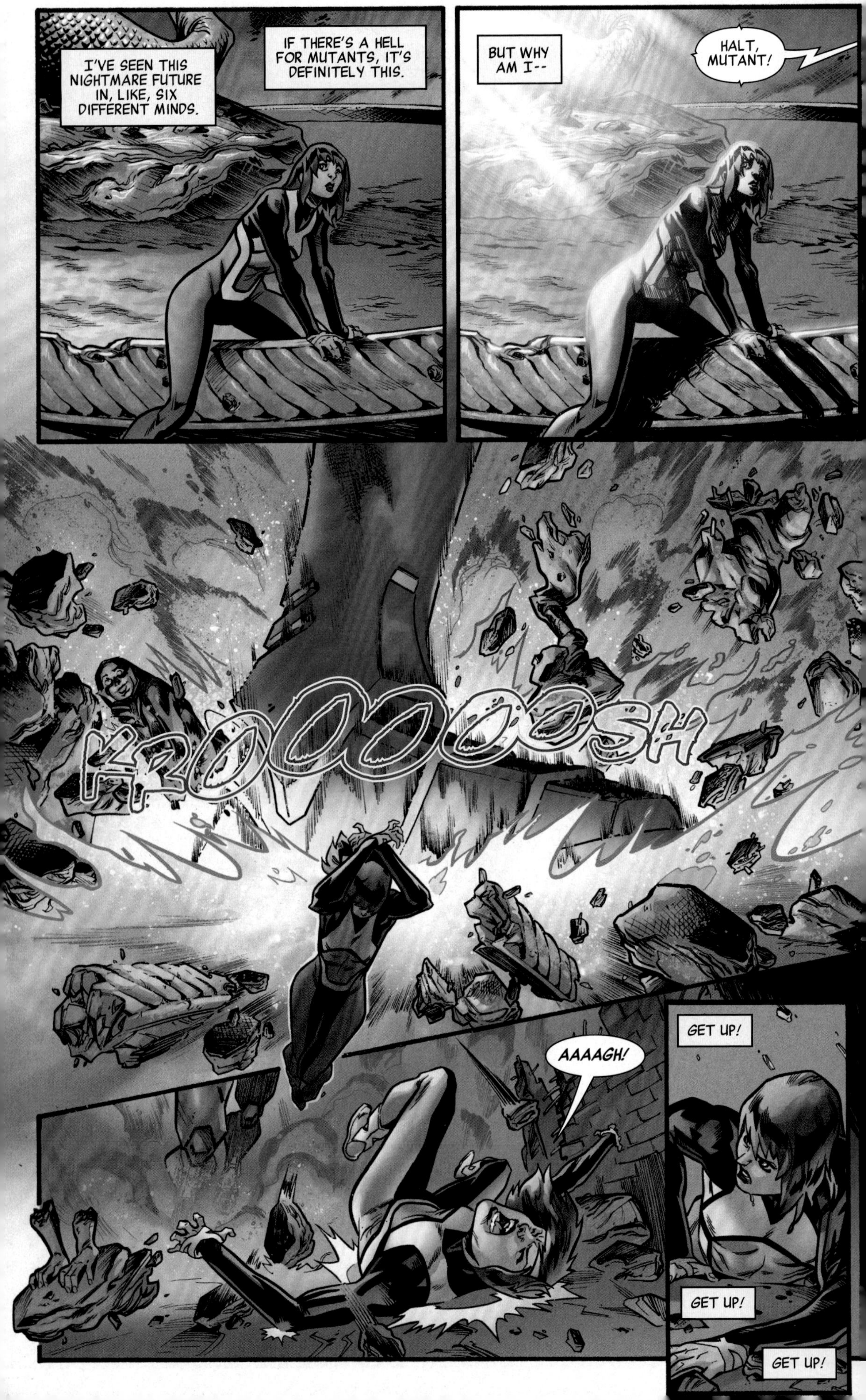
I'VE SEEN THIS NIGHTMARE FUTURE IN, LIKE, SIX DIFFERENT MINDS.
IF THERE'S A HELL FOR MUTANTS, IT'S DEFINITELY THIS.
BUT WHY AM I--
HALT, MUTANT!
KROOOOOOSH
AAAAGH!
GET UP!
GET UP!
GET UP!

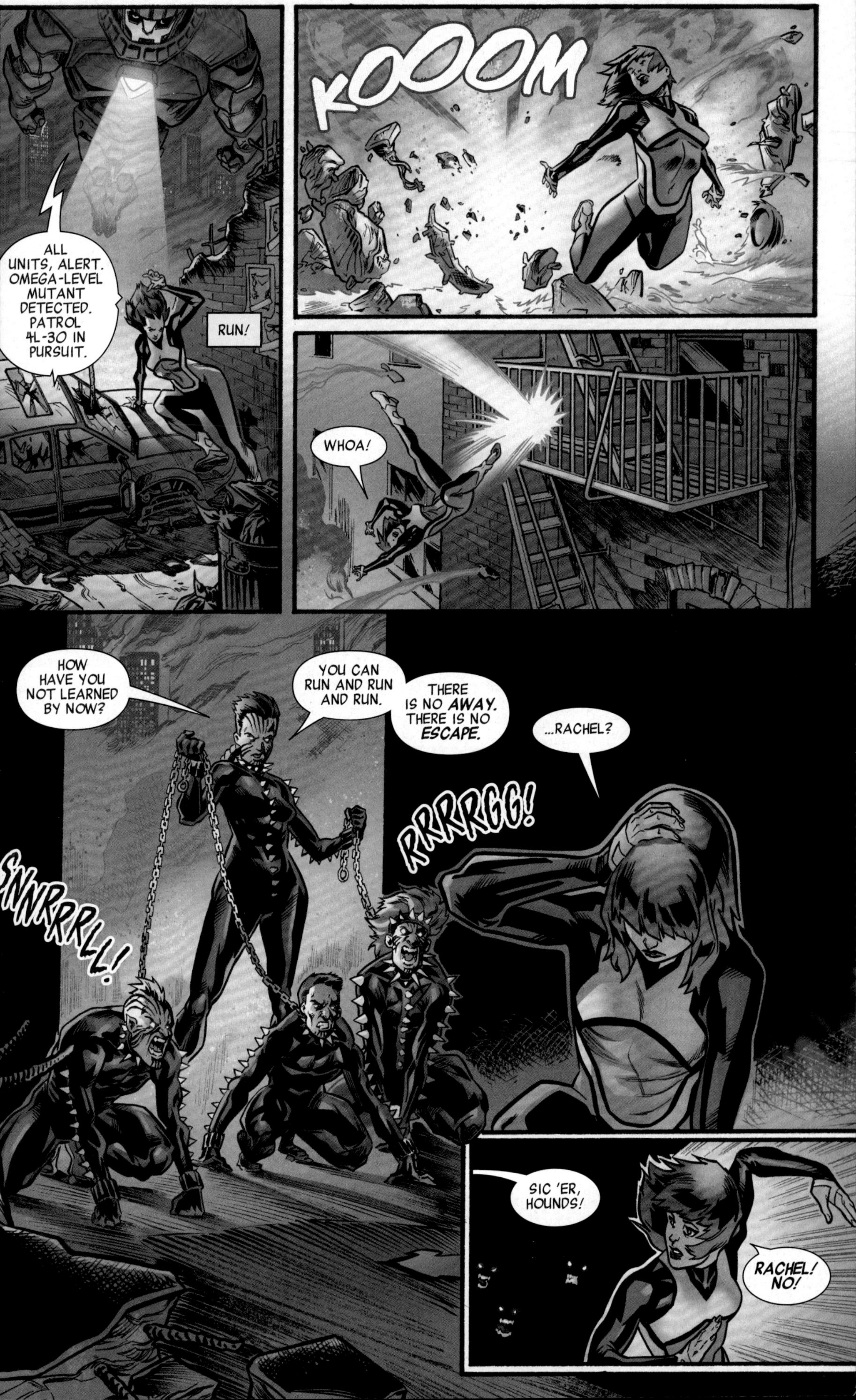
ALL UNITS, ALERT. OMEGA-LEVEL MUTANT DETECTED. PATROL 4L-30 IN PURSUIT.
RUN!
KOOOOM
WHOA!
HOW HAVE YOU NOT LEARNED BY NOW?
YOU CAN RUN AND RUN AND RUN.
THERE IS NO AWAY. THERE IS NO ESCAPE.
...RACHEL?
RRRRGG!
SNNRRRLL!
SIC 'ER, HOUNDS!
RACHEL! NO!

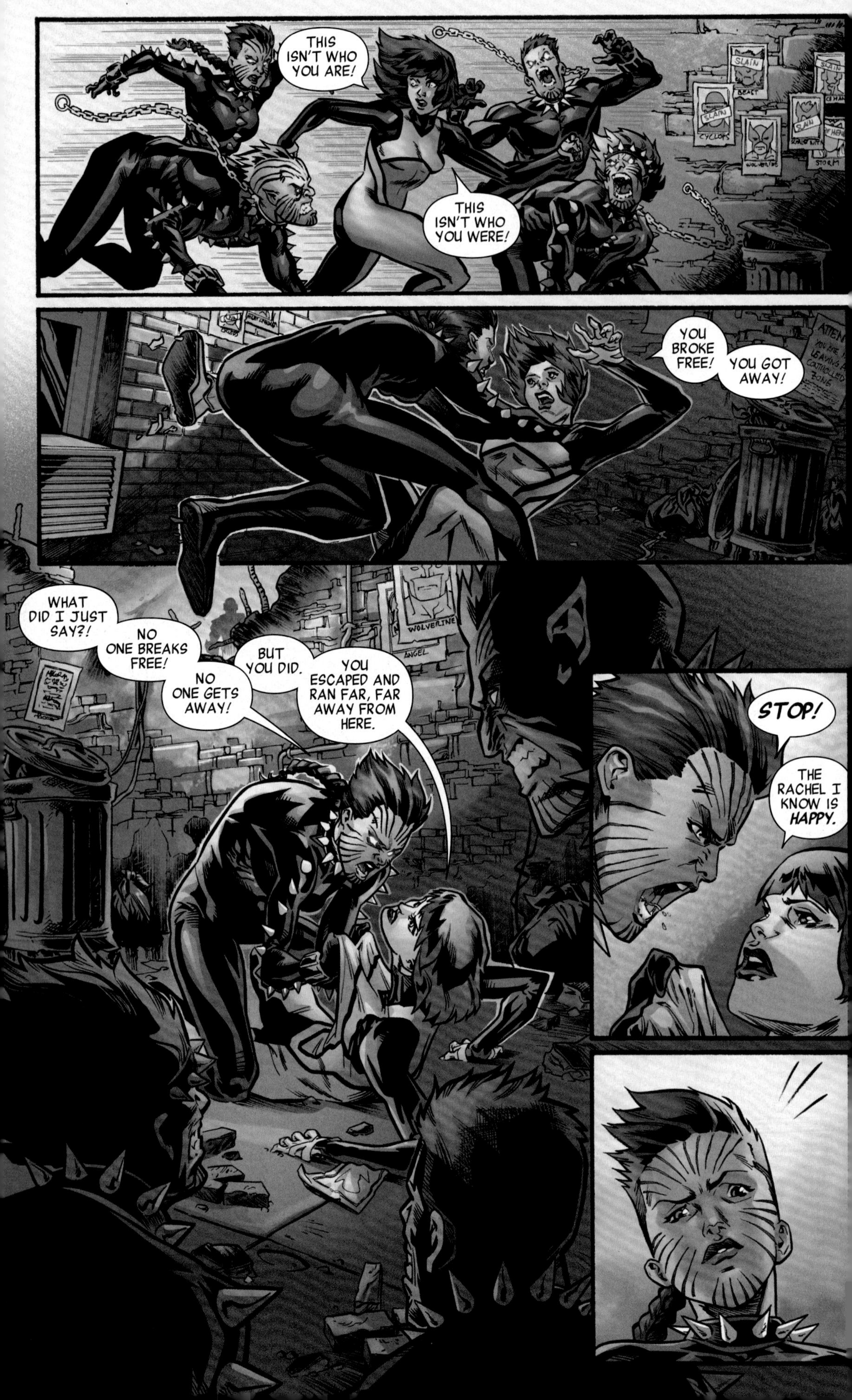
THIS ISN'T WHO YOU ARE!
THIS ISN'T WHO YOU WERE!
SLAIN
BEAST
SLAIN
CYCLOPS
WOLVERINE
SLAIN
STORM
YOU BROKE FREE!
YOU GOT AWAY!
WHAT DID I JUST SAY?!
NO ONE BREAKS FREE!
NO ONE GETS AWAY!
BUT YOU DID.
YOU ESCAPED AND RAN FAR, FAR AWAY FROM HERE.
WOLVERINE
ANGEL
STOP!
THE RACHEL I KNOW IS *HAPPY.*

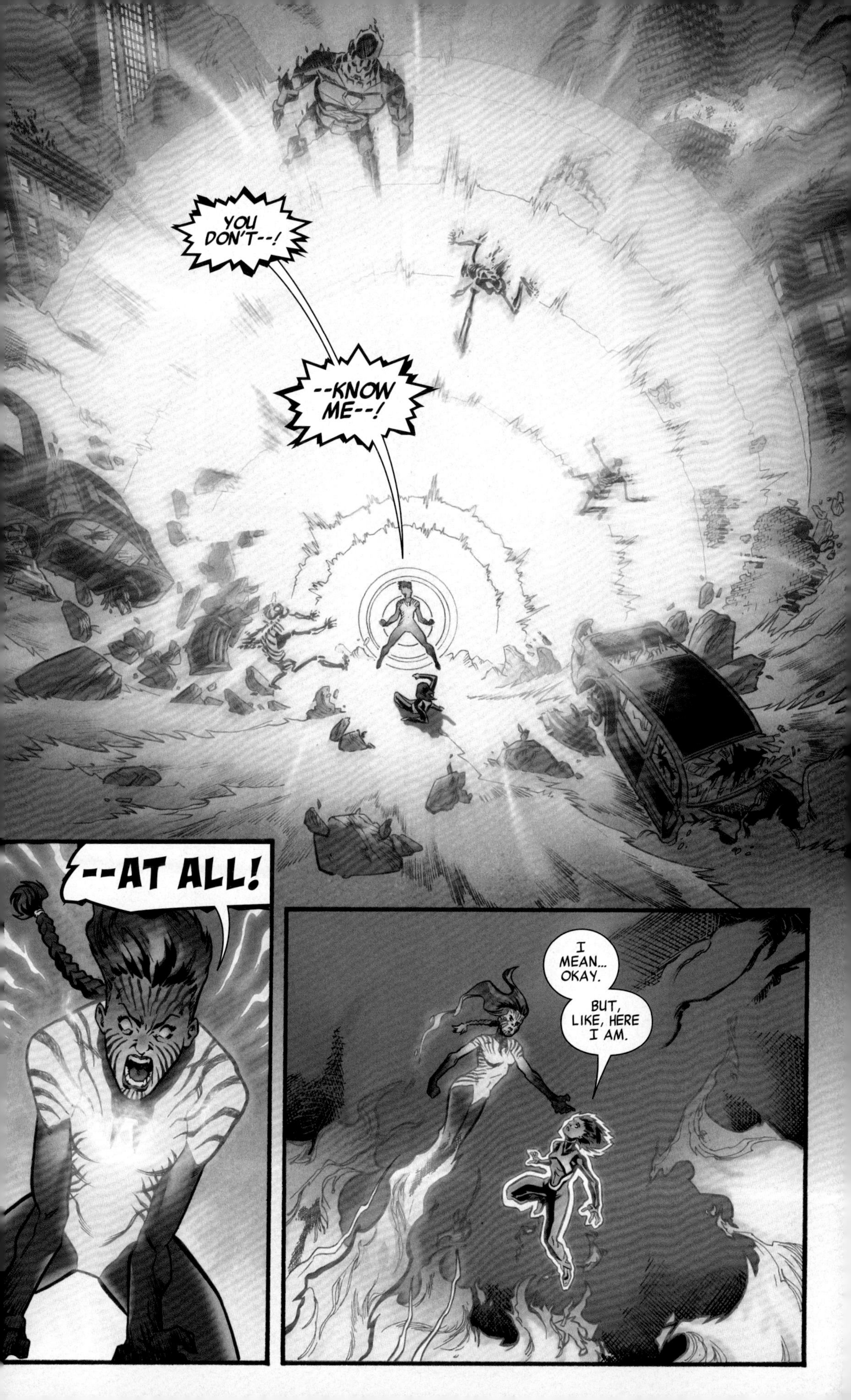
YOU DON'T--!
--KNOW ME--!
--AT ALL!
I MEAN... OKAY.
BUT, LIKE, HERE I AM.

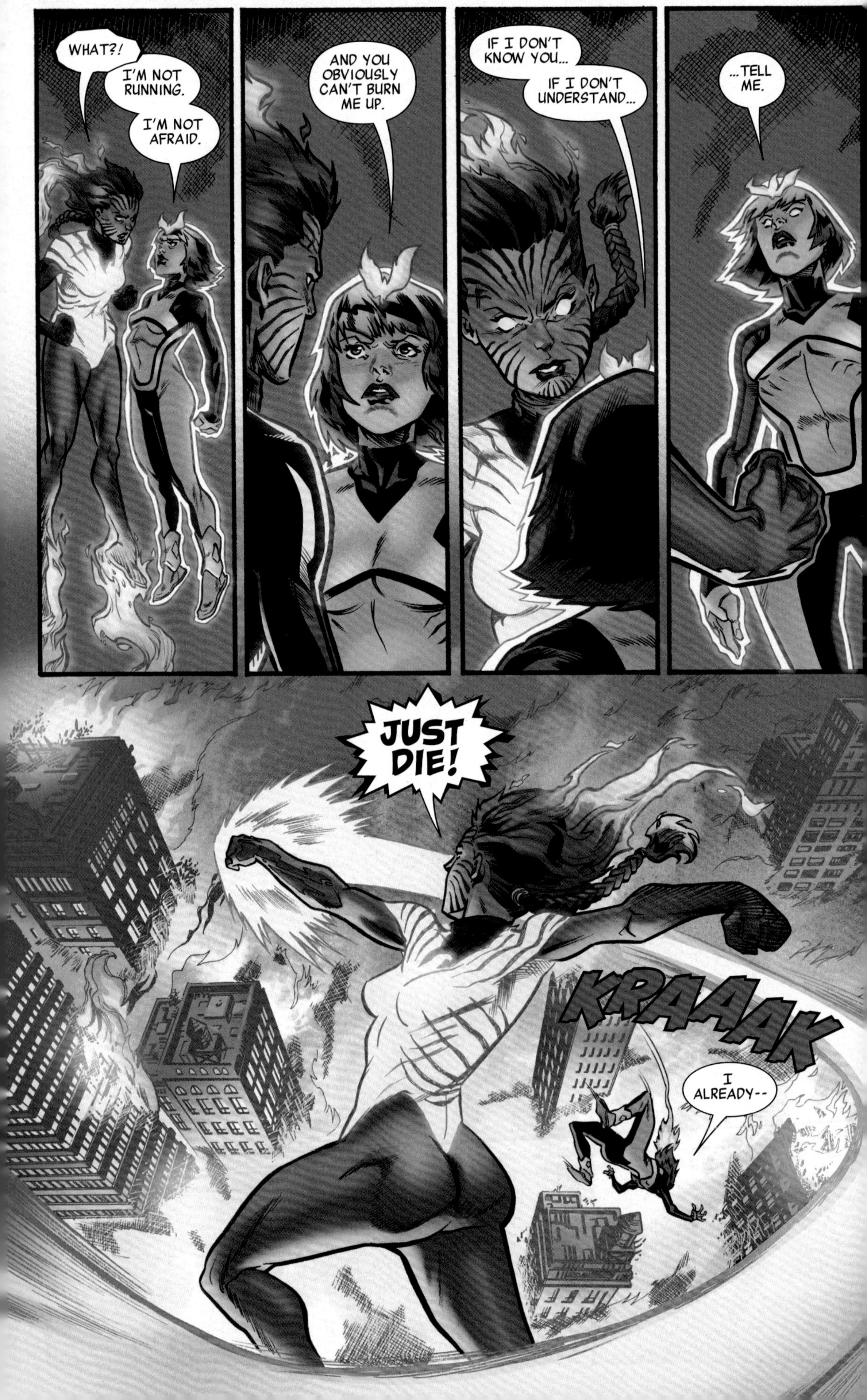
WHAT?!
I'M NOT RUNNING.
I'M NOT AFRAID.
AND YOU OBVIOUSLY CAN'T BURN ME UP.
IF I DON'T KNOW YOU...
IF I DON'T UNDERSTAND...
...TELL ME.
JUST DIE!
KRAAAK
I ALREADY--

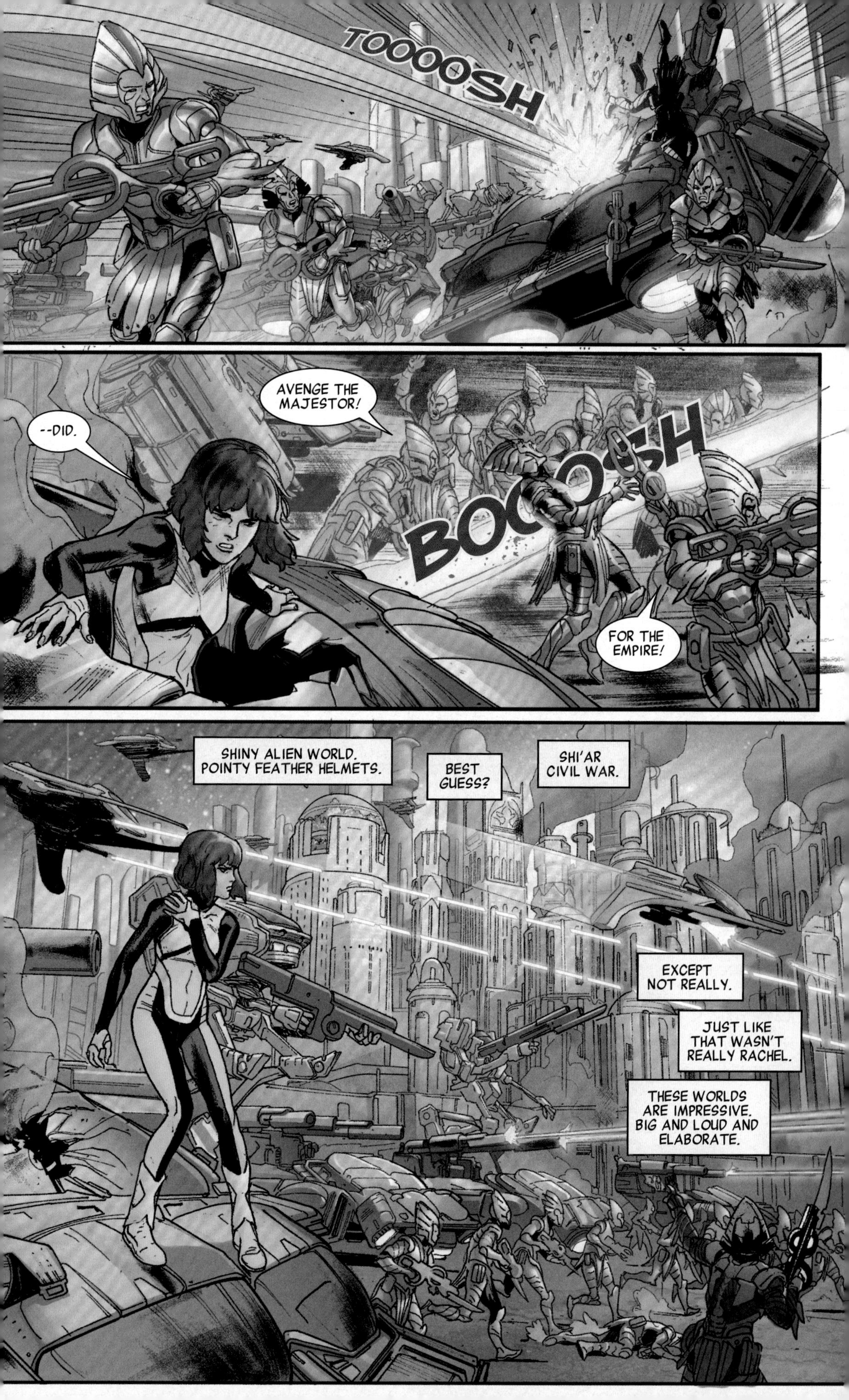
TOOOOOSH
AVENGE THE MAJESTOR!
--DID.
BOOOOSH
FOR THE EMPIRE!
SHINY ALIEN WORLD. POINTY FEATHER HELMETS.
BEST GUESS?
SHI'AR CIVIL WAR.
EXCEPT NOT REALLY.
JUST LIKE THAT WASN'T REALLY RACHEL.
THESE WORLDS ARE IMPRESSIVE. BIG AND LOUD AND ELABORATE.

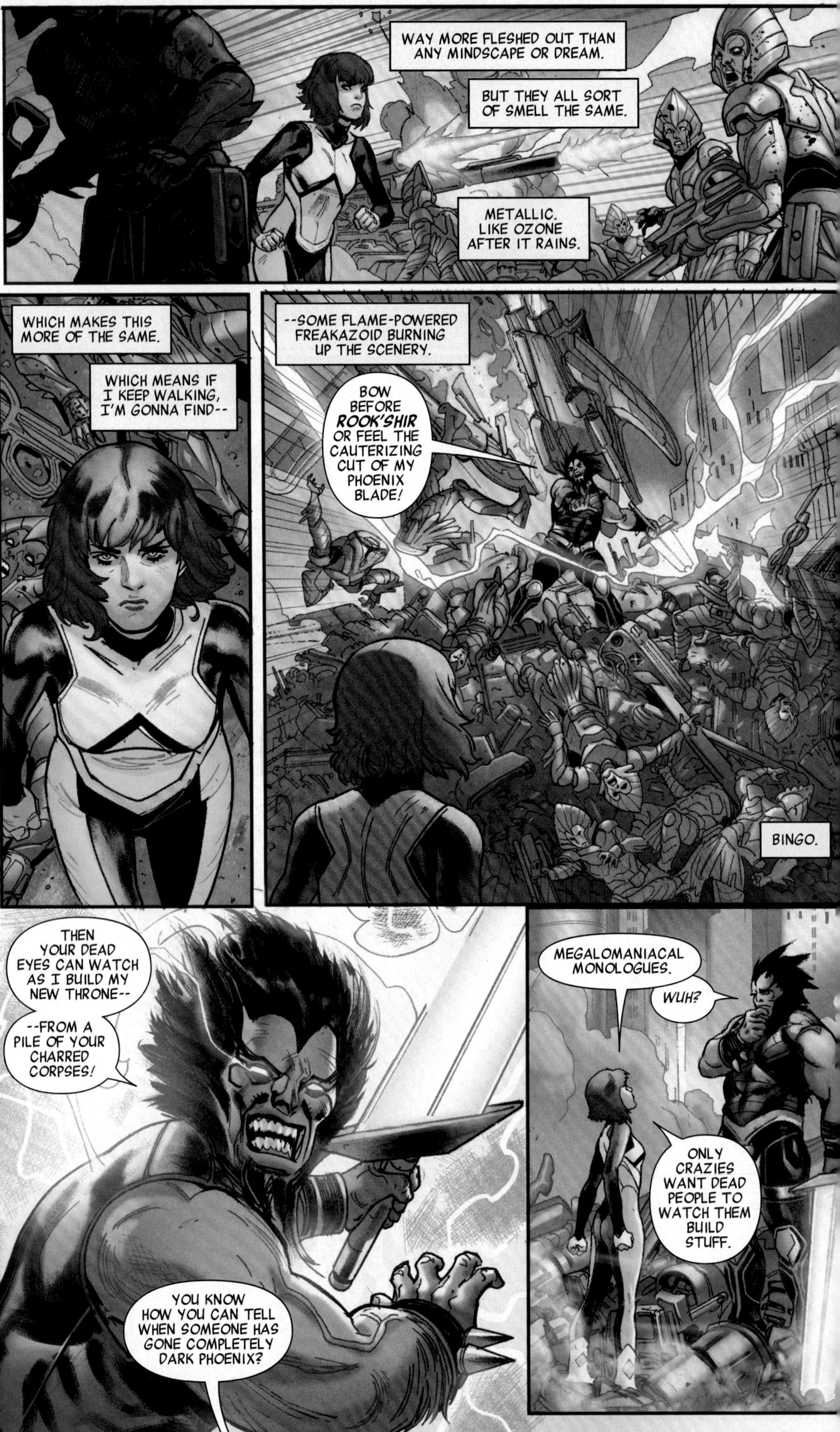
WAY MORE FLESHED OUT THAN ANY MINDSCAPE OR DREAM.
BUT THEY ALL SORT OF SMELL THE SAME.
METALLIC. LIKE OZONE AFTER IT RAINS.
WHICH MAKES THIS MORE OF THE SAME.
WHICH MEANS IF I KEEP WALKING, I'M GONNA FIND--
--SOME FLAME-POWERED FREAKAZOID BURNING UP THE SCENERY.
BOW BEFORE ROOK'SHIR OR FEEL THE CAUTERIZING CUT OF MY PHOENIX BLADE!
BINGO.
THEN YOUR DEAD EYES CAN WATCH AS I BUILD MY NEW THRONE--
--FROM A PILE OF YOUR CHARRED CORPSES!
YOU KNOW HOW YOU CAN TELL WHEN SOMEONE HAS GONE COMPLETELY DARK PHOENIX?
MEGALOMANIACAL MONOLOGUES.
WUH?
ONLY CRAZIES WANT DEAD PEOPLE TO WATCH THEM BUILD STUFF.

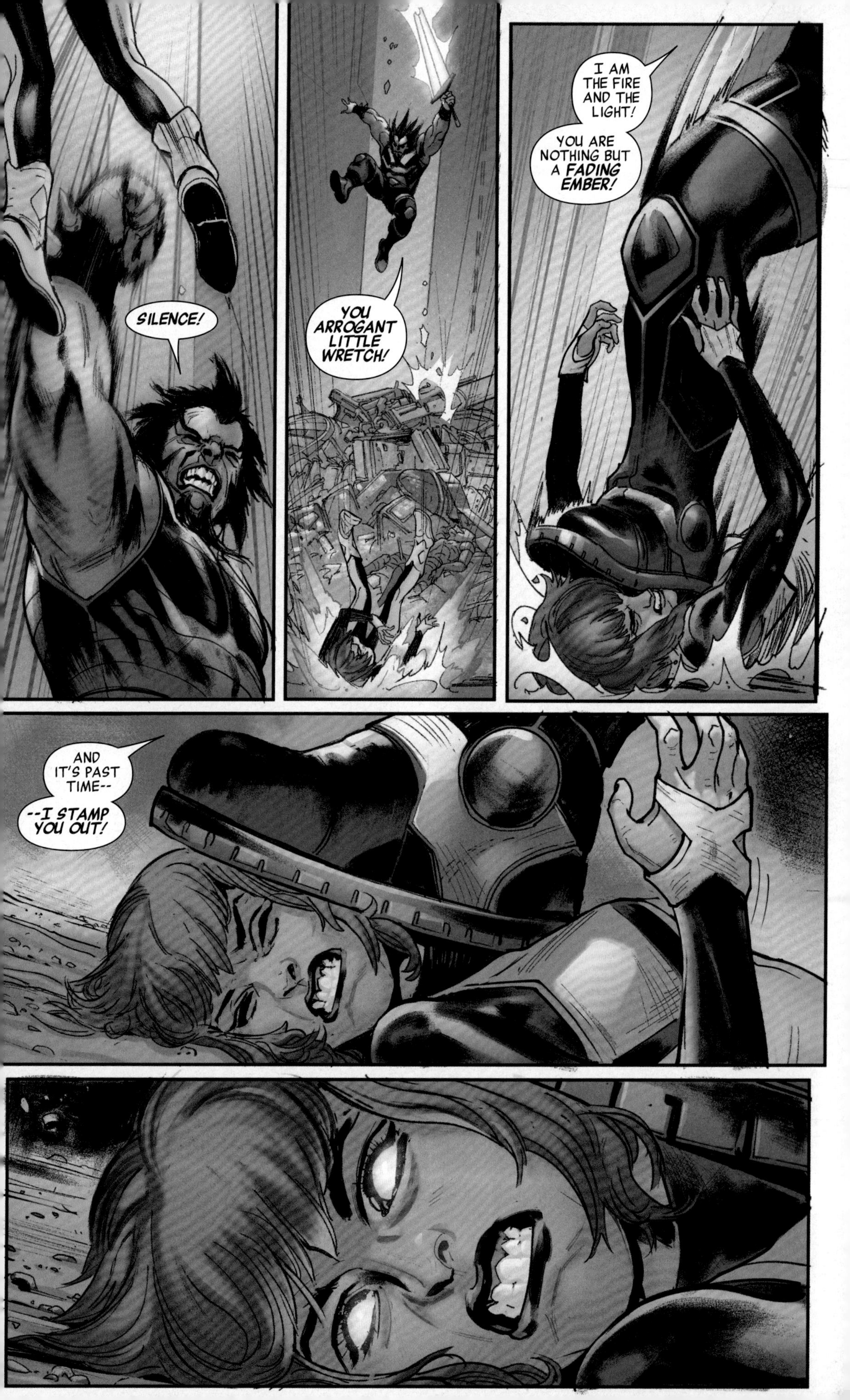
SILENCE!
YOU ARROGANT LITTLE WRETCH!
I AM THE FIRE AND THE LIGHT!
YOU ARE NOTHING BUT A FADING EMBER!
AND IT'S PAST TIME--
--I STAMP YOU OUT!

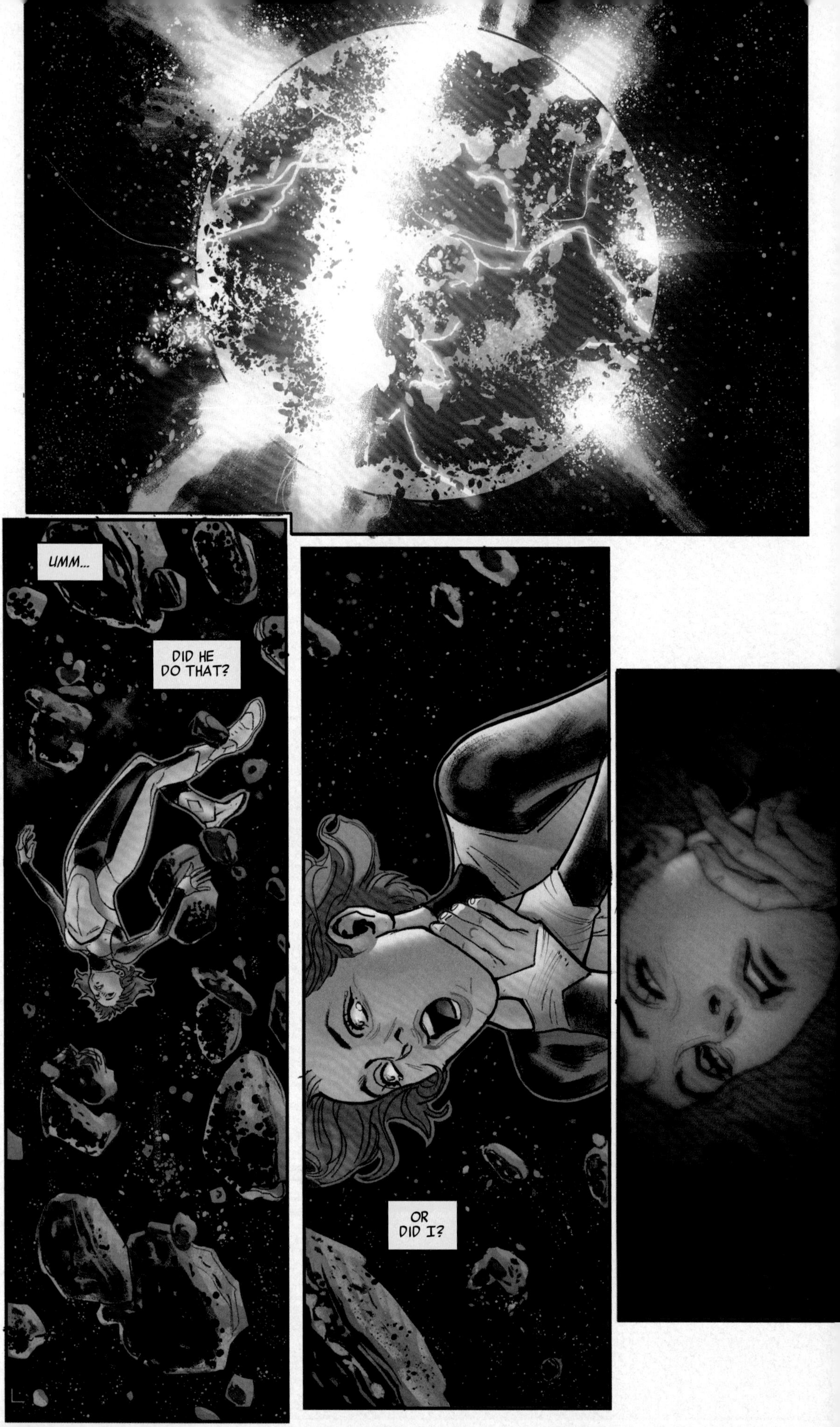
UMM...
DID HE
DO THAT?
OR
DID I?

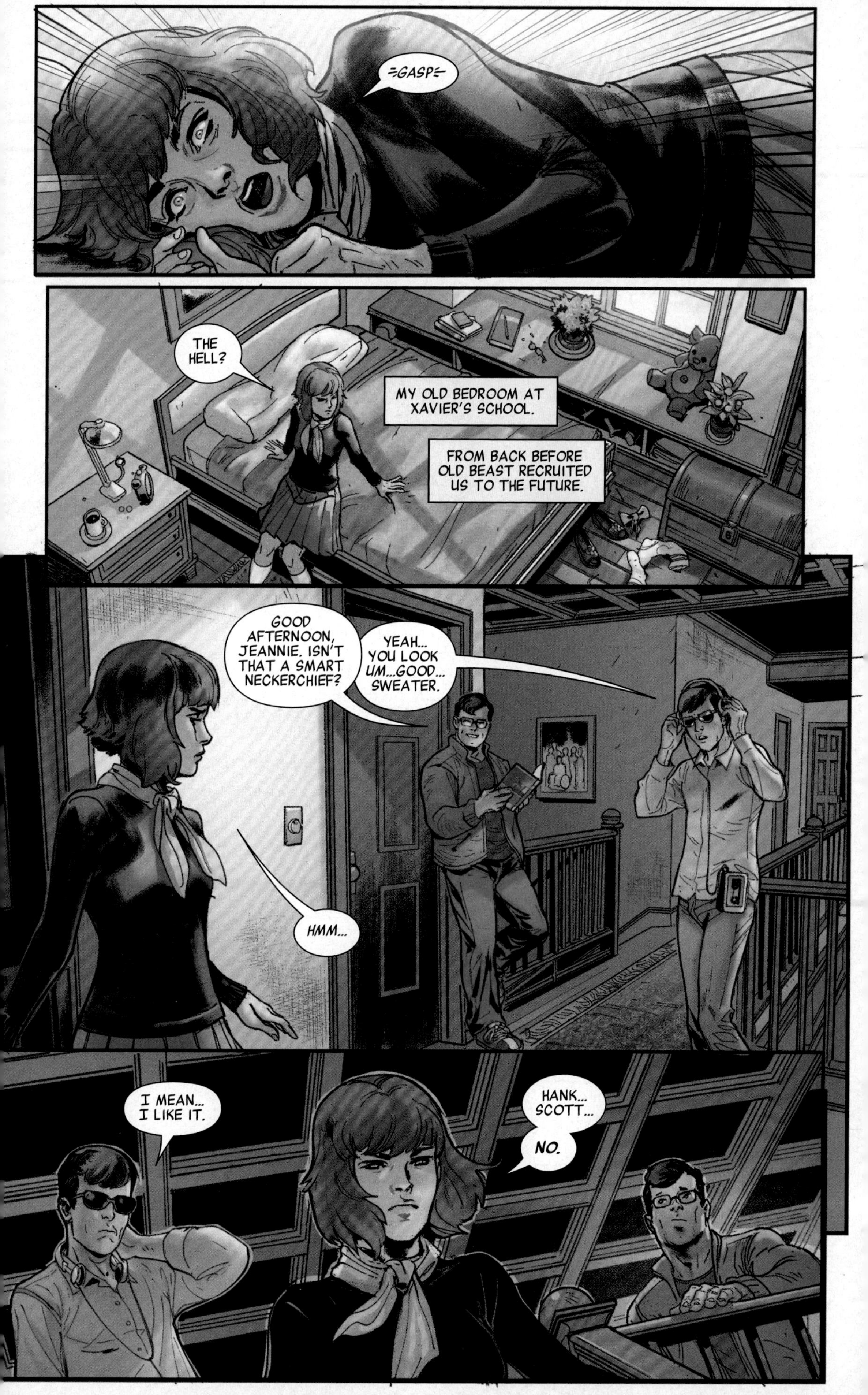
=GASP=
THE HELL?
MY OLD BEDROOM AT XAVIER'S SCHOOL.
FROM BACK BEFORE OLD BEAST RECRUITED US TO THE FUTURE.
GOOD AFTERNOON, JEANNIE. ISN'T THAT A SMART NECKERCHIEF?
YEAH... YOU LOOK UM...GOOD... SWEATER.
HMM...
I MEAN... I LIKE IT.
HANK... SCOTT...
NO.

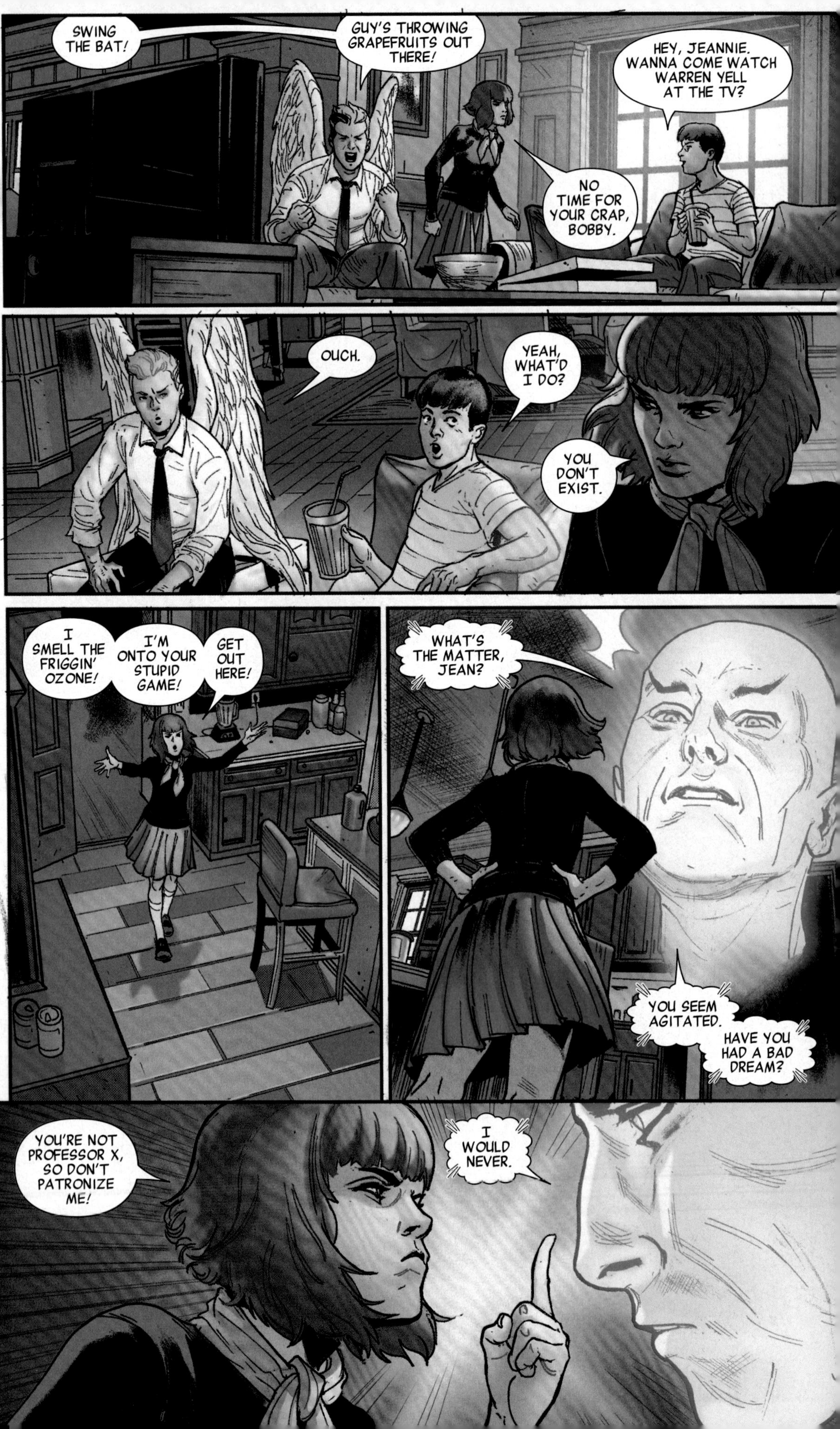
SWING THE BAT!
GUY'S THROWING GRAPEFRUITS OUT THERE!
HEY, JEANNIE. WANNA COME WATCH WARREN YELL AT THE TV?
NO TIME FOR YOUR CRAP, BOBBY.
OUCH.
YEAH, WHAT'D I DO?
YOU DON'T EXIST.
I SMELL THE FRIGGIN' OZONE!
I'M ONTO YOUR STUPID GAME!
GET OUT HERE!
WHAT'S THE MATTER, JEAN?
YOU SEEM AGITATED.
HAVE YOU HAD A BAD DREAM?
YOU'RE NOT PROFESSOR X, SO DON'T PATRONIZE ME!
I WOULD NEVER.

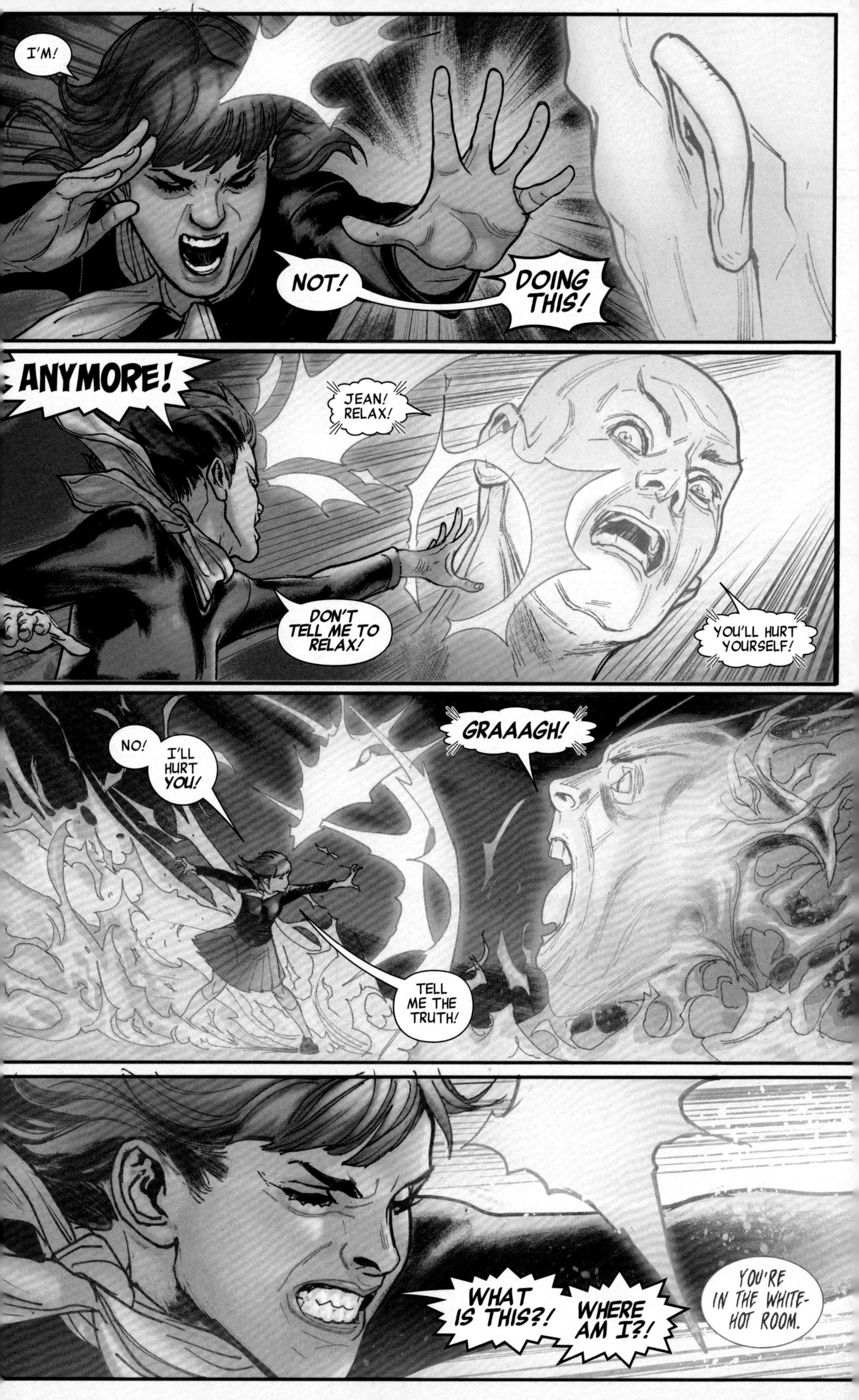

I'M!
NOT!
DOING THIS!
ANYMORE!
JEAN! RELAX!
DON'T TELL ME TO RELAX!
YOU'LL HURT YOURSELF!
NO!
I'LL HURT YOU!
GRAAAGH!
TELL ME THE TRUTH!
WHAT IS THIS?!
WHERE AM I?!
YOU'RE IN THE WHITE-HOT ROOM.

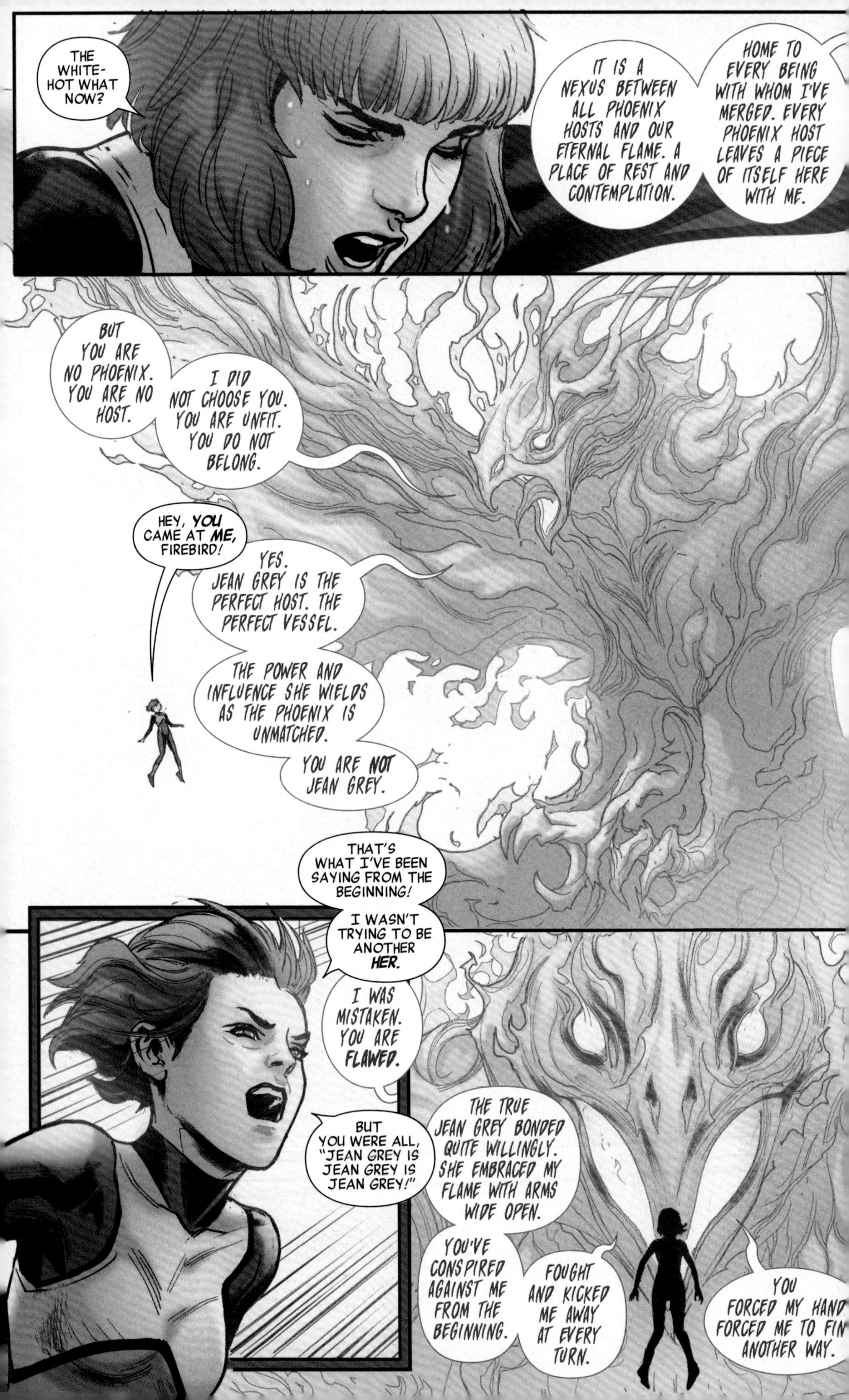
THE WHITE-HOT WHAT NOW?
IT IS A NEXUS BETWEEN ALL PHOENIX HOSTS AND OUR ETERNAL FLAME. A PLACE OF REST AND CONTEMPLATION.
HOME TO EVERY BEING WITH WHOM I'VE MERGED. EVERY PHOENIX HOST LEAVES A PIECE OF ITSELF HERE WITH ME.
BUT YOU ARE NO PHOENIX. YOU ARE NO HOST.
I DID NOT CHOOSE YOU. YOU ARE UNFIT. YOU DO NOT BELONG.
HEY, YOU CAME AT ME, FIREBIRD!
YES. JEAN GREY IS THE PERFECT HOST. THE PERFECT VESSEL.
THE POWER AND INFLUENCE SHE WIELDS AS THE PHOENIX IS UNMATCHED.
YOU ARE NOT JEAN GREY.
THAT'S WHAT I'VE BEEN SAYING FROM THE BEGINNING!
I WASN'T TRYING TO BE ANOTHER HER.
I WAS MISTAKEN. YOU ARE FLAWED.
BUT YOU WERE ALL, "JEAN GREY IS JEAN GREY IS JEAN GREY!"
THE TRUE JEAN GREY BONDED QUITE WILLINGLY. SHE EMBRACED MY FLAME WITH ARMS WIDE OPEN.
YOU'VE CONSPIRED AGAINST ME FROM THE BEGINNING.
FOUGHT AND KICKED ME AWAY AT EVERY TURN.
YOU FORCED MY HAND FORCED ME TO FIN ANOTHER WAY.

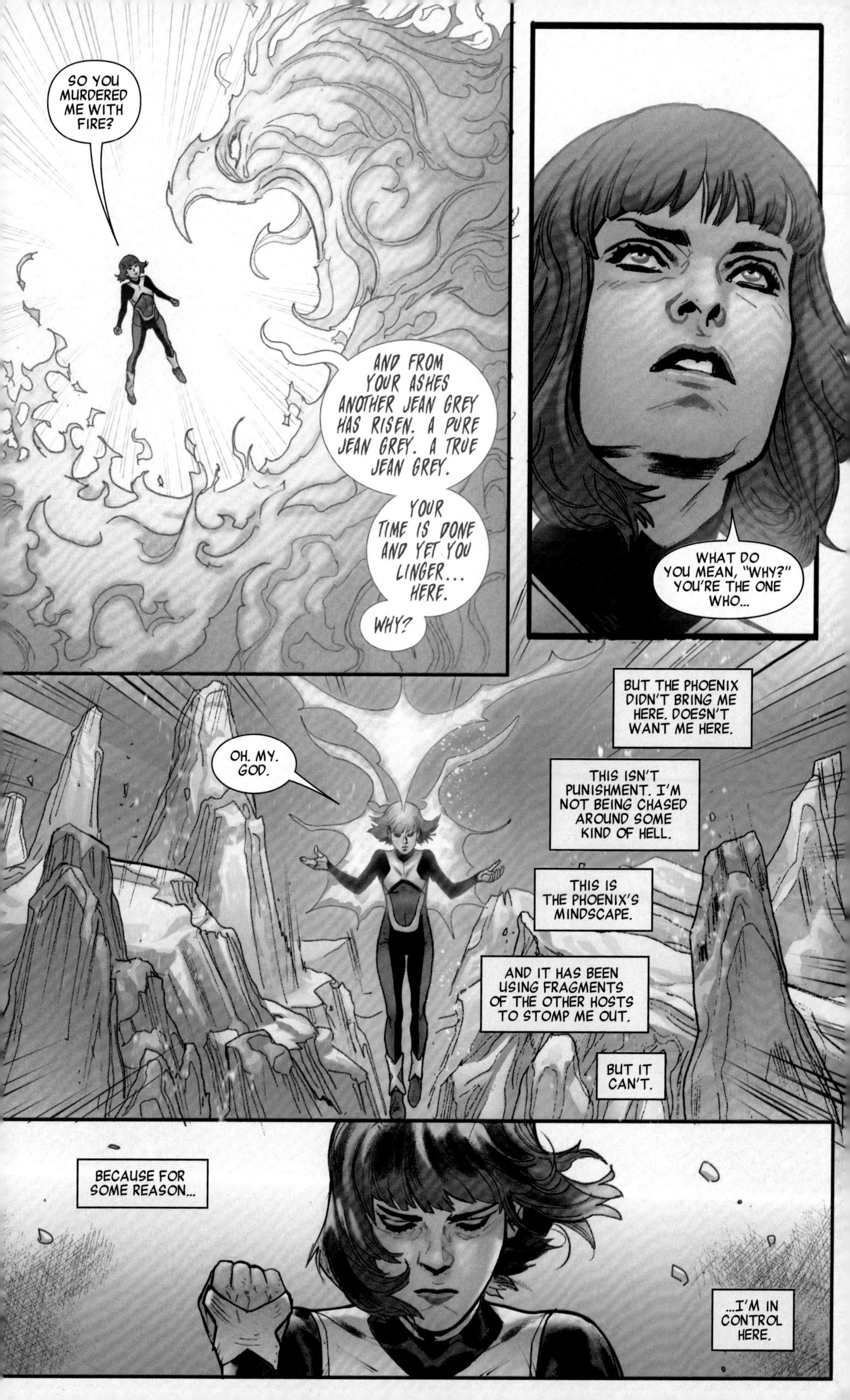
SO YOU MURDERED ME WITH FIRE?
AND FROM YOUR ASHES ANOTHER JEAN GREY HAS RISEN. A PURE JEAN GREY. A TRUE JEAN GREY.
YOUR TIME IS DONE AND YET YOU LINGER... HERE.
WHY?
WHAT DO YOU MEAN, "WHY?" YOU'RE THE ONE WHO...
OH. MY. GOD.
BUT THE PHOENIX DIDN'T BRING ME HERE. DOESN'T WANT ME HERE.
THIS ISN'T PUNISHMENT. I'M NOT BEING CHASED AROUND SOME KIND OF HELL.
THIS IS THE PHOENIX'S MINDSCAPE.
AND IT HAS BEEN USING FRAGMENTS OF THE OTHER HOSTS TO STOMP ME OUT.
BUT IT CAN'T.
BECAUSE FOR SOME REASON...
...I'M IN CONTROL HERE.

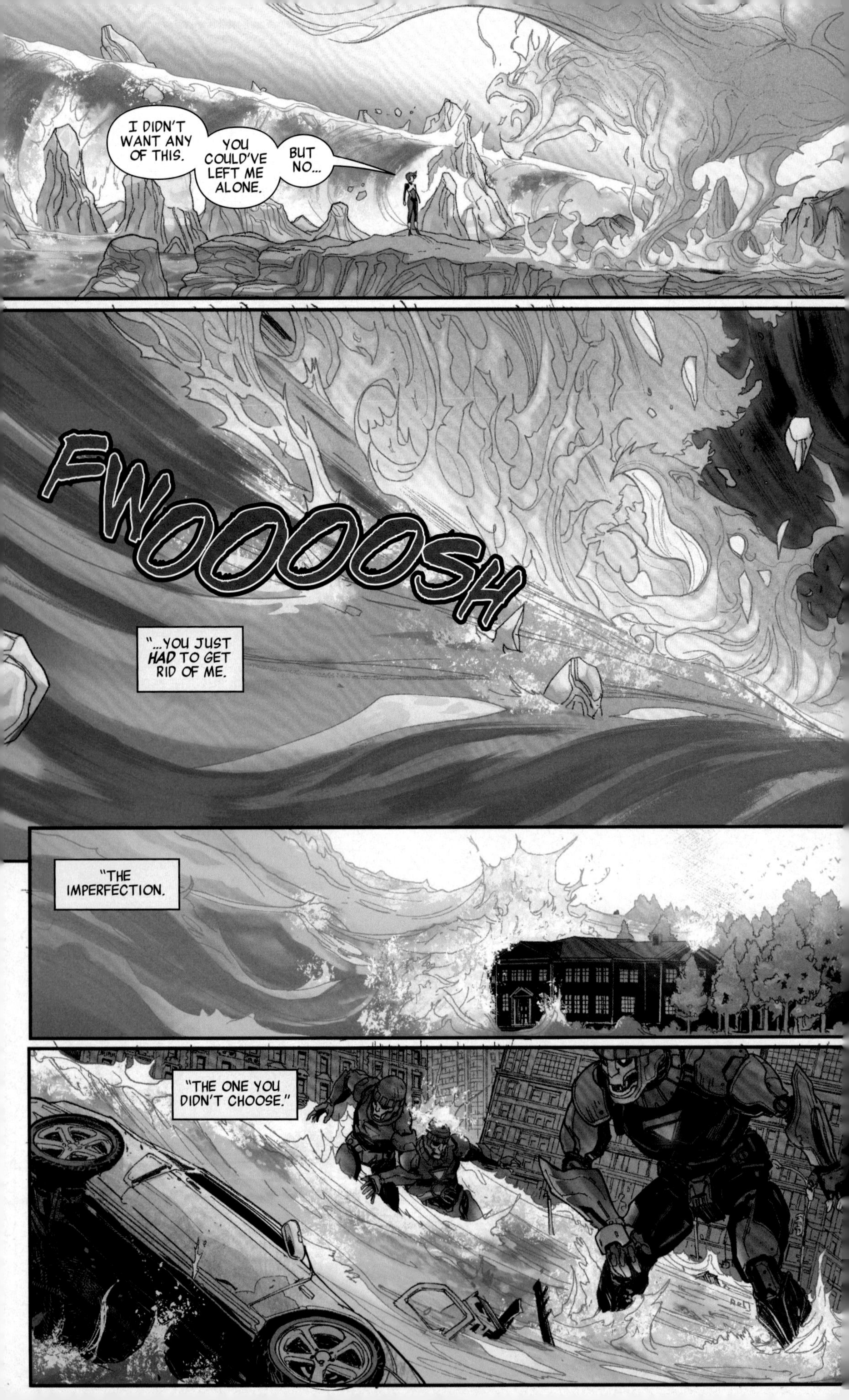

I DIDN'T WANT ANY OF THIS.
YOU COULD'VE LEFT ME ALONE.
BUT NO...
FWOOOOOSH
"...YOU JUST *HAD* TO GET RID OF ME.
"THE IMPERFECTION.
"THE ONE YOU DIDN'T CHOOSE."

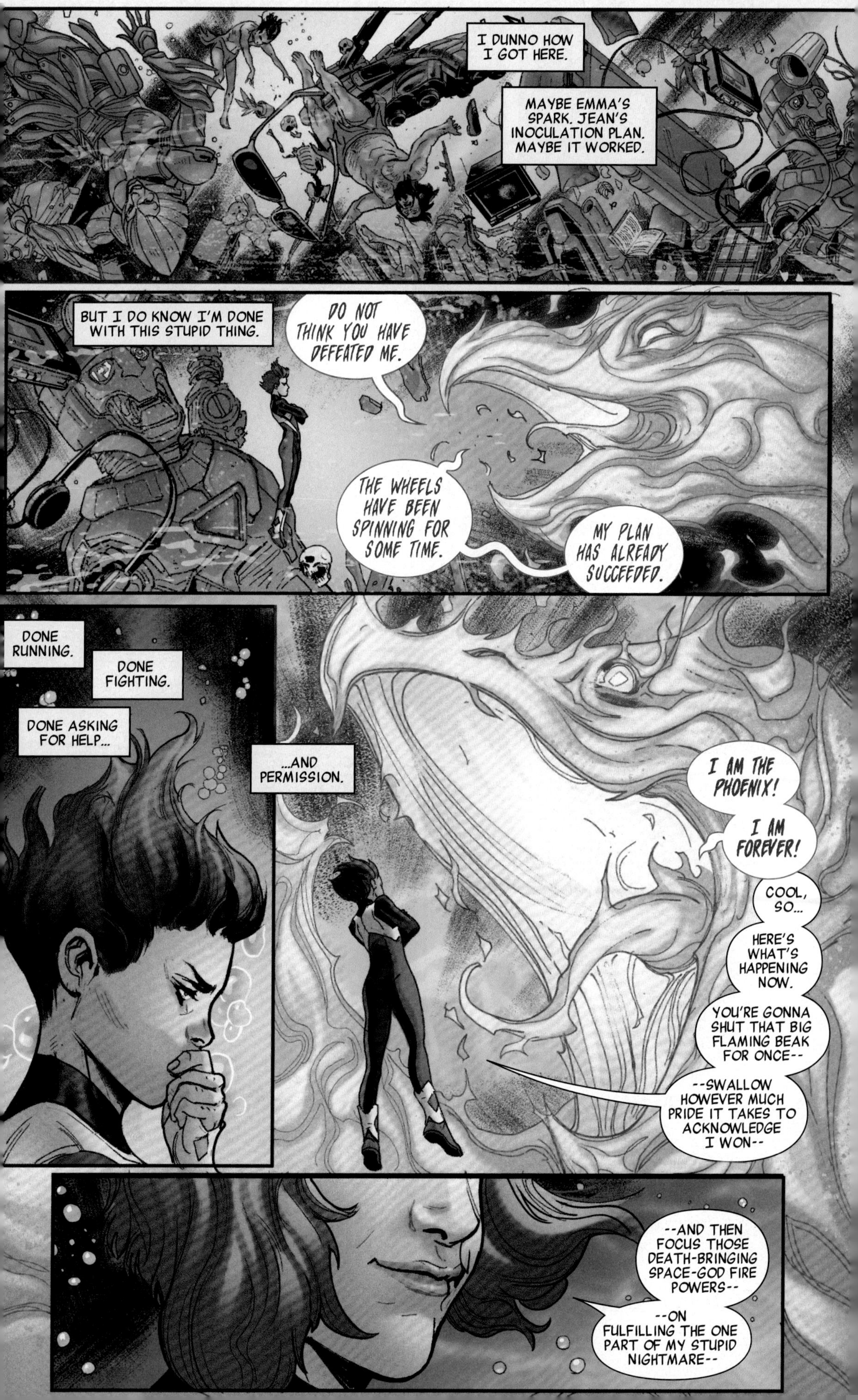
I DUNNO HOW I GOT HERE.
MAYBE EMMA'S SPARK. JEAN'S INOCULATION PLAN. MAYBE IT WORKED.
BUT I DO KNOW I'M DONE WITH THIS STUPID THING.
DO NOT THINK YOU HAVE DEFEATED ME.
THE WHEELS HAVE BEEN SPINNING FOR SOME TIME.
MY PLAN HAS ALREADY SUCCEEDED.
DONE RUNNING.
DONE FIGHTING.
DONE ASKING FOR HELP...
...AND PERMISSION.
I AM THE PHOENIX!
I AM FOREVER!
COOL, SO...
HERE'S WHAT'S HAPPENING NOW.
YOU'RE GONNA SHUT THAT BIG FLAMING BEAK FOR ONCE--
--SWALLOW HOWEVER MUCH PRIDE IT TAKES TO ACKNOWLEDGE I WON--
--AND THEN FOCUS THOSE DEATH-BRINGING SPACE-GOD FIRE POWERS--
--ON FULFILLING THE ONE PART OF MY STUPID NIGHTMARE--

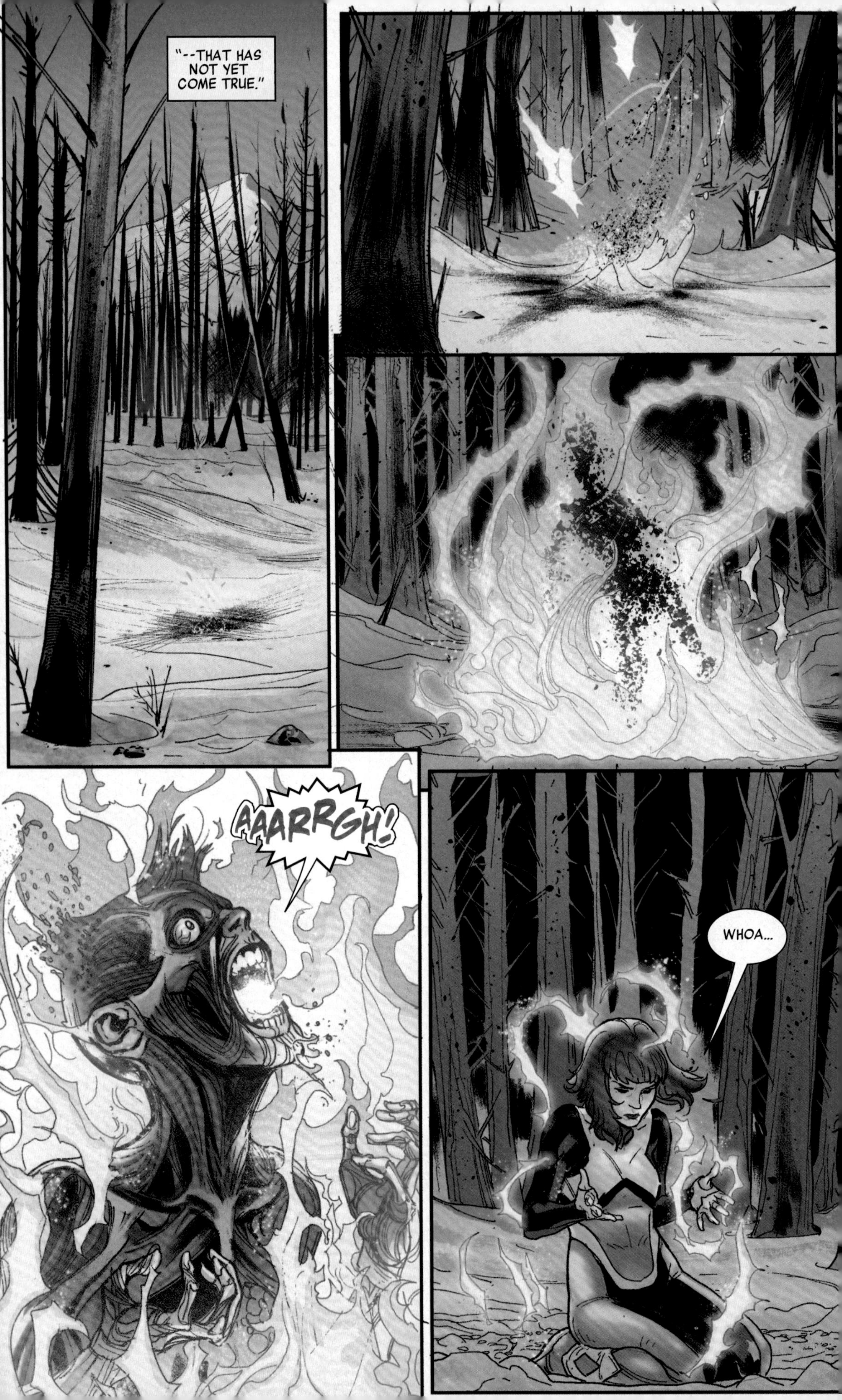
"--THAT HAS NOT YET COME TRUE."
AAARRGH!
WHOA...

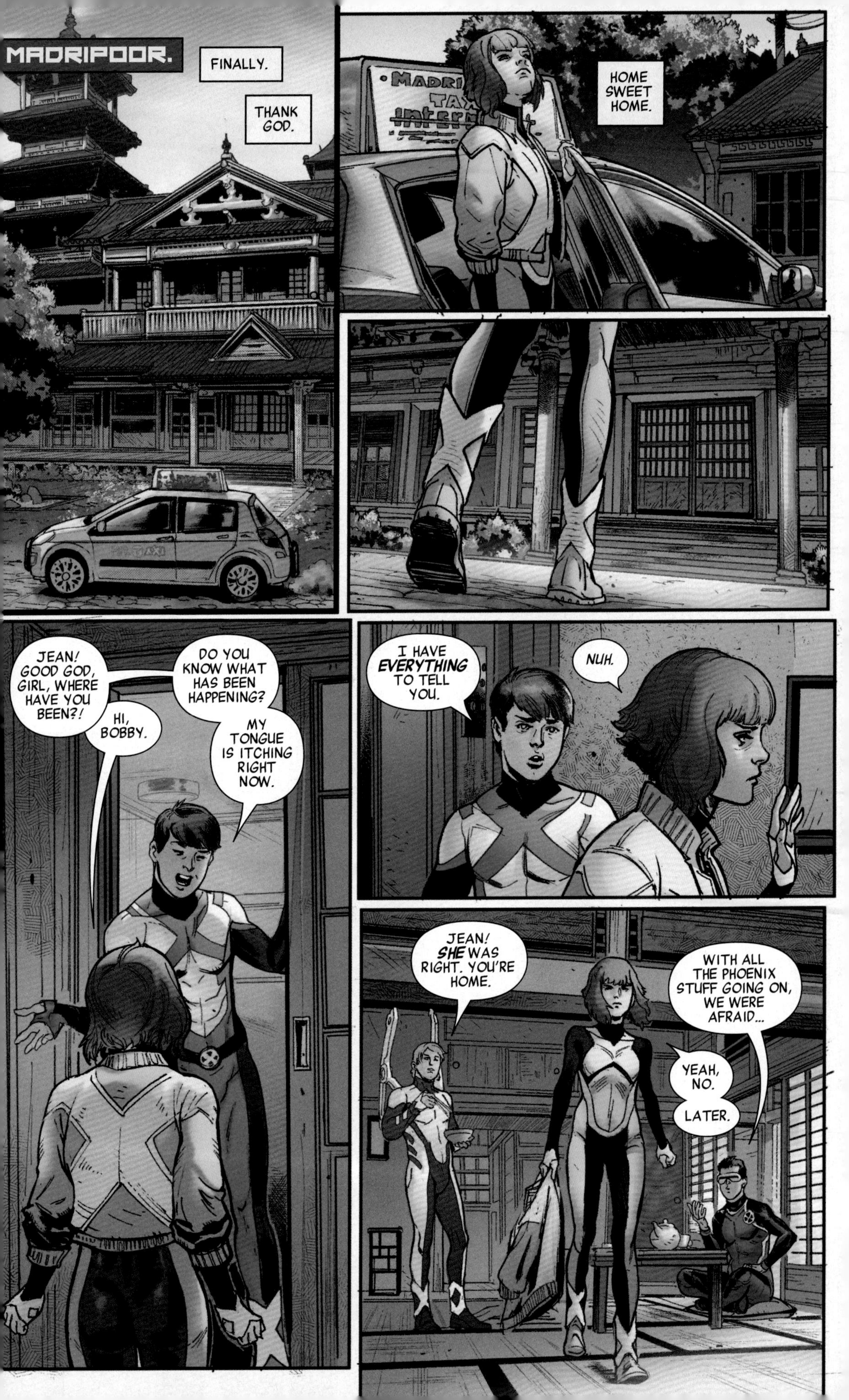
MADRIPOOR.
FINALLY.
THANK GOD.
HOME SWEET HOME.
JEAN! GOOD GOD, GIRL, WHERE HAVE YOU BEEN?!
DO YOU KNOW WHAT HAS BEEN HAPPENING?
HI, BOBBY.
MY TONGUE IS ITCHING RIGHT NOW.
I HAVE EVERYTHING TO TELL YOU.
NUH.
JEAN! SHE WAS RIGHT. YOU'RE HOME.
WITH ALL THE PHOENIX STUFF GOING ON, WE WERE AFRAID...
YEAH, NO.
LATER.

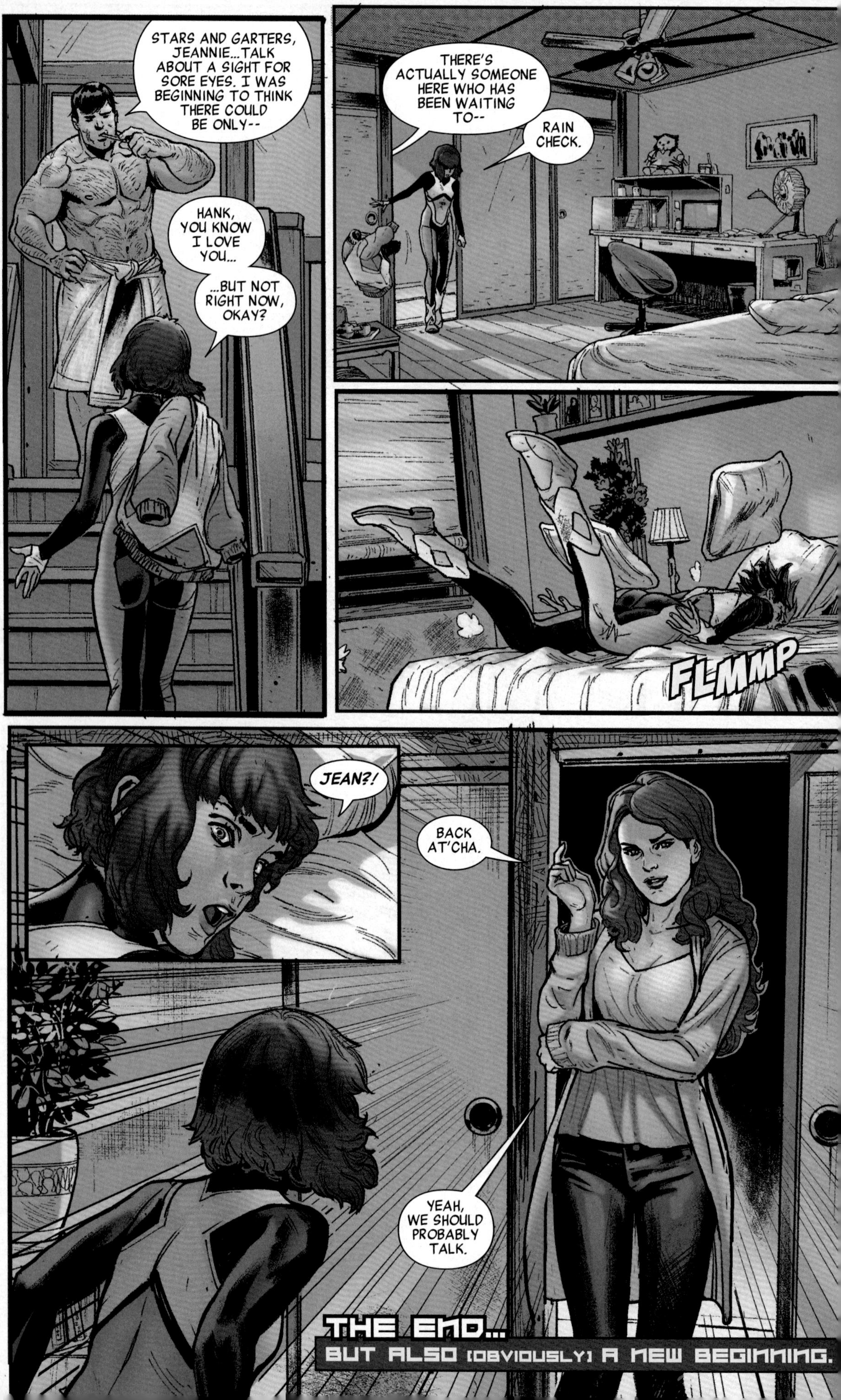
STARS AND GARTERS, JEANNIE...TALK ABOUT A SIGHT FOR SORE EYES. I WAS BEGINNING TO THINK THERE COULD BE ONLY--
HANK, YOU KNOW I LOVE YOU...
...BUT NOT RIGHT NOW, OKAY?
THERE'S ACTUALLY SOMEONE HERE WHO HAS BEEN WAITING TO--
RAIN CHECK.
FLMMP
JEAN?!
BACK AT'CHA.
YEAH, WE SHOULD PROBABLY TALK.
THE END...
BUT ALSO [OBVIOUSLY] A NEW BEGINNING.

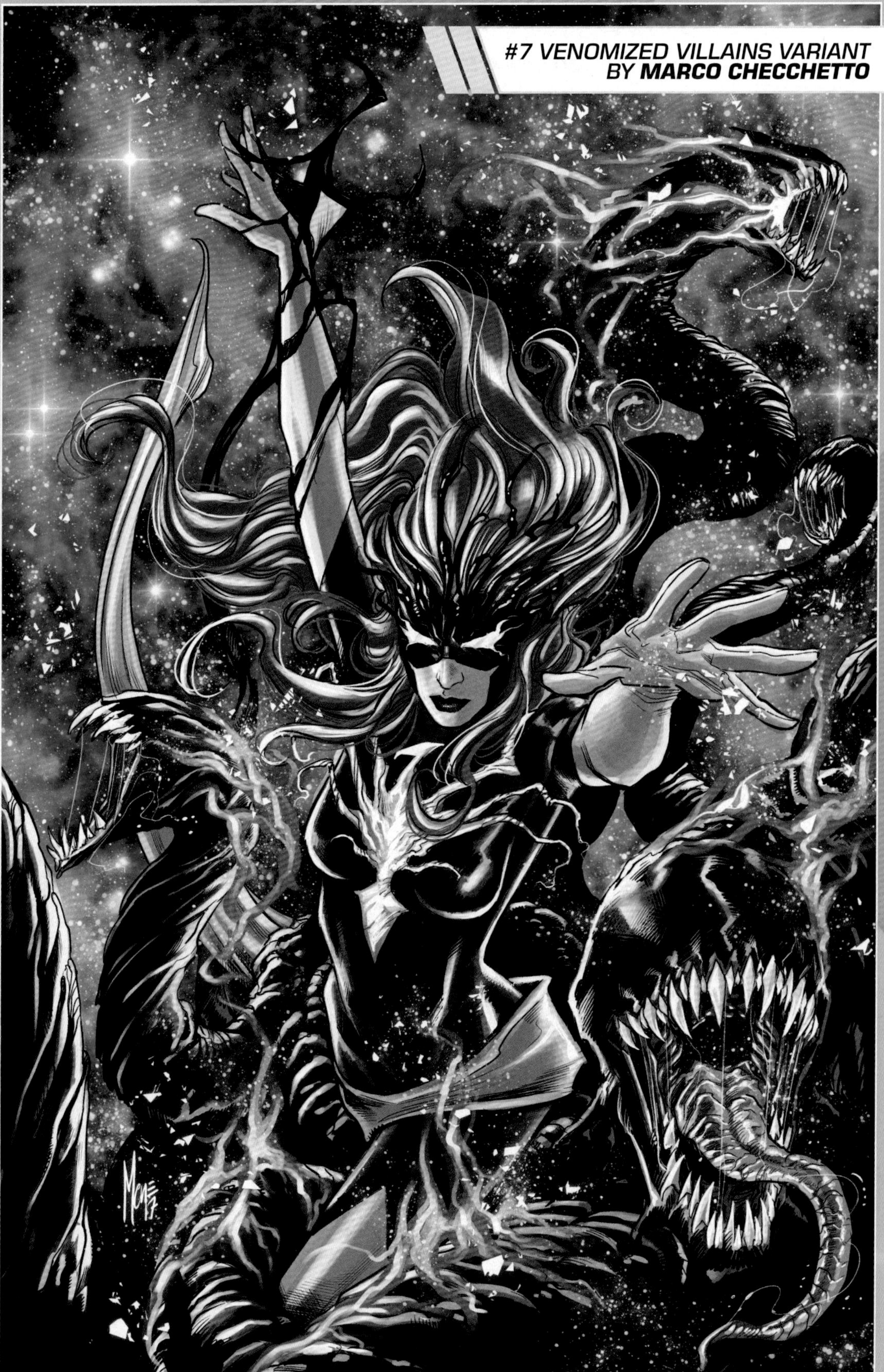

#7 VENOMIZED VILLAINS VARIANT
BY **MARCO CHECCHETTO**

#8 HOMAGE VARIANT BY **MIKE MAYHEW**

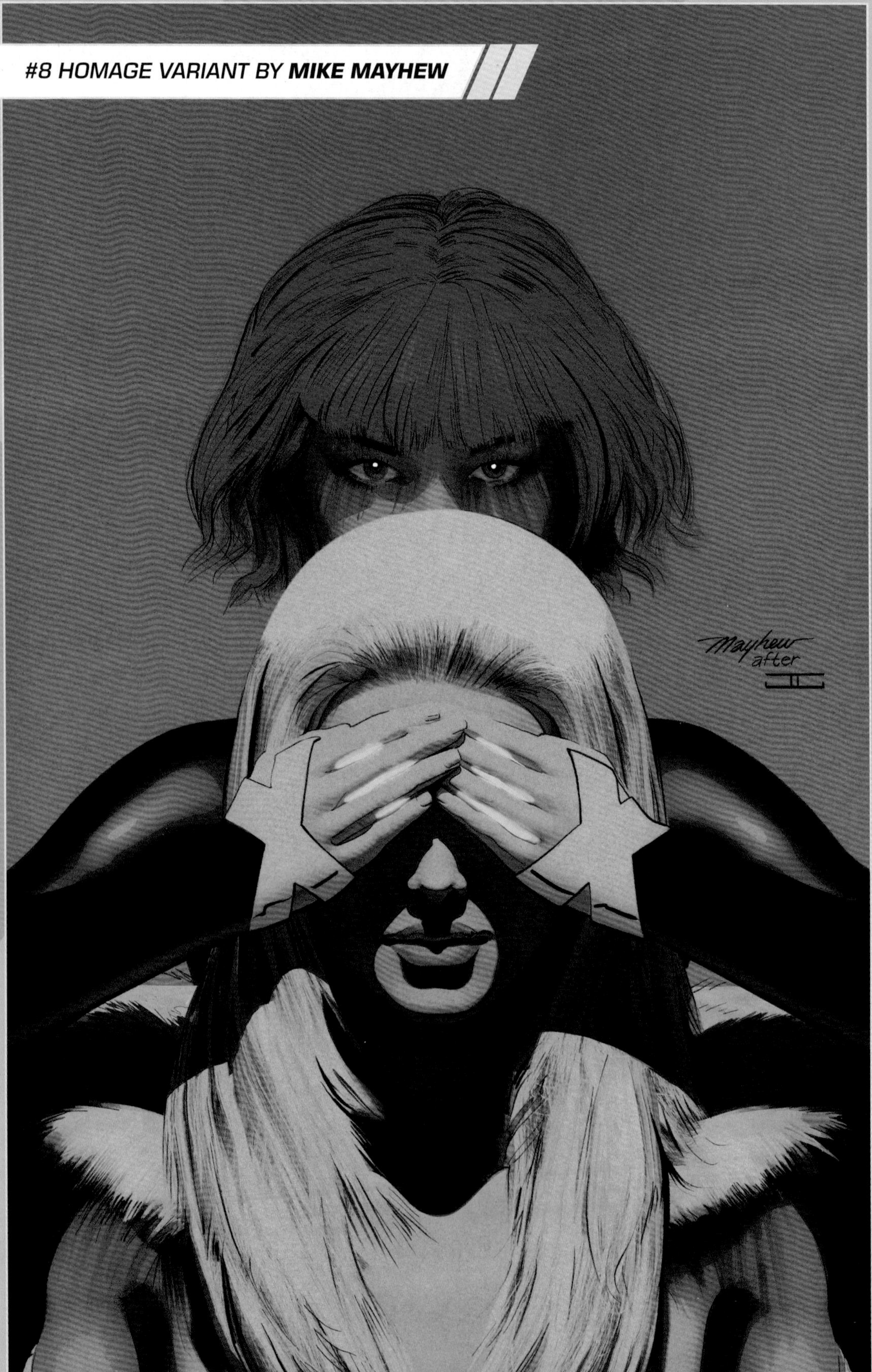
Mayhew after

#8 LEGACY HEADSHOT VARIANT BY **MIKE McKONE** & **ANDY TROY**

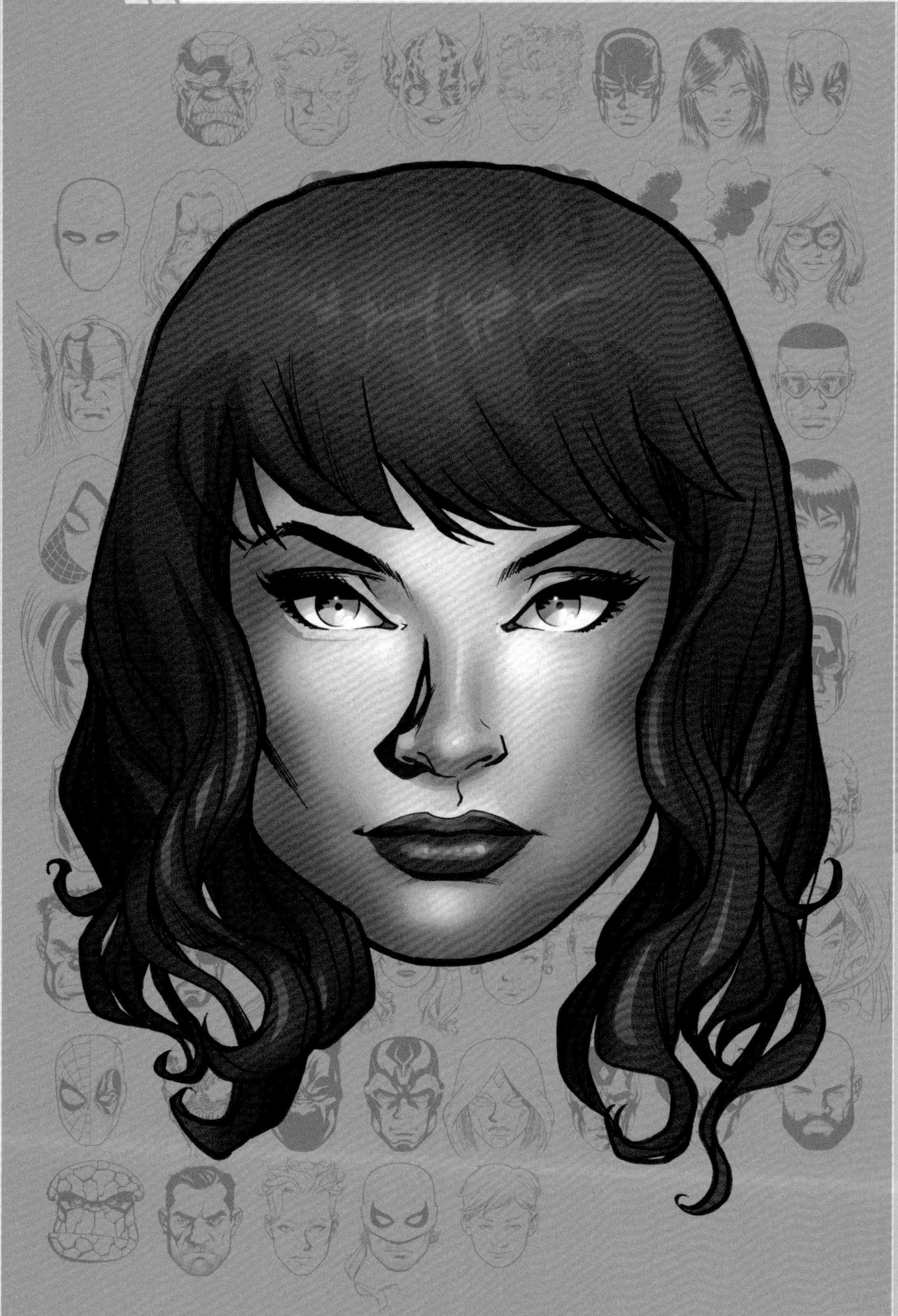

PHOENIX RESURRECTION: THE RETURN OF JEAN GREY #2
& JEAN GREY #11 CONNECTING VARIANTS BY **VICTOR HUGO**

#11 VARIANT BY **GURIHIRU**

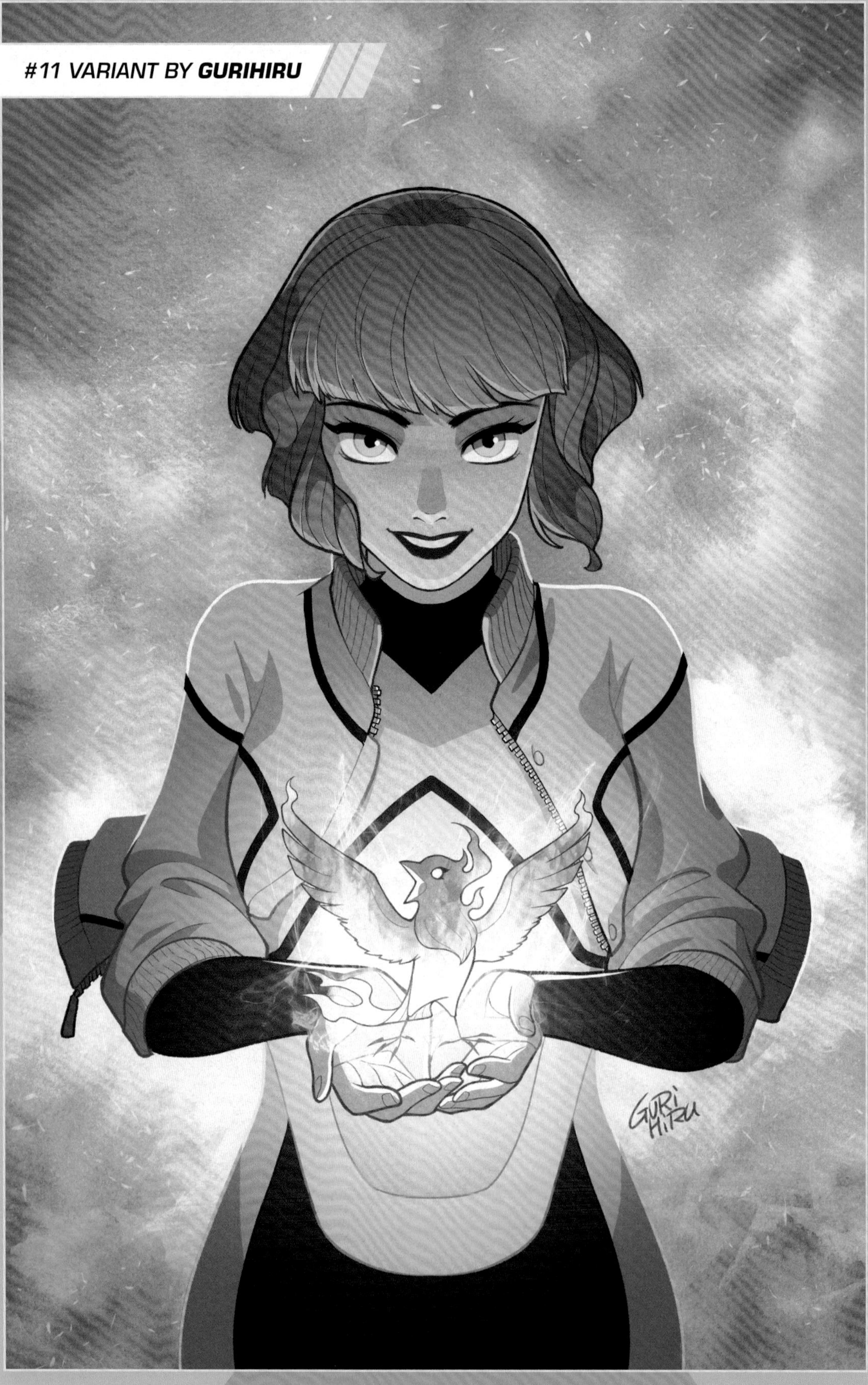
GURI HIRU

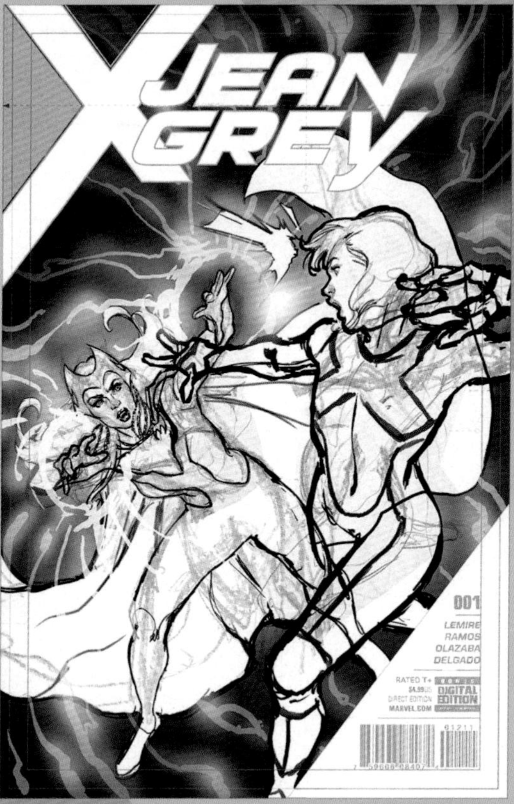
X
JEAN GREY
001
LEMIRE
RAMOS
OLAZABA
DELGADO
RATED T+
DIGITAL EDITION
MARVEL.COM

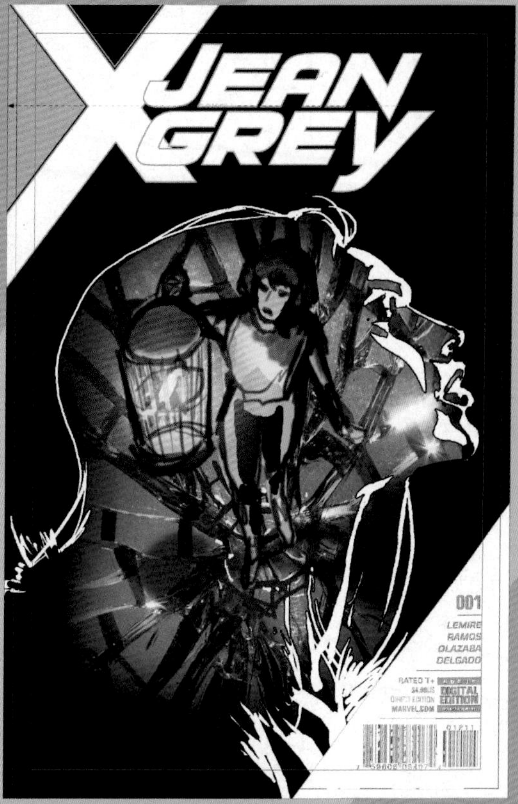
X
JEAN GREY
001
LEMIRE
RAMOS
OLAZABA
DELGADO
RATED T+
DIGITAL EDITION
MARVEL.COM

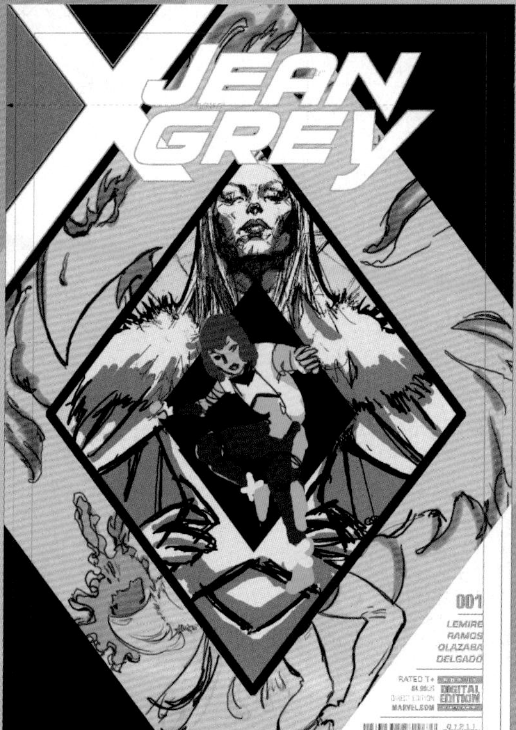
X
JEAN GREY
001
LEMIRE
RAMOS
OLAZABA
DELGADO
RATED T+
DIGITAL EDITION
MARVEL.COM

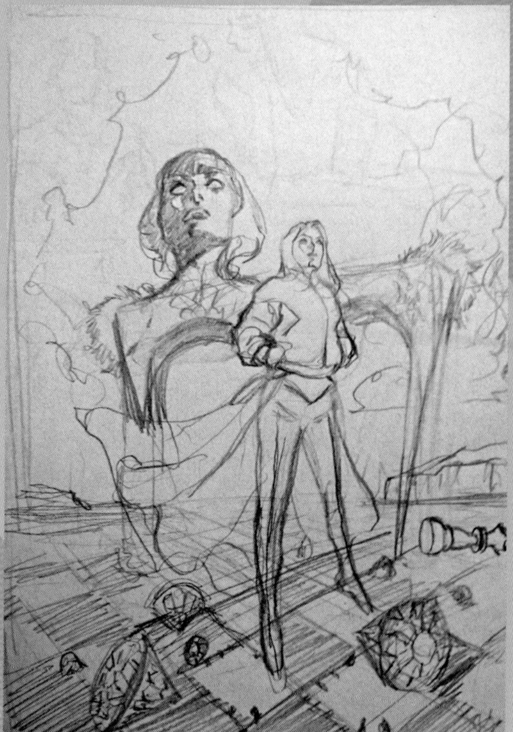

#7-9 COVER SKETCHES BY **DAVID YARDIN**

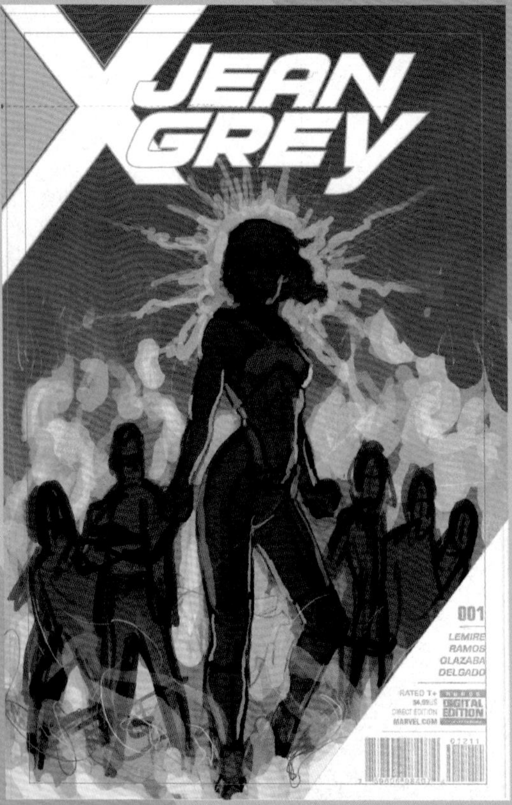
X JEAN GREY
001
LEMIRE
RAMOS
OLAZABA
DELGADO
RATED T+
DIGITAL EDITION
DIRECT EDITION
MARVEL.COM

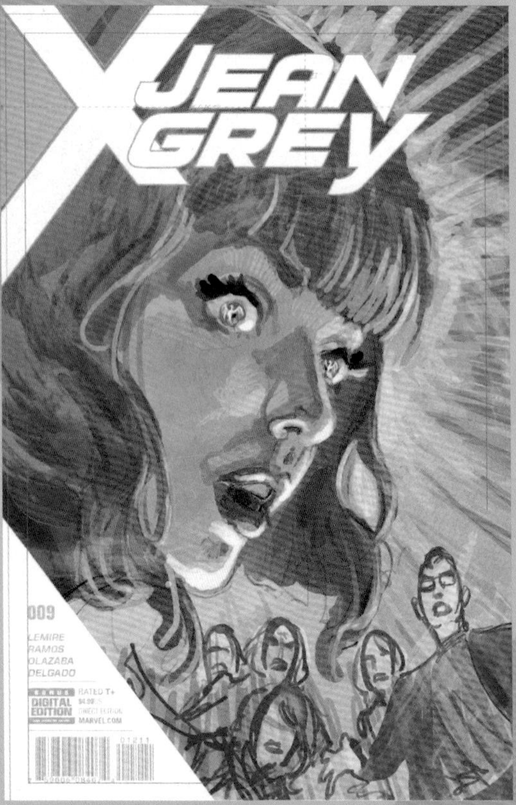
X JEAN GREY
009
LEMIRE
RAMOS
OLAZABA
DELGADO
RATED T+
DIGITAL EDITION
DIRECT EDITION
MARVEL.COM

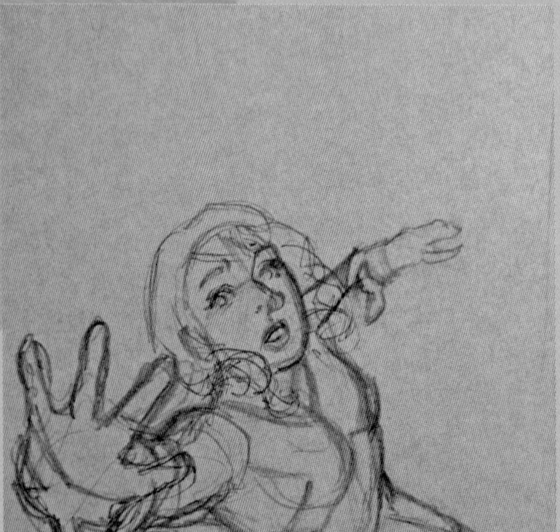

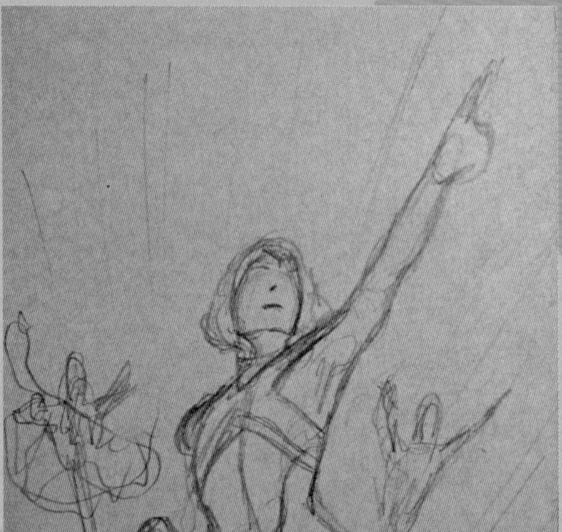

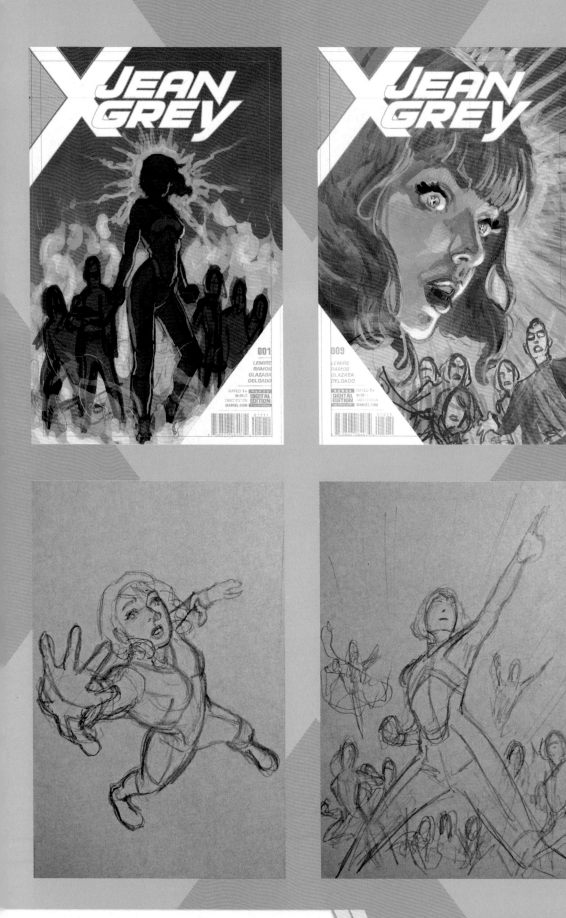

#10-11 COVER SKETCHES BY DAVID YARDIN

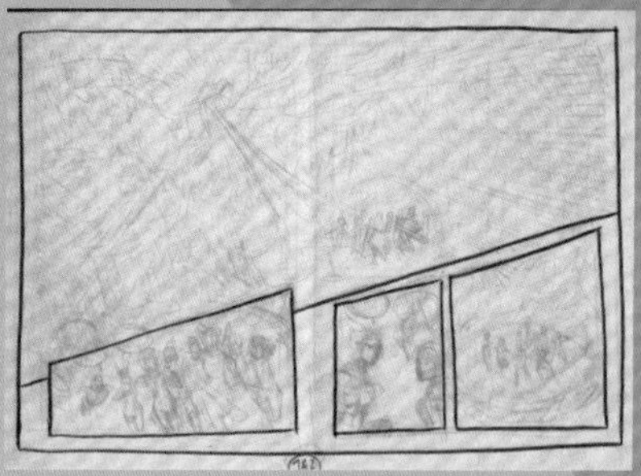

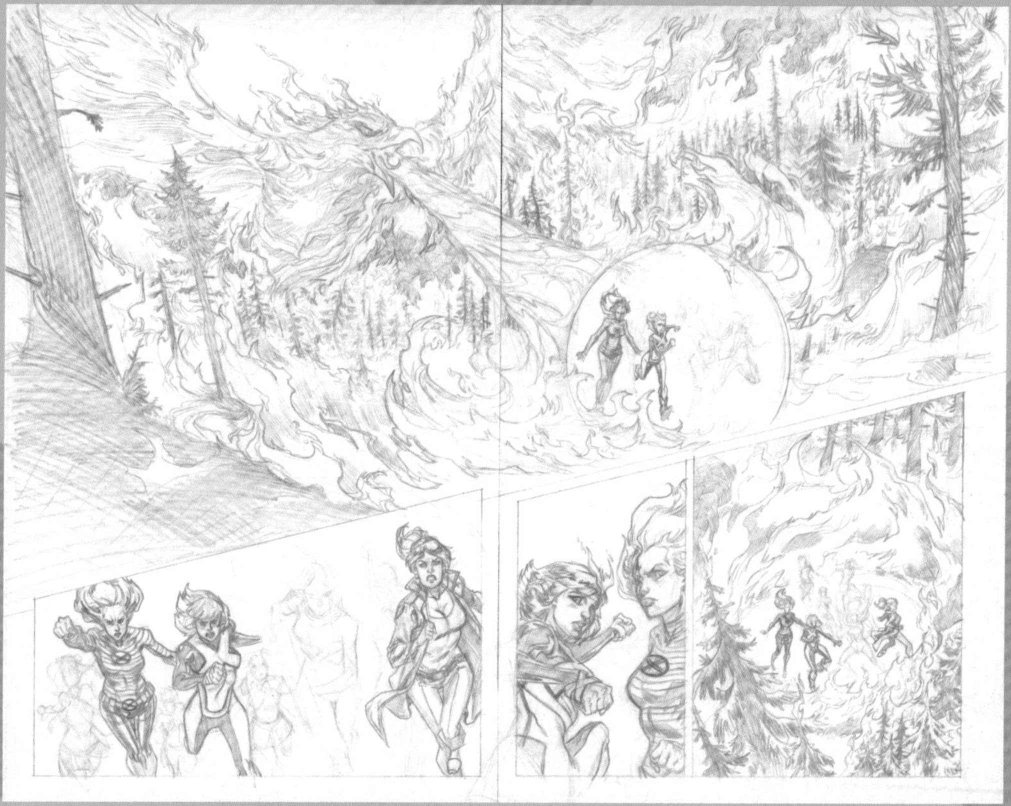

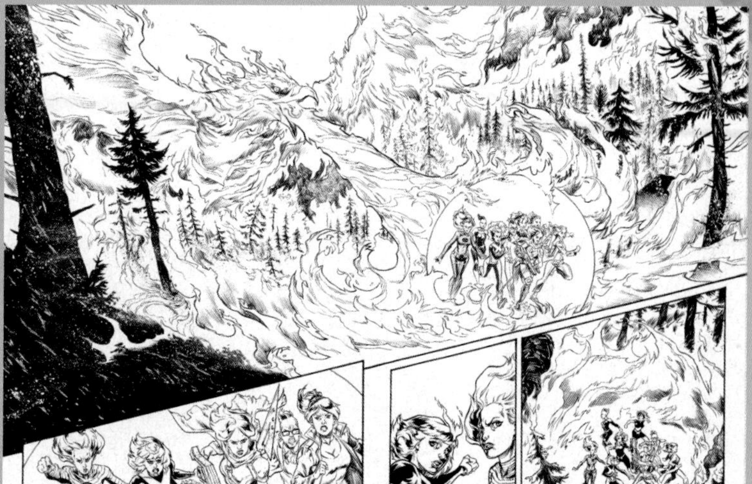

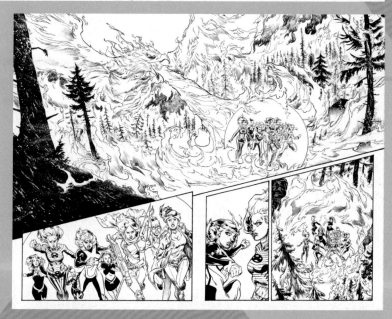

#10, PAGES 2-3 ART PROCESS BY **ALBERTO ALBURQUERQUE**

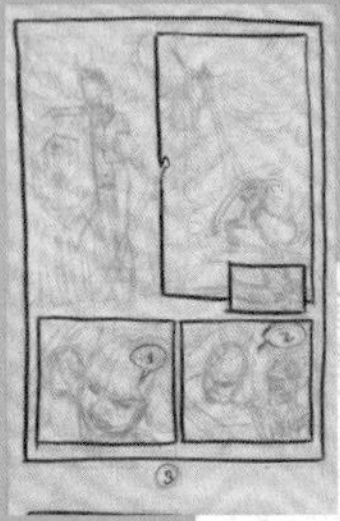

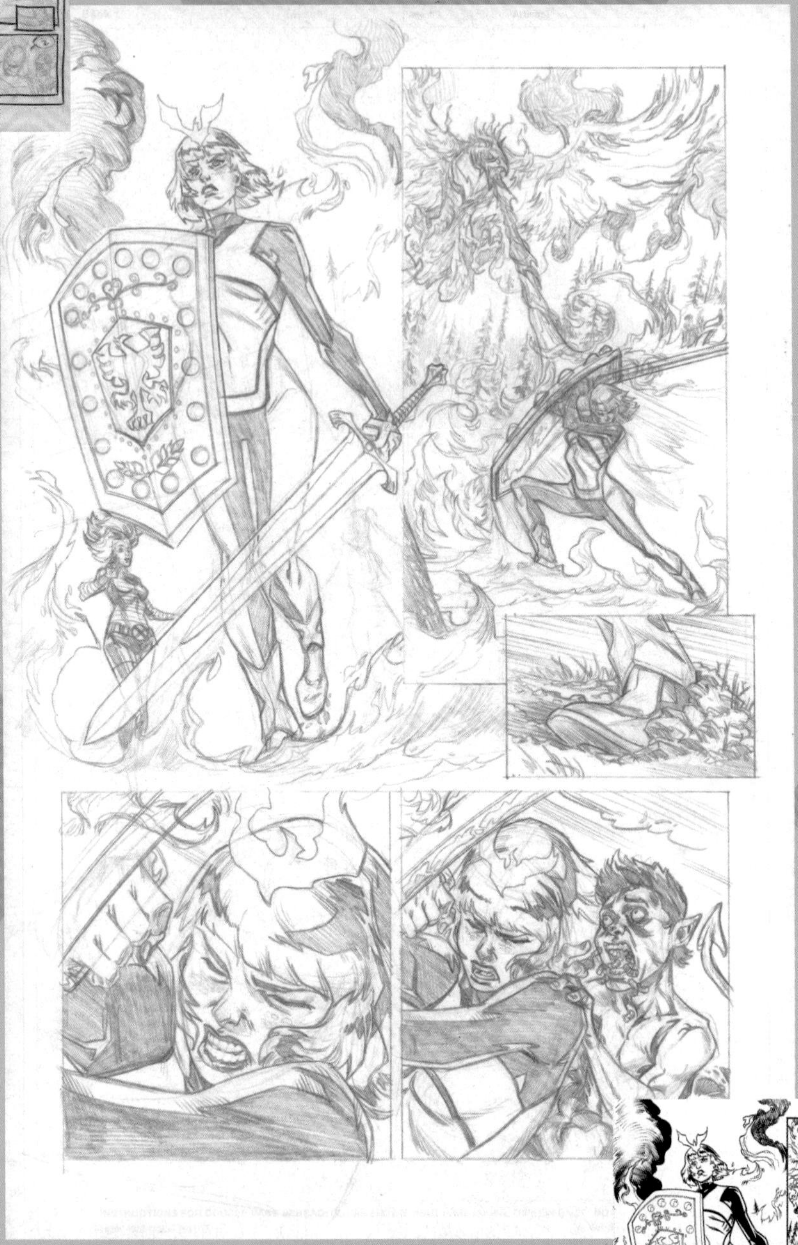

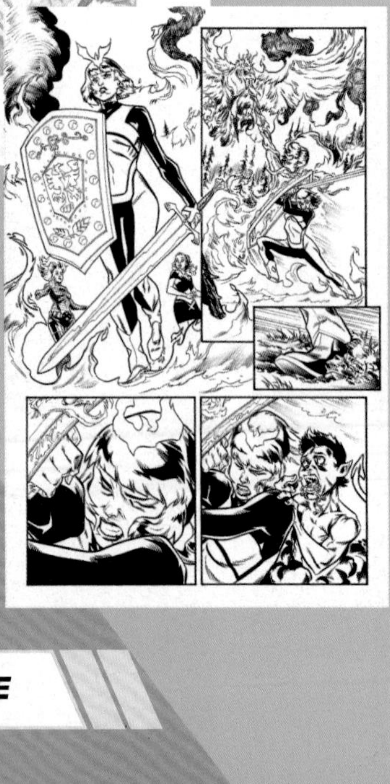

#10, PAGE 4 ART PROCESS BY **ALBERTO ALBURQUERQUE**

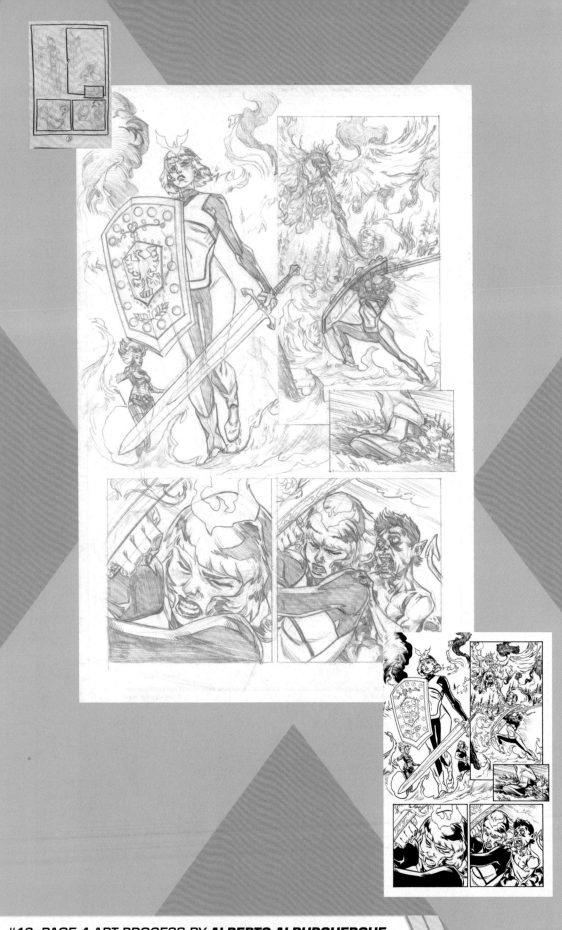